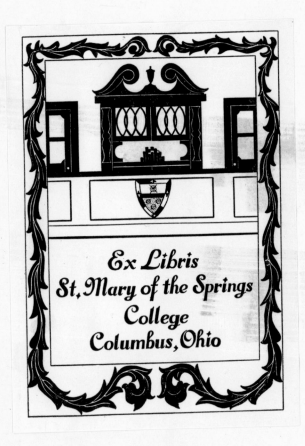

IN THE HUMAN GRAIN

IN
THE HUMAN GRAIN

Further Explorations of
Contemporary Culture

BY

WALTER J. ONG, S.J.

THE MACMILLAN COMPANY, *NEW YORK*
COLLIER-MACMILLAN LTD., *LONDON*

901.9
O 58

Library of Congress Catalog Card Number: 67-10575

FIRST PRINTING

Chapter 5 reprinted by permission of the publisher from *Darwin's Vision and Christian Perspectives,* by Walter J. Ong. Copyright 1959, The Macmillan Company. (First published in *Thought.*)

The Macmillan Company, New York
Collier-Macmillan Canada Ltd., Toronto, Ontario

Printed in the United States of America

TO THE MEMORY OF

PERRY MILLER

Cor ad cor loquitur

CONTENTS

Introduction

THE ESSAYS AND studies in this collection range widely, but all
have to do in one way or another with aspects of the human condition. An earlier volume, *The Barbarian Within,* to which this is
a sequel, treated a wide spectrum of subjects largely in terms of
interpersonal relations. This present book looks rather to various
matters in literature, technological culture, and religion in terms
of the temporal and material ground in which the human being
finds himself imbedded and which enter into the grain of his
consciousness and person. We come into being in time and
change, and time and change remain with us—uneasily always and
even uncomfortably, for their incompleteness suggests more meaning than it reveals. The world around us promises and refuses.
It teases us with actuality which insistently implies something
more than what appears on the surface, and even of such puzzling
actuality it gives us only a little at a time.

But for all their burden of incompleteness, time and change,
like earth herself, are not here identified with evil. What is temporal limits man's life and knowledge, but it also enriches them.
Time not only destroys what falls behind: it builds what lies before us.

Man's knowledge and understanding come into being within
time, though they situate man in a way outside time's bounds. In
the realm of knowledge today, time is paying high dividends. In
many fields of learning we now gain more ground in a decade
than earlier man could gain in millennia. This is because knowledge is even more than cumulative: it is self-accelerating, and
we live in an age when its acceleration has reached the point
where it must be calculated in orders of magnitude entirely new
in relationship to the life of the individual human being. There is
no way to "sum up" knowledge in a computer age.

As man moves through time and his growth in knowledge ac-

[ix]

celerates, his relationship to time itself undergoes a change. He notices time more and more. He studies it and himself in it, becoming more and more explicitly knowledgeable about his past. The further we get from the beginning of things, the more we know about the beginning. As knowledge of the past grows, focus on the present becomes more intent, for the present acquires a face of its own insofar as it can be both connected with and differentiated from a past circumstantially known. The knowledge explosion thus breeds the existentialist sensitivity to the present moment, felt as the front of past time, which marks our age.

Moreover, as time unfolds, the mind of man not only accumulates knowledge at an accelerating rate, but it also acquires new dimensions and new relations to the sensory world. The human sensorium reorganizes itself as the spoken word is reconstituted outside its native habitat of sound, relegated to space by the alphabet and then, this time with the aid of the alphabet, introjected into a new world of sound, the electronic world which dominates, though it does not monopolize, our modes of expression and consequently our thought processes today. These shifts in the media of communication entail corresponding shifts in psychological structures, creating new strains in the psyche while relieving old ones.

Though he was born into time and lives in its stream, man does not readily believe that time is good. Attempted repudiation of time is the theme of the second section of this book. Man fears time, for it lies totally outside his control. Despite anything he can do, it moves inexorably on, never reversing itself, never allowing him really to recapture a moment of his past, even when this past grows in charm and poignancy as it recedes into the distance. Science may control genetics and even the weather, but it cannot harness time. Not the least promise shows here. Worst of all, time engulfs all our decisions. A decision once made cannot really be retracted. So-called retraction or retractation means not a withdrawal of the first decision, which has already vanished down the steadily moving stream of time, but rather a second decision which we must add to the first. Instead of "replacing" a decision, we now have two on the record. Time is beyond all persuasion. It hears no pleas. This inexorability of time tempts man into illusion: he likes to think that time is cyclic, that it will return either to give him another chance or to show that he never had a chance at all—what happens happens because it had happened before, so that he has no responsibility. But this pretense is unreal, and it reveals itself more and more as unreal since the discovery of evolution, which is the discovery of the unrepeatability of all being.

The passage of time affects man's thinking about God and thus the way he construes his own situation. This is the line of thought running through the third and last section of the present volume. In the past it was easy to identify God with what man did not know of the universe. The argument ran: you cannot explain this phenomenon by your science, therefore it is caused only by God, who therefore must exist. Such a concept of God as a stop-gap, an "X" accounting for what man does not know, makes God only a temporary convenience, no more. It makes God only a substitute for physical science, with the result that, as our knowledge grows, God becomes less and less necessary. Such a God of physical explanation does not measure up to the Judeo-Christian concept of an eternal God, transcendent and immanent.

The God of Judeo-Christian revelation manifests himself in what men *know* of the universe, not in what they do *not* know. In the Judeo-Christian tradition, far from being a religious liability, increase in knowledge over the ages, including knowledge of material and secular actuality, is a boon to religion. Early man's ignorance deformed his religious sensibility and, despite the sense of the sacred to which he had access, predisposed his religion to superstition and deterioration. The expansion of knowledge, with the concomitant break-up of the enclaves hitherto locking man in isolated groups across the earth's surface, sees Christianity more widespread and more truly catholic today than ever before. The Christian dispensation is closely tied to the evolution of the material world, and to its very materiality. For the Christian, matter, changing in time, is a positive good, and the future is colored with hope.

Since religious thought registers so intimately man's place in time and his rootedness in earth, I have treated it here in conjunction with secular matters. I hope that in doing so I have kept the lines straight for those who wish to separate the religious and the secular, as we all wish to do on occasion. But at some point they have to be discussed together, since the two have been mingled from the beginning of man's history and since in the life of any one person they are always a whole.

The present essays have appeared originally in a wide variety of places in the United States and Europe. "Breakthrough in Communications" has never been published before for general circulation. It was first presented at a private Conference in the Environment of Change held by *Time* magazine at Sterling Forest, Tuxedo, New York, June 14–17, 1964, and has appeared only in the report of this Conference. "The Knowledge Explosion in the Humanities" was first published in the *American Benedictine Review* in 1964 under the title "The Knowledge Explosion and the Sciences of Man." "Synchronic Present: Modernity in Literary Study," under the title "Synchronic Present: The Academic Future of Modern Literature in America," was published for limited circulation in *Approaches to the Study of Twentieth-Century Literature*, the Proceedings of the Conference on the Study of Twentieth-Century Literature, held at Michigan State University May 2–4, 1961, and subsequently for general circulation in the *American Quarterly* in 1962. "The Word in Chains" was first published in *College English* in 1964 in a somewhat longer form as "Hostility, Literacy, and *Webster III*." "Evolution and Cyclicism in Our Time" first appeared in *Thought* in the winter of 1959–60. "Nationalism and Darwin" was first published in the *Review of Politics* in 1960 and appeared the following year translated into German as "Darwin und der Nationalismus: über die Fragwürdigkeit des zyklischens Denkens" in *Dokumente*: Zeitschrift für übernationale Zusammenarbeit (Cologne; formerly Munich). "Evolution, Myth, and Poetic Vision" appeared in 1966 in *Comparative Literature Studies*. "Religion, Scholarship, and the Resituation of Man," originally a position paper for the Frank L. Weil Institute Conference in Cincinnati, Ohio, January 17–19, 1961, was published in 1962 by the American Academy of Arts and Sciences in its journal *Daedalus*, and the following year in German translation as "Religion, Wissenschaft, und die Einordnung des Menschen" in *Dokumente* (Cologne) and in French translation as "Macrocosme et microcosme: l'homme religieux et l'effort intellectuel contemporain" in *Recherches et débats* of the Centre Catholique des Intellectuels Français (Paris).

"Post-Christian or Not?" is adapted from "The Absurdity of the Post-Christian Myth," which appeared in 1961 in *WFMT Perspective*. "American Culture and Morality" was published in 1963 in *Religious Education*. It has been revised slightly by the addition of material from the author's "Faith and Secular Learning," which was published in the *Texas Quarterly* in 1966. "The Lady and the Issue," the only study here not belonging to the decade of the sixties, appeared first in *The Month* (London) in 1951 and the next year in the United States in *Cross Currents*; it was published in German translation as "Mariendogma als Prüfstein" in *Dokumente* (Munich) in 1952, and in 1953 appeared in French translation as "La dame et l'enjeu" in *Psyché: Revue internationale des sciences de l'homme et de psychanalyse* (Paris).

With the exceptions noted above, these essays and studies are published here without change except for a few minor revisions to eliminate needless repetition, to give an occasional cross-reference, and to excise topical material where this proved to be ephemeral.

W. J. O.

Saint Louis University

At the Present Front of Knowledge

1

Breakthrough in Communications

THE DEVELOPMENT OF communications is one of the central activities of man—indeed, in one sense, it is his central activity. Not only does society depend on it; human thought as we know it in the individual himself seemingly cannot come into existence outside a communications system. A child does not learn to think first and to talk afterward. He learns both together, and the two processes of communication and thinking remain correlatives throughout life.

Communication strikes deep into the consciousness. It is inadequate to think of communication, as we sometimes do, in terms of "contact." "Contact" suggests relationship in terms of surface. Communication is not the surface of life, but one aspect of life's substance. It is not expendable decoration, something added ad libitum to existence. Rather, when existence itself reaches a certain pitch with the advent of man, it entails communication. Man is a communicating being. Communication brings the human person himself not only to knowledge of things and other persons, but also to his own self-awareness. Although I myself am unique, and in a way closed in on myself—for no other man knows what it feels like to be this "I" that I am—nevertheless I become aware of myself as myself only through communication with others.

Man communicates through all his senses, and in ways so complicated that even at this late date many, and perhaps most of them have never been adequately described. But in some mysterious fashion, among all forms of communication—through touch, taste, smell, sight, or what have you—communication through sound is paramount. Words have a primacy over all other forms of communication. No matter how familiar we are with an object or a process, we do not feel that we have full mastery of it until we can verbalize it to others. And we do not enter into full communication with another person without speech. Verbalization, speech, is at root an oral and aural phenomenon, a matter of voice and ear, an event in the world of sound. Written words are substitutes for sound and are only marks on a surface until they are converted to sound again, either in the imagination or by actual vocalization. The work of an electronic computer, too, is merely a mechanical operation like any other until it is decoded into words, and if the words are typed or printed, they, too, are only marks on a surface without meaning until their reference to sound is established. Meaning thus focuses in a peculiar way in sound itself.

The curious primacy of sound in establishing meaning, the situation which makes the primary sensory correlative of our thoughts words, events in time, is obvious enough but very difficult for us today to grasp. The original, and permanently fundamental, spoken word has become all but inextricably entwined with writing and print and even with exactly reproduced pictorial statement—printed illustrations—to which print often refers. When we talk about words, we are seldom sure whether we mean spoken words or written words or printed words or all these simultaneously, and when we talk about verbal description, we have difficulty in separating the verbal description from the visually presented illustration which so often accompanies it. We have to make a supreme effort to establish a sense of vocalization as such. And yet, if we lack this sense, we cannot understand the development of communications systems in any real depth. For this reason, to get to the roots of our condition today, we must indulge in a little cultural history.

Communication leading to technological culture has passed through three more or less clearly defined stages, marked by the media by which the word is transmitted. The first is the oral-aural stage or voice-and-ear stage, when all verbal communication was simply oral. The second is the chirographic-typographic stage, which begins with writing, most particularly (as we shall see) with the alphabet, and reaches its plenary development with the invention of movable alphabetic type. The third is the electronic stage, in which we at present live.

It is common to view these stages in terms of the accumulation and diffusion of knowledge. A purely oral-aural culture could not accumulate its experience effectively at the conscious level. Certain of the new inventions made it possible to record knowledge, to "save" it—most notably writing, print, and finally electronic computers. These same inventions, as well as the others too, have implemented diffusion. Spoken words could not be diffused very effectively, largely because, being events in sound, they could not be transported beyond the point where the voice would "carry." Writing not only stored information but also diffused it with greater efficiency, and diffusion was further implemented in various ways by the successively developed new media, printing, telegraph, radio, television, and computers. In this view, we are different from primitive man and better off than he because we have a greater quantity of knowledge and can convey it more easily to a large number of persons.

This is a valid, but extremely limited way of understanding the development of the communications media. It conveys next to nothing about the more profound and telling psychological and existential effects of the new media. It is, moreover, a dated view, for it understands the media merely diagrammatically, thinking of communication in terms of a kind of box (storage) and a spatial field (over which "diffusion" takes place). Such spatial analogies are not illegitimate, but they can be impoverishing. They are analogies encouraged by a world of writing and, even more, of print, for writing and print commit the word—or attempt to commit the word—and with it the human sensibility as a whole to space, and do so with a particular vengeance if the writing and print are alphabetic, as we shall see. In our new world, where writing and print are being subordinated to other newer, less openly spatial media, it is, however, becoming more and more outrageous to consider communication merely by analogy with boxes and spatial fields.

We know now that when changes in the media take place, the implications of what is communicated is in some way changed and often the substance of what is communicated is itself altered. What comes through in writing and print is something of a somewhat different order from that which "comes through" or, more properly, resonates in purely oral-aural communication. Changes in the media of communication restructure man's sense of the universe in which he lives and his very sense of what his thought itself is. They restructure, moreover, his own psyche (which has been defined for us quite conveniently as "what a psychiatrist deals with professionally").

For example, writing, and even more alphabetic print, helps change man from a "traditionalist," largely driven by forces which he shared with others in his society and which he accepted uncritically, to a more interiorly driven, reflective, and analytic individual. With writing, the word becomes something which can be privately assimilated: no person other than the reader need be there, only the book. The student, as we know him, is born, the learner who labors with words and concepts alone. This new state of affairs changes the role of guilt feelings in psychic drives, the structure of personal responsibility. The new media effect these changes not simply because they diffuse knowledge better but because they change man's feelings for what knowledge is and what actuality is. As the media of communication centered around the word—the ones with which we are here chiefly concerned—evolve, man's sense of his own interior and of its relationship to the exterior world evolves too.

What was oral-aural culture like? Can we reconstruct it for ourselves imaginatively? In part we can. If we take as a working figure for mankind's presence on earth 500,000 years, it was the culture which man has known for almost the entire span of his existence, since the first scripts appear only around the year 3500 B.C. Oral-aural culture has thus been a long-standing culture, but it has been a culture without a knowledge of its own history. The American Indians, for example, at the time when the Europeans arrived in the western hemisphere, had lost all effective knowledge of where they had come from. And the Europeans were not much better off. They knew that they had just come from Europe (and they hoped they could remember how to get back), but they did not know how their own ancestors had got to Europe in the first place. They had not been literate long enough to recover this knowledge—for the distant past, unlike the more recent past, is something man had to lose as a conscious possession and is now retrieving.

Oral-aural culture was of course to a degree in contact with its past. But the contact was infra-intellectual, embedded in institutions, in customs, and in language itself. Primitive man thought the way he did because of his cultural past, but he had no explicit access to this past. The only way he could find out anything he did not know from experience was to ask someone else. And the one who was asked had no records to consult. In this situation, all but the most immediate past was a wilderness in which fact was inextricably entwined with myth. And this situation set up a feed-back: even witnessed facts in the immediate past and the present were seen in a mythological context.

Words for oral-aural man were powerful things. For those who understand what verbalization is, they still are. A word is a sound, and sound always indicates an actually operating source of power, as the object of no sense other than hearing does. A buffalo need only be passively there—even dead—to be seen or felt or smelt or tasted. If he is bellowing, something is going on, he is *doing* something, one had better watch out.

Anthropologists like to make the point that for primitive man words are somehow of a piece with actuality. Primitive man commonly feels that one can use words to hurt people as one can use an arrow or spear: hence various magic formulas. But if one thinks of words as primarily and always and inevitable spoken words—as anthropologists and other scholars seldom do—the primitive's case is a little more plausible. And if his magic does not work, neither do some of the anthropological explanations of his belief in magic. Basically, he believes that words are powerful because he thinks of them always as events, as something going on, and he feels that, since they come from men, who are free agents and unpredictable, they have an unpredictable potential. He is aware, as post-Gutenberg technological man is likely not to be aware, that words, basically, are not "things" lying passively on a page, but are something someone *does*. This aspect of the word has been progressively obscured at least since Plato (as Eric A. Havelock's *Preface to Plato* has brilliantly indicated), although it is, as we shall see, being made the object of explicit attention in our day. (In the oral-aural past it was an object of keen awareness, but not of explicit, scientific discussion.)

Oral-aural man, with his keen sense of the word as an indication of action and power, tended to think of the universe itself in terms of operations and sound. For technological man, actuality tends to be an "object"—something to be seen (and to some extent touched), something passive, something man operates on. For earlier oral-aural man, actuality, his life-world, the universe, tended more to be a "word," a manifestation and a power, something one interacted with, not a passive object of visual study and manipulation. Early cosmologies, which persist vestigially through the manuscript age and into the early typographical age, present the universe as a harmony with an insistency strange to us: the late Leo Spitzer has documented the fact massively in his now posthumously published *Classical and Christian Ideas of World Harmony*, and the concept is familiar enough to us all in the classical notion of the "harmony of the spheres" and in the Old Testament, where we read, for example, in Psalm 18:2-3, "The heavens declare the glory of God, and the firmament proclaims his handiwork. Day pours out the word to day, and night to night imparts knowledge."

To experience the universe as a unity conceived of by analogy with auditory harmony is to relate it not to quiescent Platonic forms (visualist conceptualizations, encouraged by the functional literacy of the Greeks, new in Plato's day, as Eric A. Havelock has also shown) but rather to relate it to a present source of power. Such a concept of the universe remains a permanently serviceable insight, capable of supplementing our also serviceable, but ultimately limited view of the world as a picturable and palpable "object." Milič Čapek's book *The Philosophical Impact of Contemporary Physics* calls for physicists to supplement their view of the world as basically a "picture," which is certainly not all it is, and to avail themselves of auditory phenomena, with their strikingly dynamic character, as models of physical phenomena so as to open the way out of certain dead-ends in present physical sciences.

The breakthrough from oral communication to script, as we have seen, occurred only around 3500 B.C., and seemingly occurred under the stimulus provided by the need for keeping records as society became more concentrated and highly organized in the urban centers developing at this time on a limited scale. By script we mean a system of writing which in some way represents words, not merely things. Many scripts originate in picture writing and maintain some sort of immediate link with pictures, as Chinese script does. These mark advances, but not the great advance. For pictures do not refer to words as such, but to things. A picture of a bird can elicit any number of words, depending on the language the viewer speaks. The great breakthrough which has made modern technology possible came not with picture-writing but with the alphabet.

Something of the psychological revolution involved in alphabetic writing can be sensed from two facts. First, the alphabet came into being only around 1500 B.C., which means that it took man around 500,000 years to invent it. Secondly, the alphabet was invented only once: there is, strictly speaking, only one alphabet in the entire world. All alphabets in use or known ever to have been in use—the Hebrew, Greek, Roman, Cyrillic, Arabic, Sanscrit, Tamil, Korean and all the rest—trace in one way or another to the alphabet developed, perhaps in some way out of Egyptian hieroglyphic writing, in the ancient Syria-Palestine region.

Some hint of why the alphabet was so hard to come by can be gathered if we attend for a moment to the nature of the word as sound and to what alphabetization does to sound, or pretends to do to it. Sound is a time-bound phenomenon, which exists only as it is passing out of existence. There is no way to preserve sound as sound. If I stop a sound, I have only its opposite, silence, from which all sound starts and in which it ends. A word cannot be present all at once. If I say "present," by the time I get to the "-sent," the "pre-" is gone—and it has to be gone, or I cannot recognize the word. No one has ever measured sound as sound, for to measure it would be to apply to it a spatial existence which it does not have. We measure spatial equivalents of sound—

oscillograph patterns or wave lengths—but these measurements can be carried on by deaf-mutes, who do not know what sound is, quite as well as by a Mozart or a Bartók. Our scientific dealings with sound are magnificent achievements and altogether necessary, but they are always indirect.

Words exist in this mysterious realm which eludes direct scientific treatment. And, since words are the intimate sensory equivalents of our thoughts—not the "vehicles" or "clothes" of thought, but, more accurately, its matrix or even its *alter ego*—our thinking itself is intimately related to this realm of sound, a realm of existence on the edge of nonexistence, a realm of the living present instant, the only purchase on actuality we have, slender and fragile but alive and real.

Words, then, being sounds, exist only while they are going out of existence. The alphabet implies otherwise. It implies that the whole word is present at once, that one can cut it up into little segments, spatial segments (which it really does not have), and that one can reassemble these segments independently of the flow of time. I can write the letters "p-a-r-t" in that order, but pronounce them in the reverse order to get "t-r-a-p," "trap." This kind of performance is utterly unthinkable in a world of sound. The alphabet is, in other words, an elaborate pretense, in actuality untrue to the real state of affairs, as the modern science of linguistics is acutely aware.

In our culture, we are trained, generally during childhood, to believe in the alphabet. The work of Carothers, Opler, and others (note 7 to chapter 4 below) has shown the effect of this training on the psyche. Massive repressions are set up, which differentiate literate from illiterate man, detribalize him, force him back upon himself, and encourage reflection, analysis, and a large store of guilt feelings different from those of illiterate man. Literate man often characteristically seeks relief from his tensions in schizophrenic delusional systematization, setting up a self-consistent dream world into which he can retire from anxiety. Illiterate man, a large number of studies show, is rarely capable of such withdrawal. Under comparable tensions, he seeks relief from them by a sudden outburst of overwhelming anxiety, fear, and hostility, externally directed and terminating in violence: this is the rioting Congolese soldier, or the old illiterate Scandinavian warrior gone berserk, or the Southeast Asian warrior run amok (it is significant that there are in oral-aural cultures terms for this characteristic pattern of behavior). In other ways, some of which Marshall McLuhan treats in his remarkable book, *The Gutenberg Galaxy*, illiterate man discernibly faces outward, toward the tribe, and literate man inward, toward his own ego, shrouded in new defenses, defenses necessary if society is to move on in its evolutionary course, but entailing strain.

The invention of letterpress printing or alphabetic typography, as I have attempted to show elsewhere, extends and intensifies the reduction of sound to space which was initiated by the alphabet. Significantly, it too was invented only once, in mid-fifteenth century central Europe. Elsewhere, even when breakthroughs to alphabetic type appeared inevitable, they failed to occur. The Koreans had both the alphabet and movable type, but they failed to go beyond word type: it did not occur to them to put separate letters on separate pieces of the type material. The same was the case with the Uigur Turks. On the threshold of a world-shaking invention, they were immobilized. We are obviously here in the presence of another breakthrough which entails a tremendous reorganization of the psyche, although, brought to maturity in a typographical culture, we are unaware of the reorganization to which we ourselves have been subjected, and we take the strains it entails as normal dimensions of life. The alphabet situates words in space, or attempts to do so. Printing literally attempts to lock them there, after interposing between the spoken word and the locked up form eight or so operations in space and another five or more between the locked-up form and the printed word ready to be restored to the world of sound. These operations are described in chapter 4 below.

The emergence of alphabetic typography is associated with a great intensification of spatial awarenesses in the European culture where alphabetic typography developed. The fifteenth and subsequent centuries mark the age of full linear perspective in painting, of maps and the concomitant sense of the earth's surface as a spatial expanse to be covered by exploration, of Copernican cosmology and Newtonian physics, which plotted the universe with charts more than ever before and reduced the old nature philosophy in the physical sciences to ineffectiveness. It was the age which made an issue of observation—that is, of the application of sight or of other senses conceived of not as they are but by analogy with sight. (One cannot "observe" a phenomenon with one's ears: one can only *hear* it.)

The heightening of the importance of vision which accompanied typography changed man's sense of the universe about him. Vision depersonalizes. This truth can be grasped rather immediately if we reflect that to stare at another person, to treat him merely as an object of vision, is intolerable, for it reduces the other to a mere thing. One can, on the other hand, look at an individual as long as one wishes provided one talks to him at the same time. Speech personalizes. The movement from the old oral-aural world to the new visual world of alphabetic writing and typography can be understood largely in terms of this polarity between speech and vision. The old oral-aural culture was highly personal, nonanalytic, dramatic, oratorical, full of hostilities, some natural and some cultivated—cultivated, for example, in the practice of dialectic and rhetoric, to which the academic system clung for almost all its teaching, despite writing and print, until the advent of the romantic age. The newer chirographic culture, matured by typography, and at long last relatively victorious, depersonalized the world.

In terms of this polarity of hearing and sight, the oral and the visual, where are we now? The introduction of electronic communication has certainly realigned the worlds of sound and sight and has brought the former into a new prominence. Communication by letter and print is now supplemented and in many areas overwhelmed by the telegraph, telephone, radio, and television, which give sound a new ascendancy. Significantly, the physical operations central to all these media, the movement of electrons, lie outside the range of sight. The speed of electronic communication has given a new meaning to the present, a meaning reflected in our newly explicit preoccupation with decision making, commitment, and an "existentialism"—to use an expansive but serviceable term—which focuses on the reality of the present moment instead of on the immobile and timeless essences once so largely the preoccupation of a culture which spatialized and visualized the word by means of writing and print.

The point has been made by Marshall McLuhan that chirographic and typographic culture is "linear" in the sense that it encourages the habit of assimilating matter in sequences, one item after the other—the Aristotelian insights into causality were achieved in a chirographic culture. Oral-aural culture by contrast encouraged a sense of simultaneity, of paraphenomena, multi-related events occurring not in chains but in clusters. Vision presents its objects in relatively disjointed, strung-out fields: one has to move one's eyes or turn one's head to catch visually the actuality with which one is surrounded, which means that one catches it in series, linear sequences. By contrast, hearing registers everything in every direction simultaneously. Our electronic culture in its reinstatement of sound certainly favors a sense of simultaneity.

It does so partly, no doubt, because of the new ascendancy of sound in the new electronic media just adverted to. But there is no "return" here to an earlier sound world. Time is one-directional. There is no road back. The simultaneity of our present culture is qualitatively different from that of our oral-aural beginnings.

Simultaneity today is more sweeping both in space and in time. For the first time in human history, events happening all over the surface of the globe are objects of immediate or near-immediate attention for all well informed individuals. The man in touch with actuality has running through his head each day current happenings in Washington, Paris, Shanghai, Moscow, Rome, Buenos Aires, and Cambridge, Maryland, and/or any number of other places. All cultures are present within us today simultaneously—if they are not, we are to that extent today unrealized human beings. But our attention is caught not merely in all corners of space, over the surface of the globe and out through the stars. It is likewise focused through time in ways unknown to earlier man. Many statements about our lack of contact with our past are themselves out of contact with the reality of the present and past both. They mean merely that connections, mostly inarticulate, which individuals once felt with a regional segment of humankind no longer bulk so large as they used to. An adult can no longer feel his whole being as immersed in Concord, Massachusetts, or in Dublin. James Joyce focuses on Dublin, it is true, but he brings into his focus vast segments of humanity of which tribal culture in Dublin or elsewhere was never aware. And so with other major literary works today. The experience caught in Pound's *Cantos* starts in Idaho, zeroes in on the troubadours, and works around to Chinese ideograms. The problem for modern man is not that the past has evaporated but rather that it has grown beyond immediate comprehension. Never has man had anything like the detailed and circumstantial and sweeping contact with his past which he has today.

Moreover, this contact with the past has come to have an immediate bearing on the present. Our controlling interest in the past is no longer antiquarian. Our sense of time, as explained above in the first chapter here, has become synchronic: we see the past as formative of the present. Because we have the accumulation of knowledge about the past which we now enjoy, we can see the present as something distinctive, which both resembles and differs from the past in a myriad of ways: in terms of the classical tradition, the Hebrew life-world, the early Christian sensibility, the Middle Ages, the Renaissance, the Enlightenment, and so on ad infinitum. Self-study in terms of our past is an enterprise which no other age of man has been able to undertake, for it did not have the requisite kind of possession of human antiquity. Moreover, our possession of the past is growing: the further we get from the beginnings of our universe itself, the more we know about them. We are constantly structuring more and more of the past into the present.

Furthermore, knowledge of the past is as a trajectory terminating in the present which leads us to plan for the future, so that our sense of presence now involves future ages as it hitherto never has.

The past and future so construed, it might be argued, are so vast as to be meaningless to the individual. For who could have the skills necessary to recover all that we know? But we do have the skills, and their development through computerization and other electronic media has been one of the most remarkable features of the period since 1950. For individuals with adequate training, access to knowledge previously totally unfamiliar to them, can be virtually instantaneous and total. This is not true of all knowledge, but the fact that it is true of some and becoming increasingly true of more and more restructures the psyche of every sensitive and informed person and gives man collectively a new sense of presence in and to the world.

This new sense of presence is paradoxical regarding the exteriorization and interiorization of man's life. The popular criticism of the media of communication—and there is a lot of it—shows awareness, widespread if not very perceptive, of some of the exteriorizing effects of the new media. We are told over and over again that man's life has been depersonalized by the machine and by mass culture. Data processing machines are the last in a long line of inventions which have reduced man himself more and more to a mere object, a thing, exteriorly manipulable, instead of honoring him as a person whose most valuable source of action is his own interior. The new media have extended man's senses. They have made his reach into time and space longer. But the result has been that the tips of his fingers are farther from his heart. What is truly human has been eliminated: a breathless superficiality governs too may relationships between individual and individual. This is the popular mythology, finding expression in George Orwell's *Nineteen Eighty-Four* or Aldous Huxley's *Brave New World* or Vance Packard's *The Naked Society*.

There is of course real reason for concern about the mechanization of life and the consequent minimization of human values centered on love and free choice. But before we accept this critique as exclusively valid, other considerations warrant attention. First, the implication that matters are getting worse needs to be challenged (although the challenge need not imply that matters are particularly good). Professional cultural historians are not notably prominent among those who view with alarm modern communications and the technological society which they implement. A circumstantial understanding of the past—such as, for example, one finds in the work on the history of the family in the West by Philippe Ariès, *Centuries of Childhood*—does not leave one convinced that there was wide opportunity for personal fulfillment in less mechanized ages. Or, if one wishes to match fiction with fiction before 1984 arrives, neither do the novels of Charles Dickens. The attitude warranted by our present situation is, I believe, deep concern but not alarm—or, let us say, not more alarm than the human situation always has called for.

Secondly, the exteriorization enforced by the modern media of communication and the social organizations which they implement has as its dialectical complement a new interiorization or humanization of life. Writing, as we have seen, brings man to consider the world around him more "objectively" and less personally. In the verbal media, the new resort to sound, which is related to actual speech and thus to personal exchange in a present, "existential" context, today personalizes in a new way the world which writing had to a degree depersonalized. Writing and printing parked or stalled life in space, removed it (in a way) from time. Sound revalidates time and the present. The new personalism, of course, is not exactly like the old: it is less instinctive, more reflective and deliberate. But this very fact makes it in its own way more human.

The most evident instance of reflectiveness concerning the human person is modern personalist philosophy itself—the kind of thinking focused on the human person as such which we find in Emmanuel Mounier, Gabriel Marcel, Martin Buber, and now many others. A personalist philosophy is quite as typical of our present century as our technology is. No other century has had either. Present-day talk about an "I-thou" relationship, dialogue, commitment, and intersubjectivity has become so common as to be at times mere cant, but the awareness which these expressions register represents a new psychological breakthrough.

We should not forget the connection of Freud's work with personalism, even though we may not subscribe to all the implications which Freud professed to see and even when we are aware of the mechanistic models with which depth psychologists often do their thinking—"drives," "outlets," and the rest, as though consciousness and the subconscious were plumbing systems. The focus on sex developed by depth psychology and so typical of our age is, despite its aberrations, one form of the retreat from a mere object-world to one of persons. Sex is for human beings an interpersonal phenomenon in the last analysis, unless it is in some way immature or deformed.

Art and letters manifest their own interiorization, even when they are taken up with less obviously human subject matter than was the work of Reynolds or Renoir. The complaint is often heard that present-day art and poetry are concerned only with individual, private meanings. Picasso, even in a political painting such as *Guernica*, does not use the public mode of presentation which we find from Michelangelo or Raphael through Louis David and Delacroix. But it is precisely the private meanings which interest those concerned with the arts today. The same collectors who purchase Rubens or Velazquez out of the past purchase out of our own age Picasso and Jackson Pollock and Mondrian. If the painters have retired into their own interiors, that is exactly where we ourselves feel at home. There is nothing we enjoy more than being alone together. As I have attempted to show in *The Barbarian Within*, man can identify with the outsider today with an intensity and sympathy hitherto generally unrealizable. The outsider has become a cult object, so much so that to be "way out" today is synonymous with being "in." The beatnik communicates by his very withdrawal into himself, even when it is only a pretended withdrawal. No one interests us more. Recognition of the interiorization of the person is at the root of our recognition of our social problems.

The new media of communication most often accused of promoting all the vices of mechanized, exteriorized, mass culture are, under close inspection, at times found to be involved at the same time in unexpectedly interiorizing human experience. We can mention only television and the computer here, and one instance for each. The role of television at the time of the assassination of President Kennedy has often been commented on. And the point has been made, and deserves making, that the immediate participation in the events following on the assassination brought the country together in a kind of intimacy unknown and impossible previously in the history of mankind. Here public affairs became suddenly personal and intimate, without losing their public relevance, in an utterly novel way. In the case of the computer, we have only to recall one of its best known effects: data processing is often simply a prelude to decision making. The computer means that decisions hitherto a matter of guesswork, in which the decision maker was all too imperfectly aware of the issues and situations involved, have many of them become more intellectualized and to that extent freer. The fact that one knows explicitly all the elements, or virtually all of them, involved in a decision means of itself that the decision is more human. If it is also more agonizing, if the mere possibility of a decision to push the button launching an atomic war seems almost more than man can bear, that is another problem. The decision maker will at least know what—in detail—he is deciding. And if this very knowledge is a strong incentive not to push the button, it is a direct incentive to react humanly and humanely after all. It is noteworthy that the "hot wire" connecting Washington and Moscow represents an attempt to restore decision making to a context of person-to-person relationships.

In the interior of the sensitive person the past and present and future of the human race around the globe thus dwell with an immediacy which is a new and arduous experience, unknown to our ancestors, and still resisted strenuously in certain sectors of society. Our race relations problems, in their brighter and gloomier aspects, have their basis here. Experience of community with those of other races is unavoidable today. Some find the experience a call to generosity and joy. Others find it a call to fear and hate. The dialogue among religious groups has roots in the same inevitable opening of interiors necessitated by modern communications media. Each man finds more and more that his interior life includes and must include that of his brother in other religions, even where he disagrees with his brother's religious tenets.

The crisis which developments in communication have imposed on man today is thus not one of the mere depersonalization of life. It is at least equally that of the intense interiorization of consciousness. Or, better, it is the tension between a growing exteriorization and a growing interiorization. The problem, insofar as it is a human problem, must of course find its more radical solution from the interior, from within. We must have more and more machines in our communications processes, but we must at the same time master them more and more by growth in our interior resources. The way to this mastery of necessity involves fuller understanding of the history and structure of communications in relation to the human psyche.

2

Synchronic Present:
Modernity in Literary Study

WITH MODERN LITERATURE understood as the literature of our
own time—roughly twentieth-century literature, but especially
that written after the beginning of World War I—a discussion of
the study of modern literature can well begin with the fact that
intense academic study of the literature of one's own time is something new. A hundred years ago the study of the then contemporary or near-contemporary literature was not taken to be at
all the concern of formal education. It was carried on by writers
for the *Edinburgh Review*, the *Quarterly Review*, the *Westminster
Review*, the *Athenaeum* and *Blackwood's* in ways which, if not
always genteel, had at least the advantage of appearing relatively
casual.

The state of affairs is different now. Today the work of the
serious writer—and often of the fifth-rater, if he is of sufficient
sociological or pathological importance—is not merely picked
over at random by chance critics but pinned down in the lecture
hall and, in accordance with principles stated in the university
catalogue and approved by accrediting associations, is devoured
alive before entranced undergraduates or even graduate students
all duly registered for the course. Scholarly bibliographies of
studies on Joyce and Faulkner vie with bibliographies on Shakespeare, and while the former of these two modern writers did not
live to see the appearance of the periodical devoted entirely to the
study of his work, the latter outlived one devoted to the study of
his. Institutions of higher learning work under constant harass-
ment from new developments and trends. The interest in modern
literature has repercussions throughout the curriculum. As current writing is gathered into university halls, following Mr. Eliot's
recipes in "Tradition and the Individual Talent," the dons are

obliged constantly to reassess their assessments not only of the present but of the past. Jostled by the new Ulysses of James Joyce and Nikos Kazantzakis, scholars must have another look at Homer. "Agonizing reappraisal" has entered into the vocabulary of literary scholarship just as much as into other vocabularies of our time.

To understand our present situation, we will do well to examine the quite different situations which preceded it. We can do so only in the rough, for, although Stephen Potter's *The Muse in Chains* engagingly reviews aspects of the teaching of English in British universities up to 1937, so far as I know, no full-scale history of the teaching of English literature has been written, and a fortiori no history of the interaction of academic practice and literary creativity. This is regettable, for such a history would carry us into the very center of the cultural developments which have produced our modern world, particularly the modern West, and most particularly the United States. Our present fascination with the literary production going on around us is no incidental, fortuitous matter. It is as characteristic a product of the twentieth century as technology itself.

Insofar as literature is indeed literature, it is of course ineluctably associated with the academic world. For the concept of literature is built up around the use of *litterae* or letters of the alphabet, and the academic world has taken the alphabet under its strict surveillance in those cultures which use this remarkable invention. Indeed, the teaching of the alphabet and its uses forms the hard core of formal education in all alphabetic cultures, where even the whole of formal education tends to be described, at least in its initial stages, as "letters." Ordinarily, a person is opened to the influence of literature only by passing through the academic world over one or another route. Under these circumstances, it is not surprising that protests against too little academic influence on literature and too much academic influence alternate through literary history. The alliance between literature and the academy is too close to be other than uneasy.

As a result of this alliance, for centuries all but a few specially schooled persons have thought of even the oral performance of completely illiterate peoples as their "literature," implying that oral composition is merely a makeshift for the writing one learns in school—although this is not what oral composition is at all. The idea of nonliterary verbal composition totally uninterested in and unconscious of any program of visual fixity has been occluded by our academic institutions, which, abetted by typography (itself a by-product of the academies), have welded together the concepts of verbal production and letters. Even though our present-day creative writers may be more consciously aware of the nonliterary, oral-aural creativity which Professor Northrop Frye in *The Anatomy of Criticism* quite rightly urges us to think of as "epos," through the past centuries generally the prestige of literacy has brought more and more workers with words to hanker after the literary rather than the original oral epic form. Even Virgil is not Homer.

If at so profound and elemental a level there has been for centuries an interaction between academic activity and creative ambition, and if other interactions can doubtless be traced over the centuries, interactions between the academicians and the creators have nevertheless in our own age, and particularly in the United States, become so intense, so deliberate and so self-conscious as to demand altogether special explanation. Today the literary innovators are desperately hard put to keep ahead of the academic analysts. With the appearance of Thomas Parkinson's *A Casebook on the Beat*, even the undergraduate is being moved out into what he can feel to be the front line, where from the coign of vantage provided by the academic world, he can perhaps even predict what purportedly unpredictable maneuver the beleaguered beat will have to resort to next. The next step would appear to be automation academically controlled. And some would have it that automation of literary productions is not far away. A recent article explains how an electronic computer could conceivably be programed with not only all the previous productions of an artist, but also with the interrelationship between the productions, the patterns according to which each new creation is related to what preceded it and the patterns according to which these relationships themselves change from the early creations to the latest, so that ultimately the computer can compose the composer's next creations before he does—or even whether he does or not.[1]

This interaction between academic study and contemporary creativity was long in coming. Early literary cultures do not manifest it. Their academic work tends to be focused on the past. Although Aristole is by no means an antiquarian and occasionally refers in passing to contemporary or near-contemporary practice, his *Poetics* is concerned basically with a literature already standardized by time.[2] Other ancient writers such as Dionysius of Halicarnassus and, later, Quintilian, appear to be rather more interested in contemporary performance, and Suetonius notes that the grammarian Quintus Caecilius Epirota, a freedman of Cicero's friend Atticus, began the practice of reading Virgil and other then modern poets.[3] But the most contemporary-focused of such writers lack the urgent sense of present goings-on to which we are accustomed today. The reasons for this are obvious enough. Education and learning had at so early a date enlisted the efforts of relatively few individuals. Information was scant, communication difficult. The intellectual penetration of the past was still shallow, and the present, which shows up as truly the present only insofar as we set it against huge backdrops of the past circumstantially conceived, hardly had a distinctive character of its own.

Through the Middle Ages and the Renaissance formal study of all subjects was focused on Latin and a few Greek authors, largely represented, with varying degrees of exclusiveness, by the writers of classical times. What there was of formal literary study in the Middle Ages was basically past-focused. It was even more so at the height of the Renaissance. In the Renaissance, it is true, contemporary Latin writers such as Politian or Mantuan were compared with the ancients and might even be studied in the schools, as Mantuan was within a few years after his death. But the Latin which such writers composed was only partly their own, being a language chirographically and typographically controlled, and thus, even when spoken, isolated from ordinary oral development.[4] The vernaculars, which had no literary antiquity, were given no attention whatsoever in the schools—unless we consider the sort of attention which we find in Richard Mulcaster's *Elementarie,* where English is indeed treated, but only as a suitable subject for tiny youngsters in what we today would call chiefly a kindergarten program, consisting, in Mulcaster's own words, of "reading, writing, drawing, singing, and playing."

The great change-over from Latin-centered to vernacular-centered instruction which presaged the subsequent drift of interest within English to the contemporary field, has come much later than most persons—sometimes even scholars—are aware. There are some rather unsteady references to lectures on English (and even American) literature in American college catalogues of the mid-nineteenth century,[5] but these are atypical and the vernacular literature remains no more than a casual ornament in a Latin-dominated curriculum of higher education until the very late nineteenth and early twentieth centuries.[6] English leaked up into the universities from the lower levels of the curriculum, first as a language of instruction to replace Latin and then as an object of study. But when English first came in, the language was studied, not the literature, and the older forms of the language—Anglo-Saxon and, at a somewhat later date, Middle English—received the lion's share of attention,[7] partly because they were more like Latin, at least in relative antiquity and remoteness from ordinary speech.

The forces working for the introduction of English into the universities were often quite oblique. Nationalism was, indeed, one direct influence, but another less direct although perhaps equally strong was the presence of women, who had been newly admitted to the universities and who were traditionally far less schooled in Latin than men had been.[8] Indeed for several decades after the introduction of a full course in English at the English universities, the women, although a minuscule proportion of the university population, were more numerous as students of English than the men, apparently because the men had an established tradition of not studying it.[9]

In the academic setting, moreover, English was often treated philologically and schematically when it was not being actually read or discussed as literature, outlines of English literary history and critical statements about the value of various works appear often to have preceded the actual reading of texts,[10] and often a university which provided for examinations in English literature had not provided for instruction in the subject.[11] At least some reasons for this situation are obvious enough. The early teachers of English, themselves trained in the classics, would be likely to approach English literature somewhat indirectly, treating it by a kind of extrinsic analogy to Latin and Greek. Thus we find editions of Milton's *Paradise Lost* designed explicitly with the hope of classroom use in the early nineteenth century, when there are no anthologies of English literature available for such use.[12] *Paradise Lost* fitted into the curriculum after a fashion, not because it was English but because it was an epic like the *Aeneid*, the *Iliad* and the *Odyssey*.

A century ago, when the study of English was in its infancy, the directions which scholarship had to take were obvious enough, at least many of them. Editions had to be prepared, dictionaries of national biography compiled, bibliographical tools of all sorts devised or improved, the *New English Dictionary* constructed, histories of English literature written. Anthologies had to be got together—and good ones were latecomers on the scene, since their subsidiary biography and bibliography and criticism could only retail material got together through more basic research.

As basic research continued, more or less exhausting the earlier materials—although never quite doing so, of course—it tended to let its focus of attention wander more and more from the Anglo-Saxon and Middle English through the Renaissance and seventeenth century, the eighteenth century and even the nineteenth. Scholarship is always a voracious thing, but through the past hundred years the number of scholars was increasing by leaps and bounds, and the efficiency of their work was being stepped up by rapid transportation and other technological aids. The earlier periods of English literature were soon pretty well picked over, and, however constant the need for revisionist history always remained, more recent literature, and eventually contemporary literature itself, proved highly enticing. Moreover, as the study of English literature matured, those who studied it were less and less familiar with the Latin required for an adequate approach to earlier English literature, not only in the Middle Ages and Renaissance but also well through the seventeenth and even the eighteenth centuries. Later English was more English English, and more accessible on this score to an English-trained generation.

Furthermore, the intensive work on the past had made the present more accessible. Although it stresses "originality" to a degree and in ways unknown in oral-aural cultures, literature has to be studied within a tradition. The effort to secure a scholarly hold on the English literary past by providing texts of earlier works, commentaries on them, literary histories, monographs and massive special studies and a wealth of bibliographical tools, was tremendously successful on the whole, however imperfect in many details. As a result of this effort, the opening years of the twentieth century came into possession of earlier literary tradition in a more reflective and detailed way than any other age had known. The context out of which contemporary literature had arisen and was arising had been charted. With the possible exception of Neo-Latin literature written after the work of the great sixteenth-century classicists who founded modern literary scholarship (a literature of a special sort, with special limitations), no active literary tradition had ever before been in such complete reflective possession of its past as the literary traditions of English and other major West European languages were by the early years of the present century.

The relationship of the study of modern literature to the past is thus twofold. First, the study of modern literature simply terminated the movement which has carried the focus of academic literary interest first from Latin to English, and then forward from Old English through the intervening ages into the nineteenth century and thence to the present. *Victorian Studies* has been duly founded, in accord with this diachronic pattern. The foundation of a full-scale academically supported *Twentieth Century Studies* should follow, and quite shortly, for the movement of focal interest from the past to the present accelerates through its successive stages. There are already entire publications, such as *Twentieth Century Literature*, not to mention a wealth of articles scattered through various journals, which have prepared the ground. The earlier periods are by no means used up, and they never will be, but they are indisputably more picked over than the literature just rolling off the presses or not yet written. The Promised Land of scholarship lies ahead.

Secondly, as already hinted, the study of modern literature is related to the past in the sense that it has been made possible and has been given body by our developed knowledge of the past. It is quite impossible to study the present in isolation. We can study the past precisely because we have as a constant point of reference our own present from which the study of the past is being made, even when we do not consciously advert to our present. Conversely, to study the present, we must hold it up against something. So absolute is the necessity for a point of comparison that if nothing else is available, we inevitably project an idealized image of the past to meet our need. But an accurately constructed image is much to be preferred. And this, thanks to the various kinds of historical studies which have become possible in the past few hundred years, we are approximating more and more, despite the persistent tendency of doctrinaire interpretations to foul the picture.

Because of its dependence on the circumstantial reconstruction of the past, only recently become possible to man, the focus on the present which marks modern literary studies is not exclusively a literary phenomenon. Indeed, a present-centered historicism, the natural culmination of any well-developed historicism, is one of the characteristic marks of any informed outlook in our times. Ours is the age which has more detailed and circumstantial knowledge of the past than any earlier age had. In our age the study of the past continues to grow, and indeed, as is evident in the development of biblical archaeology and of paleontology, not to mention astrophysics, continues to penetrate further and further into the past, but the focus of interest is no longer there. The past is studied with reference to the present in which it terminates. We study biblical archaeology not merely for antiquarian purposes but to understand ourselves and where we are. We study paleontology for comparable reasons. Astrophysics carries us into ever vaster reaches of past time, but it also helps us prepare for the future—for the advent of the little green men from outer space or for the next ice age.

The interaction of past and present in the study of literature is nowhere more strikingly illustrated than in a recent book on Homer and the oral tradition, Albert B. Lord's great monograph, *The Singer of Tales*,[13] which brilliantly develops the earlier work of the late Milman Parry. Here we find an interest in Homeric epic form moving into a comparative study of present-day Yu-

goslavian singers of tales, who, it is found, are *effective only insofar as they are illiterate*. From the point of vantage secured by
Parry's and Lord's painstaking interviewing and recording, where
literacy registers as not merely irrelevant but as a definite disability because of the special cultural squints which it entails, it
becomes possible to evaluate manuscript cultures and our post-
Gutenberg typographical cultures with singular detachment. The
book's sensitive preface, written by Harry Levin, who found himself as an observer close to the work at its inception and through
its completion, alertly picks up the implications here and ties
them in with lines of thought developed elsewhere, most notably
in some of their aspects by Marshall McLuhan (himself a sixteenth-century scholar now domiciled in the twentieth century
but much given to commuting).[14] These lines of thought force us
to see ourselves through the Homeric-modern Yugoslav complex,
making us aware of the fact that we are living in an era when verbal activity, including of course literature, is largely dominated
and determined by typographical practice and of the further fact
that this era is in some measure drawing to a close under the impact of the electronic media of communication. The Parry-Lord
investigation, at first faced into Greek antiquity, appears at this
point as faced into our own future.

What is more, we encounter here not merely an impact of past on
present or of present on past but a true interaction. There can
hardly be any doubt that Milman Parry's special type of interest
in Homer was made possible by the fact that he lived when the
typographical era was breaking up: the older presuppositions of
an all but exclusively typographical outlook were no longer tyr-
annizing over the more alert minds. One can see this same
breakup back of the tremendous twentieth-century progress in
biblical studies. And it would not take a great deal of work to
correlate the breakup of the typographical outlook with the
growth of historical awareness generally, for as men have acquired the detailed knowledge of the past which is history, they
have been forced to see, as earlier men could not, the circumstantial differences between one age and another. It is ironic that
the acquisition of this detailed knowledge of the past has depended largely on typography, so that our awareness that the
typographical outlook establishes its own special perspectives for

viewing actuality has been brought about by typography itself.

In Lord's book, which is both brilliant and typical of today's brilliance, we can see how twentieth-century penetration of the past intensifies interest in the past, while this interest itself in turn implements a critique of twentieth-century culture which gave rise to such interest. We should perhaps note here that we are not dealing with a cyclic phenomenon. There is no "return" to the past here. Quite the opposite. For every excursion into the past forces a greater concentration on the present. The situation is curiously like that of the individual stories within the tradition of tales which Professor Lord's singers sing. Here each rendition of a story exists only once within a tradition of which it itself and others like it—but never quite the same—are the epiphanies.

From one point of view the shift of focus in literary study from the past into the present would seem to imply no more than that we have arrived at a kind of live dead end. We have pretty well worked over the accumulation of earlier material and are now reduced to using up new material as fast as it appears, but, since it apparently is going to appear indefinitely and in ever-increasing bulk, we can reassure ourselves with the thought that there will always be work to do.

With this kind of thinking there goes a great deal of uncertainty, of course, as to the nature of the work to be done. It has been suggested by R. W. B. Lewis that "contemporary literature is not really a subject for scholarship," and that although "it can be a subject for criticism," such criticism is "only of a provisional kind," since "in a deep and insuperable sense, contemporary literature must always be unfinished business."[15] And another writer, Fred B. Millett, has urged that if the term scholarship

has any meaning in relation to contemporary English literature, it is a very different meaning from that it has in relation to the Renaissance, the eighteenth century, or even the Victorian period. The term *scholarship*, in the sense of a careful scientific manipulation of literary documents, is only rarely applicable here, although it may be exhibited by the best biographies of twentieth-century literary figures.[16]

These statements, quite true in the sense in which they are intended, do not fully register the uniqueness of the present situation. Our relationship to the literature of our own time, as against that of past ages, is not defined simply by the fact that we are closer to this literature than to that of the past. We cannot define this relationship in what may be called a simple diachronic view, imagining a line protracted from the past into the future and considering ourselves as moving along this line depositing literature as we go and improving our view of what we have done as we move to a greater distance from each deposit—somewhat as a painter might stand back after applying a brush of color to a canvas. Time gives distance.

There is, of course, some relevance in this analogy. Certain gains are realized by the passage of time, since we can improve our reactions by reflection and comparison, which take time, and since occasional aberrations in judgment—not so common on the part of skilled readers as popular mythologies about literature and art suppose—can be corrected by reflection and comparison.

Nevertheless, this simple linear construct will not do. It does not enable us to register certain essential facts in our relationship and that of literature to time. Time has different densities at different points, since the interaction of past and present varies both in manner and in intensity not only at various times but in various civilizations at various times. For example, within approximately the past two generations, at a certain point within Western civilization, billions of years removed from the beginning of the universe and apparently hundreds of thousands of years removed from the appearance of the first man, it has become apparent that our universe has an age of some five to ten billion years. The mere knowledge of such a fact concerning the past and its consequences regarding our extrapolations into the future fills our own age with time in ways unknown before. The time sense achieved at this point in time by the West is now spreading mercurially or has spread across the entire globe, but the various civilizations to which it comes are themselves at various tempos because of their relationship to past time, and they are affected by this time sense variously. Persons in the West are aware of this fact, or should be, and this awareness in turn complicates their own sense of time. And what has been said here with reference to cosmic history applies proportionately to the other historical senses developed within the past few hundred years, most particularly for our purposes to the sense of the historicity of literary forms.

The purely linear sense of time, what we have called the purely diachronic sense, the sense that events are strung through time and no more, fails to do justice to the present situation because one of the characteristics of the present is the way in which it appears to have caught up into itself the entire past. Our mid-twentieth-century sense of time is synchronic—and that in at least two ways: first, it feels the present as the front of a past which was vastly different from itself and yet with which it is in a multitude of ways continuous; secondly, it feels diverse fronts of the past as existing in the present in terms of the various cultures across the face of the earth which are variously related to the past and thus to the present, but which are now all part of us since, with our global awareness, all cultures are more and more present to one another.

Although, as Professors Millett and Lewis have indicated, the concept of scholarship applies to the present in a sense somewhat different from that in which it applies to the past, the synchronism of our sense of time is such that the sense of scholarship, even as applied to the past, is going to have to be revised. The adjustments in our concept of scholarship when the concept is applied to the present on the whole represent gain rather than loss, enlargement and enrichment rather than sheer limitation. We are not only the first age which has happened to study intently its own literature. We are the first age which has been able to do so. And we have been able to do so because, whereas earlier ages may have been necessarily shortsighted with regard to their own times (and we shall always labor to some extent with this disability), we are "depth-sighted" with regard to ours, or at least in our most alert minds we can be so "depth-sighted."

Depth-sightedness confers advantages not merely on the present, where as we have seen our synchronic sense is at its most intense, but also on our study of the past. For having developed a synchronic immediacy within the present, it is only natural that we should develop a similar immediacy insofar as possible in our approach to the past. There is no particular virtue, except

from the narrowest point of view of a blindly typographical culture, in having masses of accumulated manuscripts and decades
of leisure to mull over them if, regarding the past which they
represent, we lack the immediacy of perception which we can
bring to our own age. And, having tasted this immediacy in the
best scholarly and critical work on our contemporary literature,
we should never again be satisfied with the kind of scholarship
which had not known it. The work of scholars in Renaissance
times—not only the schoolmarmish Ascham, or on the Continent
the suave and precious Rudolph Agricola, the loquacious Scali-
gers, or knowledgeable Adrien Turnèbe, but even the highly sensitive Vives and Colet and Erasmus, for all the latter's historical
sense in the presence of a text—falls short of the kind of sensitivity we look for today in dealing with the past because, through
no fault of their own, men of so early an era could not yet react
to their own age with full historical sensitivity. Two or three centuries later Dr. Johnson or Hugh Blair still had insufficient reflective grasp of their own milieux if we go by standards which
we must impose on ourselves today. We today sometimes fail to
approach earlier work sufficiently on its own terms and are otherwise not always at our best, but when we are, our reflective sensitivity to our own problems plus a freedom of movement from
present to past and back again gives a suppleness and an insight
into the past which is, by all standards, remarkable. I have in
mind work such as Eric Auerbach's *Mimesis*, M. H. Abrams'
The Mirror and the Lamp, or the work of Leo Spitzer or Charles
S. Singleton or Helmut Hatzfeld, or the criticism of Blackmur or
the critical theorizing of Wellek, Wimsatt and Brooks, or, at another level, the work on the literature of the ancient Hebrews and
their milieu done by William Foxwell Albright. These writers and
others—of whom there are many now—exhibit an ease of movement back into the past and an insight there such as man could
hardly have at earlier periods when society was less reflective and
articulate about its present.

   The way in which focus on the present sets up tensions which
are highly productive can be seen in the case of the "New Criticism." Although this criticism to some extent concerned itself
with older works, there is no mistaking the fact that by comparison with the criticism which went before it, it was contemporary

in its focus. To see this one has only to examine the selection of poems in Brooks's and Warren's *Understanding Poetry* (first published 1938), which has put the "New Criticism" and its principles in reach of every college-trained person in the land. Of the 229 poems in this volume (1953 edition), almost 40 per cent are from twentieth-century authors. It is impossible to find any similar textbook in previous periods at all comparable to this in its emphasis on contemporaneity. The early sponsors and/or Great Archetypal Symbols of the New Criticism—persons such as Richards, Leavis, Pound, Eliot or John Crowe Ransom—were deeply involved in the creative activity of the age, even when they were as academically committed as Dr. Leavis. Leavis' *New Bearings in English Poetry* and *Revaluation*, not to mention *Scrutiny,* were about as programmatic as criticism, academic or other, can well be.

As the opposition to the New Criticism formed (to no one's surprise, for the New Critics were certainly inviting opposition), one detects beneath the other issues the disagreement between the older, established academic mind, accustomed to dealing academically with the past as past, oriented strongly toward Latin and Greek, and the present-focused mind. The Milton issue in great part turned on this disagreement. For one group, Milton's Latinate expression was good, for the other bad. But Milton was a symbol of the past in more than his Latinate expression. He stood for a feeling for English literature which went back to the time before English was an academic subject, for he was one of the earliest authors to be introduced into the classroom, where he had fitted even when Latin with its attendant Greek was in full control because, although he had written English, he had produced an epic consonant with Virgil and Homer. The Milton question was seldom set expressly in these perspectives, but they were there to guide the drift of argument none the less. Eliot focused the issue by nominating as Milton's polar opposite James Joyce, who was a mere parvenu but who, we were told, was more glorious than Milton because Joyce's "rhetoric" and "music" could not be imitated.[17] This deft statement wiped out Milton's partisans with the man himself and gave a neat advantage to Joyce's contemporaneousness, for there had in fact hardly been time for any Joyce imitators to mature. Eliot's reservations about

Milton were far more restrained and nuanced than was commonly recognized by those who thought of him as a "debunker" of Milton, but the reservations did evince a present-focused mind in at least one of its phases.

Other key maneuvers in the battles over the New Criticism suggest similar alignments in terms of past and present. The differences between *Scrutiny* and other groups at Cambridge often, although not always, involved a difference between an English-language literary outlook and a somewhat Latin-oriented one. Perhaps the concentration of the militant opposition upon Pound and Eliot was due in part to the feeling that they were old enough to know better: both had been educated when English was just barely established as an academic discipline, and before the academic focus of interest in English had moved even close to the present. Significantly, both Pound and Eliot had been in and out of the academic world, finally choosing to be out—possibly because as a result of the movement which they had sparked, they could now be assured of continued close contact with the academic world simply because they were among the leading writers of the century.

As everyone is aware, the tension between the New Critics and the historical scholars has by now diminished to the point of virtual disappearance. But the effect of the earlier contest on both sides had been considerable, and it remains. The New Critics, or their epigoni, have assimilated vast amounts of historical and other scholarship—for which, on the whole, they had had no positive dislike, but simply, as some of them thought, no time. But everyone, meanwhile, has assimilated a great deal of the best in the New Criticism—its close attention to literary effects rather than to sheer detail,[18] its concern with circumstantial discrimination, its psychological awareness, its ability to be articulate about some all but ineffable aspects of interior organization, its determination to get inside a work of literature on the latter's own terms and to wrestle with the knottiest issues instead of caroming off such things in a shower of impressionist similes.

The fact is that the extremely minute detailed awarenesses with which the best literary scholarship today operates were developed in great part through the New Criticism's attention to modern literature. At their optimum, they appear impossible in the case of literature other than one's own contemporary vernacular. No one can achieve a responsiveness to literature of the past, no matter how hard he works, quite so comprehensive, so total and so immediate, as that which the same person can achieve with regard to the literature of his own living linguistic world—although once again we must remind ourselves that a familiarity (and the greater, the better) with literature of the past is a necessary condition for full reaction to the present. It is not strange that close attention to present-day literature has produced an articulateness and penetration in literary criticism such as we have never known before, nor is it strange that this same articulateness has sharpened the issues in literary scholarship generally outside the critical field as such, and that it has brought a new depth (not without occasional distractions) to the study of earlier literature. There is no doubt that criticism and literary scholarship generally today, whatever their real difficulties (such as the complication of issues, tendencies toward special vocabularies and mere massiveness, perhaps overproduction, not to mention the inevitable complement of imperceptive or poor work), are far more articulate than was ever the case in the past, when, generally speaking, the most exquisite awareness of literary effects and the most sensitive and total reaction to them was accompanied by critical analyses and literary theory surprisingly underdeveloped.

Our articulateness today even about the past can in great part be traced rather directly to the New Critics' concern—not exclusive at all, but intent and real—with contemporary literary activity. Rosemond Tuve's *A Reading of George Herbert*, for example, is unthinkable without the New Criticism and its interest in the present literary front. Miss Tuve's prelude to this book was her own *Elizabethan and Metaphysical Imagery*, which revises present interpretations of the past and in doing so agitates and reagitates all the preoccupations and techniques of our own literary performance, using the study of modern literature to show by comparison and contrast the niceties of the real issues in the sixteenth and seventeenth centuries. Professor Richmond Lattimore, Father Herbert Musurillo and others are busy now on classical Latin and Greek, in which they are opening many areas with the help of awarenesses sharpened on modern literature.

At this point it becomes evident that the New Criticism is considerably less mysterious than it has sometimes been made out to be. It really does not replace anything in particular. Insofar as it is new, it is simply the criticism which is generated at the point when academic attention is turned first on the vernacular and then finally on contemporary productions in the vernacular. The New Criticism was the product of the first age when thousands of persons became intent on academic, and ultimately scholarly, analysis, as penetrating and painstaking as academic procedure can make it, of the literary activity actually going on around them.[19]

In an age given to lamenting its own overspecialization, it is ironic that among the most striking phenomena in the study of literature should be the interaction, often deliberately encouraged, of literary study with various extra-literary awarenesses and lines of thought. Yet it would appear that such interaction is one of the characteristics of our time. For the pulling together of temporal perspectives which has resulted in our synchronic sense is accompanied by other convergences, as ranges of activity which had earlier separated are brought together again. Literary scholarship and criticism as well have availed themselves of the resources not only of philosophy and theology and cultural history, but of psychology, sociology, anthropology and the physical sciences, not to mention technology, the practical ultilization of which began many years ago with the appearance of the printing press and has currently matured in the use of electronic computers for the collation of literary texts.

There are those who decry this rapaciousness of literary scholarship and criticism, but it has been going on from the very beginning. We are no more untoward in availing ourselves of Freud or of Malinowski than earlier writers were in making use of the faculty psychology, the old four-element physiology, or the Stoic or semi-Stoic physics which we find underlying the quasi-critical writings of the age of Sir Philip Sidney. Indeed, we have if anything more warrant than before for utilizing a great variety of approaches—provided always that we know as far as possible what we are doing when we are doing it—since there is a valid sense in which fields such as psychology and anthropology are themselves becoming more articulate about man's interior in its relation to the exterior world. With the development of phenomenological psychology and of the anthropology and semantics on which it draws, the problem of expression is becoming a preoccupation of a great number of disciplines and is interpreted more and more explicitly as a central problem of human existence. Many disciplines are converging more and more on the depths of man's interior, where literary creation takes place, even though this creation is in a sense a process of exteriorizing the interior. The creators of literature themselves have deployed their own interests as variously and as often as scholars and critics have, and they have done so in the past as well as in the present. The kind of knowledge finding its way into *Finnegans Wake* is more elaborated, but essentially no more diverse than that threaded through *The Anatomy of Melancholy*. Cicero's prescription that the orator should know everything to be a good orator must always apply with equal force to the literary scholar, who operates at the communications center of humanity and who today lives in the age of "area" studies and interdisciplinary programs of learning.

Another pulling together which today parallels the synchronization of temporal awarenesses is that which assimilates the academic and extra-academic worlds to one another. There has always been considerable kinship between politics and the academic world, of which almost from the beginning lawyers have been denizens. But the extra-academic world of modern industry and business has lately been assimilated to the academic as it has become in profound ways more scholarly, more reflective, than milieux concerned with material productivity and commerce have ever been in the past. The migration of personnel back and forth between the universities and industry is ample evidence of this fact, and while this migration affects the physical sciences most, it is by no means restricted to them. The extra-academic world is more reflectively involved with communications than ever before. Even at the engineering level the involvement can be highly sophisticated, as when architects, city planners, anthropologists and professors of English get together to study media of communications in modern urban centers.

Within the field of literary study itself perhaps the most significant phenomenon accompanying the synchronization of temporal and other awarenesses has been the growing together of the academic study of literature and the writing of literature. What has happened, at least in the United States, is not merely that academic investigation has caught up with present trends so that it can talk about them, as we noted earlier, as soon as they develop. There is a positive interaction which goes beyond this. There is so much study of literature close to its point of production that the production itself is intimately affected by academic activity and affected directly as it has never been before. The creative artists are paying attention not only to what the critics are saying but also to what the professors are saying, if indeed a distinction between the two is still feasible. The effect on Ben Jonson of his master Camden was one thing—parental, personal, somewhat retrospective, inspirational. Camden had initiated Jonson into the life of literature. But the effect of the academy has today extended far beyond this. The consciousness of literary structure which an intelligent undergraduate turning professional writer can bring from the classroom to the writing of short stories would put Edgar Allan Poe to shame. From his Aphthonius and other authors, Shakespeare could learn a great deal about writing, and did. But he had not studied in school the plot structure of Kyd and Marlowe nor psychoanalyzed the audiences in the bear pits. We must not forget the narrowness of early literary study, however we admire its intensity. Until the advent of vernacular literature, almost the sole structural form which was taught as a whole in the classroom was the structure of the oration—a structure applied in one or another author from antiquity through the Renaissance to virtually everything from poetry to letter-writing.

The present intimate effect of academic activity on literary production presents new problems, moral problems, which we are far from even stating satisfactorily, let alone solving. If academic activity is directly influencing much writing today, what responsibility does it have to society to develop writing programs suitable for mankind and for individual men? All writing, Allen Tate has said, is programmatic. But how does one program a writer's vision? How far can what is programmatic about writing be rationalized and evaluated in advance? It has been, to some extent, by the founders of *Poetry* magazine, the Southern Fugitives and many others, although generally in language so apocalyptic as to be relatively meaningless at the time to those outside a small group.

The role of scholarly activity in influencing production extends far beyond that of the midwife, presiding over literary works at their birth. Scholarly activity today has a direct effect on sales. The publishing success of Faulkner is certainly in great part academically induced. When *The Town* first appeared, it was informative to see how it shot immediately onto the list of best sellers (rather far down) and almost as immediately dropped off. The Faulknerians, who are, one suspects, largely in the colleges and universities or not too long out of these institutions, were more alert than less academic readers: poised en masse, they knew exactly what they were looking for, and their joint purchases catapulted onto the list for a moment a writer normally too demanding on his readers to qualify for long as a best seller. Someone might do a study of where James Joyce would be without the American universities and colleges. Or Wallace Stevens. Or William Carlos Williams. Or where Dylan Thomas might be today if the academicians had not stopped bothering with him.

The situation was never quite like this before. Despite a certain real and inevitable interlocking of interests between the academic and literary worlds, neither in Chaucer's day nor in Shakespeare's nor even in Keats's were vernacular productions thus dependent upon academic attention, which, as we have noted, did not extend officially to vernacular literature at all, much less to current vernacular literature. Academic influence on the formation of taste was real enough to engender quarrels, such as the ancients-and-moderns controversy. But the sense of a community of teachers and writers—if not always too peaceable a community—which overpowers one in reading studies such as Alfred Kazin's *On Native Grounds* or the comments in Kimon Friar's and Malcolm Brinnin's anthology *Modern Poetry* cannot be matched in earlier ages. Although Pope and Theobald were both sensitive, each in his own way, to some of the real problems which Shakespeare had to face, neither was capable of stating the literary problems of his own age with the circumstantial finesse with which those of our own age are regularly articulated today in the better quarterlies. Literary history had not been so developed as it is today, and the psychological, sociological and general cultural matrices of literature had not been so thoroughly studied and related to literary production in the way which leaves us in our present *embarras de richesses*.

One of the noteworthy aspects of the present situation is that complaints about a so-called academic style are heard today not only in extra-academic circles but probably even more often in the universities and colleges themselves. Being academic is obviously not what it once was—at least in the United States it is not. Academic writing is not writing done in the way those teaching literature want. It may well be writing done in the way those teaching literature cannot help. But who is not teaching literature these days? Those whom we study always teach us, no matter how much we turn on them our critical guns. When twentieth-century American universities and colleges put some of their best efforts to learning directly from the poets and novelists around them as well as from the past, can it be helped if they learn too much for their own good? Perhaps we should enlarge Douglas Bush's suggested moratorium on productive scholarship[20] to include a moratorium on study of contemporary literature. Such a suggestion might possibly be taken seriously were it not that it has already been acted upon. For this neglect of real study of contemporary work is approximately the beat poets' program, and the results have not always been impressive.

In the last analysis, there appears to be nothing to do academically about contemporary literature which does not involve a closer and closer study of contemporary literature. By this I do not mean that any student, much less all students, should be encouraged to study contemporary literature to the exclusion of other literature. Far from it, for our ability to interpret contemporary literature will remain a function of our ability to interpret the literature of the past. On the other hand, we shall in the future have to study the literature of the past with the contemporary more and more at our elbow. Mere antiquarianism is a luxury which can no longer be tolerated in an age in which planning ahead has become a central human concern, an age in which change has become institutionalized. Those of us who are concerned with the past must examine it more closely than ever before, but with the full knowledge that in a world as unified as our own the synchronic sense of time is at least as important as the diachronic sense, of which the synchronic sense is of course the necessary outcome.

The stage at which we have arrived, where modern literature can be experienced as the front of a massively reconstituted past, is destined to change in many ways, of course, and ways which we can hardly predict. No one today can safely forecast what the genres derivative from the modern novel will be fifty or a hundred years from now, much less ten or twenty thousand years hence. Yet because of our accumulation of knowledge and our reflection on it, these productions of the future would perhaps not astonish us too much. We have reached the point at which we can comfortably think in a constant matrix of historical change. We are in somewhat the situation of the Irishman who had transcended the stage where he could be surprised: "I didn't sell my pig for as much as I thought I would, but I didn't think I would."

The urgent sense of the future which overpowers us today derives from our sense of the fullness of our own present, charged with the past. The academic mind at its very best is perhaps more charged with the sense of this fullness of the present than any other mind in our society. It is for this reason that modern literature, the literature being created around us now, appears to be and is a matter of such serious concern. In it the reflectiveness of this reflective moment in history becomes present to itself. At this moment the flight into nostalgia and the past, which always threatens those concerned with literature because of the connection between literature and the mythologizing tendencies derivative from the psychosomatic alliance between the human organism and the (more or less) cyclic seasons, becomes peculiarly deadly. In *The Two Cultures* C. P. Snow, speaking more of British than of American culture, notes that the humanities have failed to orient themselves toward the future with the explicit dedication that marks the physical sciences of today. Perhaps it is not quite so bad on this side of the Atlantic as Snow makes it out to be on the other. Our new and thriving academic interest in modern literature—remarkably robust by comparison with what obtains elsewhere in the English-speaking world—is, I hope, a sign that we are alive to the future which challenges our time.

NOTES

1. Fred Attneave, "Stochastic Composition," *Journal of Aesthetics and Art Criticism,* XVII (1958–59), 503–10. This and two other related articles are reported on under the heading "I.B.M. ozart's 42nd Symphony" in *Review of Research and Reflection,* I (1960), 45–50. The problem of programing the computer is, however, somewhat dismaying: one would have to work out in advance all the "rules" or "possible varieties of lawfulness" in musical composition. Although the "possible varieties of lawfulness" are potentially infinite in number, Mr. Attneave states that the varieties of lawfulness which the human "perceptual machinery" will "register" are limited and can be classified "economically" (p. 509).

2. Aristotle mentions, for example, that the tragedies "of most modern poets" *(ton neon ton pleiston)* involve no character study, although they do have plot—*Poetics* vi. 15. 1450a, in *Aristotle, the Poetics; "Longinus," On the Sublime; Demetrius, On Style* (The Loeb Classical Library, eds. T. E. Page *et al.;* Cambridge, 1953), pp. 26–27. But the poets and tragedians with whom he chiefly deals by name were all deceased before his time.

3. Both Dionysius of Halicarnassus, in his various treatises on rhetoric and on the style of individual authors, and Quintilian, in his *De institutione oratoria libri XII,* are concerned with the practical business of training the orator, and their investigations of literary effects are regularly subservient to this practical end. On Dionysius, see S. F. Bonner, *The Literary Treatises of Dionysius of Halicarnassus* (New York, 1939), esp. pp. 98–104. See Suetonius, *De grammaticis XVI,* in *Suetonius,* ed. and trans. J. C. Rolfe (Loeb Classical Library; London, 1914), p. 421.

4. See Walter J. Ong, *The Barbarian Within* (New York: Macmillan, 1962), pp. 177–219; "Latin Language Study as a Renaissance Puberty Rite," *Studies in Philology,* LVI (1959), 103–24.

5. *Amherst College, Catalogue of the Corporation, Faculty, and Students, October, 1827* (Massachusetts, 1827), p. 15, "Lectures: English and American Literature"—these lectures do not appear in the November 1835 catalogue, but in the 1840 catalogue we find (pp. 21–22) "Lectures: Rhetoric, Oratory, and English Literature, second term." *A Catalogue of the Officers and Students of Dartmouth College, 1835* (Claremont, N. H. [1835]), p. 23, states that in the Junior year the Rhetorical Department treated "The history and characteristics of the English language" and provided "critical examinations of portions of English authors in Prose and Poetry." *The Catalogue of the Officers and Students of Brown University, 1850–51* (Providence, 1851), pp. 26–28, lists a department of Rhetoric and English Literature which, however, confines its work to "the third year of the regular course," providing in the second term of this year instruction out of Whately's *Rhetoric* "followed by lectures on the History of the English language and its Literature . . . from Anglo-Saxon . . . to the present time" which lectures give "biographical sketches of the principal authors, together with criticisms of their writings." There is no mention of the students' reading of the authors for whose writings they are provided criticisms. Texts, of course, were rare and hardly suitable for most undergraduates. For ferreting out the foregoing and related

information, I am indebted to Sister St. Mel Kennedy, O.S.F., of Saint Louis University.

6. See Stanley A. Matyshak, "From Rhetoric to Literature: The Establishment of English as an Academic Subject" (Master's thesis, Saint Louis University, 1960); Walter J. Ong, "Latin and the Social Fabric," *The Barbarian Within*, 206–219. Richard Foster Jones, *The Triumph of the English Language* (Stanford, Cal., 1953), treats attitudes toward English up to the Restoration, but is not for the most part directly concerned with the teaching of English. One must recall that the most voluble enthusiasm for the language could coexist with complete indifference as to whether the literature or even the grammar be taught in the classroom—in *The Defense of Poesy* Sir Philip Sidney is still conjecturing as to whether English could be fitted with a grammar, and dismisses the thought with the pronouncement that "it needs it not." Howard Mumford Jones, *The Theory of American Literature* (Ithaca, N. Y., 1948), provides some incidental material concerning the introduction of American literature into curricula in the United States. Like R. F. Jones, he is concerned with more than academic attitudes.

7. See Matyshak, "From Rhetoric to Literature," pp. 60–69, esp. p. 68.

8. See Thomas Woody, *A History of Women's Education in the United States* (2 vols.; New York, and Lancaster, Pa., 1929), I, 51, etc. It should be noted that in Woody's Appendix IV, "Textbooks Mentioned by Women's College Catalogues Since 1850," *ibid.*, II, 474–80, the quantity of titles under a particular curriculum subject is not always an index of the attention actually given the subject. A large number of titles might simply mean that a great many textbooks were available and that the program for the particular subject was so unsteady that choice of texts was random and scattered. Thus textbook titles for Greek, which certainly was not mastered so well as French in women's colleges, outnumber those for French—and Latin! For information on English teaching to women, I am greatly indebted to an unpublished paper, "Women in the Tradition of the Teaching of English Literature in America," by Wayne A. Knoll, S.J., of Saint Louis University.

9. See George P. Krapp, "Literature, English, Teaching of," *A Cyclopedia of Education*, ed. Paul Monroe (New York, 1911–13), IV, 52.

10. Matyshak, "From Rhetoric to Literature," pp. 146–59.

11. George P. Krapp, "Literature, English, Teaching of," *A Cyclopedia of Education*, IV, 51.

12. See, for example, *Milton's Paradise Lost*, with explanatory notes by Rev. J. R. Boyd (School and Academic Ed.; New York [*ca.* 1800]; *The First Four Books of the Paradise Lost*, with notes critical and explanatory . . . for the use of schools by Rev. J. R. Major [with] a critique upon the Paradise Lost by Mr. Addison [abridged] (London, 1835)—both listed in David R. Stevens, *Reference Guide to Milton* (Chicago, 1930).

13. Cambridge, Mass., 1960.

14. See particularly the periodical *Explorations*, published from 1953 to 1959 at the University of Toronto under the editorship of E. S. Carpenter, McLuhan and others.

15. R. W. B. Lewis, "Contemporary American Literature," in *Contemporary Literary Scholarship: A Critical Review*, ed. Lewis Leary (New York, 1958), p. 203.

16. Fred B. Millett, "Contemporary British Literature," in *Contemporary Literary Scholarship: A Critical Review*, pp. 187–88.
17. T. S. Eliot, "A Note on the Verse of John Milton," *Essays and Studies by Members of the English Association*, XXI, collected by Herbert Read (Oxford, 1936), pp. 37–40; see also Marvin Magalaner and Richard M. Kain, *Joyce: The Man, the Work, the Reputation* (New York, 1956), p. 270.
18. For the difference between attention to effect and to detail, see instances in William Van O'Connor, "Modern Literary Criticism," in *Contemporary Literary Scholarship: A Critical Review*, pp. 221–22.
19. See Walter J. Ong, "The Vernacular Matrix of the New Criticism," in *The Barbarian Within*, pp. 177–205.
20. Douglas Bush, *The Renaissance and English Humanism* (Toronto, 1939), p. 132.

3

The Knowledge Explosion in the Humanities

IT IS THE commonest of commonplaces that man's position in the universe today is drastically changing. But it is not so common to note that the basic changes are less in the exterior universe than in man's mind.

The world is different today not merely because the visible effects of man's work are different but even more because the content of man's consciousness is different from what it used to be in earlier ages. First what man knows and thinks about changes, then come the changes in the outside world. This is true wherever man has instigated change. Superhighways, high-rise buildings, television sets, spacecraft, all are possible only by reason of the tremendous interior networks of consciousness which we call "physics" or other "science" and which must precede the exterior achievements. Man first penetrates even outer space through his own interior, organizing his thinking into constructs which alone can guide him into the distant material world beyond this globe. Our health is better and we are longer lived not because of something outside us but because of what we know. The population explosion occurs because a knowledge explosion occurred first.

Once we think about it, it is obvious enough that the changes in the physical world signal a knowledge explosion. Often, however, we are inclined to be aware of the knowledge explosion only as it shows directly in the world outside. Typically, we think of advances in knowledge as taking place chiefly in the physical sciences, with their adjunct mathematics, particularly at the point where these sciences affect technological change. But the spectacular and easily reportable nature of certain results of discoveries in these fields should not blind us to the concurrent explosion in knowledges having to do with man himself, his place in the universe, his activities, and his creations.

We have no adequate term for this knowledge. Sometimes we refer to it roughly as the "humanities" in the largest sense of this term or as "the humanities and social sciences." This designation is not very satisfactory, if only because the term "humanities" itself is hardly any longer a sufficiently manageable term. It appears often as a defeatist concept, perpetually on the defensive, suggesting genteel amateurishness and indecision, if not outright inconsequentiality. One trouble is that the term defines a body of knowledge by function (by the "humanities" we mean knowledge serving cultural purposes), leaving content vague and subject to endless dispute. The humanities cannot be set off effectively against the physical sciences, since these, too, can serve cultural purposes, and do. The related term "liberal arts" labors under much the same disabilities, which ill-informed references to the Middle Ages do nothing to cure. The seven liberal arts, bequeathed to medieval educational ideology in Martianus Capella's *Marriage of Philology and Mercury,* to the best of our knowledge never as a whole really governed any actual curriculum as a whole: the trivium of grammar, rhetoric and logic was generally extant only in a contorted form, and the quadrivium of arithmetic, geometry, astronomy, and music was represented by something even less categorically organized, generally known as "arts" or "philosophy," and made up largely of logic and "physics."

In lieu of using the terms "humanities" or "liberal arts" or the composite "humanities and social sciences," it would perhaps be more accurate to designate this area of knowledge set off against the physical sciences by the term anthropological knowledges or sciences ("sciences" here in the large sense of more or less unified bodies of knowledge). By the anthropological knowledges or sciences we would thus mean the various disciplines concerned with man as man, his place in the universe, his activities, and his creations. In this sense, the anthropological sciences include the study of language and literature, education and psychology, philosophy (if it is indeed a love of wisdom), the social sciences generally, and, among the latter in a special way, history in all its forms. Parts of the anthropological knowledges can approximate the physical sciences in frame of mind and method more than other parts can. They can use exact measurement and mathematical procedures. They regularly make use of the physical sciences—geology, for example, in locating man in time and space. But they are anthropological sciences insofar as they are concerned with man as distinctively man, a being who in our day must be thought of not merely in terms of nature (human nature) but in terms of personality, a being in whom even inanimate nature is integrated into a personal consciousness, unique for each individual.

I propose this distinction between the physical and anthropological sciences without real hope of securing tenure for it. We shall probably be living for a long time with the standard dyad "science" and the "humanities." The distinction can, however, help make clear what I mean by the humanities here, for I use the term in its largest sense, to mean what I have here described as the anthropological sciences or knowledges.

It is in the humanities, in this large sense of the term, that the recent growth of knowledge has been most prodigious, psychologically if not technologically speaking. Practical educational problems regarding the humanities—what to do about freshman English, what to do about art history, how to introduce a student to a humanistic psychology or to metaphysics—have blinded us to the really overwhelming problems which have taken shape around us: What does all the knowledge we have about man and his place in the universe come to as a whole? How are we to view it all? How, indeed, is one man to conceive of its chief points in any meaningful way?

The explosion of knowledge in the humanities has been a matter of both detail and penetration.

To get a sense of what this explosion of knowledge has come to, let us glance briefly over the field of language and literature. Until the seventeenth century, for all practical purposes, scholarly knowledge of literature and languages in the West was restricted to Latin, Greek, and Hebrew, with some slight excursions into Near Eastern languages such as Aramaic and Arabic. Today, scholarly work in languages extends to hundreds upon hundreds of languages from antiquity to the present, not to mention dialects. Study of additional languages has cast new light on familiar ones. Knowledge of aspectual verbs in Hopi gives new meaning to aspectual Hebrew verbs and casts new light upon nonaspectual tense systems. The vast new science of linguistics has been born, expanding language study far beyond grammar—which historically and psychologically has always been oriented toward writing— to the study of speech as such, that is, of speech as sound. Linguistics ties language study closely to anthropology and depth psychology, and strengthens earlier connections of language study with philosophy and cultural history. Linguistics is still growing by leaps and bounds, and it is only beginning to get under way. The amount of new linguistic knowledge accumulated nowadays in the course of a year, by any acceptable standard of measurement, probably far surpasses that accumulated over centuries in the past.

In the study of literature a parallel and even more complicated situation obtains. Until the Romantic age, the formal academic study of written works had been restricted almost entirely to the Bible (which was, however, hardly studied as literature) and the classics. Study of vernacular literatures had been strictly amateur, extracurricular, and sporadic. Today, while the classics remain a sizable and growing field and biblical studies have expanded to hitherto unimagined size, largely although by no means exclusively through attention to literary form (*Formegeschichte*), a study of vernacular literature has grown even more, reaching back farther and farther into the literary past and simultaneously giving more and more attention to the present.

The "1962 Annual Bibliography" published by the Modern Language Association of America in the May, 1963, issue of *PMLA* is a severely restricted bibliography. It is concerned with modern European languages and literatures (whatever their geographical locale—Europe, America, Australia, or elsewhere), but its coverage of Eastern Europe is sketchy, so that in fact it specializes largely in Western European languages and literatures, including a bit of Neo-Latin. Moreover, even for Western European languages and literatures, this bibliography is selective, passing over by design many less significant studies. With all these limitations, it still lists articles from some 1,150 periodicals together with individual books, to a total of 15,679 entries. This is only a small part of the year's work in language and literature study, since hundreds of languages, including some of the largest in the world, are entirely beyond the scope of this compilation. Moreover, in this bibliography the vast field of oral communication and performance is represented only incidentally.

I cite the instance of language and literature, for it is readily accessible to me. The conditions which obtain here could be paralleled in history, education, psychology, and virtually any other humanistic field.

Many of the items in bibliographies such as that I have just cited are concerned with details and minutiae of scholarship. But not all of them are. Our increase of knowledge concerning man has been a matter not only of detail but also of complication and penetration. It would be a mistake to think that only an accumulation of detailed facts has marked our age, although loose talk about the fragmentation of knowledge suggests to many that this is the state of affairs. In fact, while certain areas of knowledge remain more or less estranged from others, there are intense interactions, and at times whole chain reactions, between seemingly disparate areas of discovery. Countless examples can be cited. Johan Huizinga's study of the play element in culture in his *Homo Ludens* combines material from anthropology, sociology, cultural history, literary history, art history, semantics, philosophy, and much more. (Huizinga began as a philologist, and philologists have often been among those with the most sweeping command of diversified learning.) Perhaps with less adroitness, if with no less verve, Wyndham Lewis' *Time and Western Man* attacks the Bergsonian time-sense by pursuing its infiltration into the contemporary sensibility at a dizzying number of points: literature, the Russian ballet, sociology (the child cult in contemporary society), psychology, historiography (Oswald Spengler), and theology. Freud's study of the significance of humor is another, rather different, instance of the explication of a specific phenomenon in the light of a great many others. Scientific or semiscientific writing is not the only place where we find an interaction of knowledge from diverse fields. Instances in literature are not hard to come by, the most striking being James Joyce's *Finnegans Wake*, where masses of earlier literature in countless languages, together with depth psychology, philosophy, history, and much more erupt into and out of the nocturnal consciousness of one man.

The works I have just cited have diverse aims and diverse excellences or degrees of excellence. What is apropos of our present purpose, however, is the fact that none of them could have been conceived in an age much earlier than our own. They may have some sort of roots in the encyclopedic age which began in the late Renaissance and came to a head at the end of the eighteenth century, but neither Bayle nor even Voltaire nor any of their contemporaries could perform as any of these writers perform. Even when earlier writers were learned men, they did not know enough.

The earlier writers may have been the ancients, but we are older than they. We belong to the part of the human race which has had their experience and more. The result is that, even when it is partly wrong-headed, perceptive analysis of the human condition today can have a depth denied to earlier analysis. Earlier man's knowledge had depth and resonance, beyond a doubt, and this depth and resonance was at times so profound as to be virtually limitless. Plato's dialogues invite and nourish endless exploration. Early simple-sounding gnomic formulations sometimes caught distillations of great wisdom—*gnōthi seauton, gnosce seipsum,* know thyself, or *qui docet discit,* he who teaches is learning, or *quidquid recipitur per modum recipientis recipitur,* whatever is received is received according to the capacity of the receiver, and countless other such formulations which have come down to us. But earlier thinkers could not, even within a gnomic framework, relate detail to detail with the rich resonance possible for contemporary man. Their powers of recognition and response were far beyond their powers of articulation. When their literature is rich, their ability to talk about it is impoverished, even when their analytic procedures are implemented with the most intricate classifications of syllogism, enthymeme, trope, and figure.

Commentators such as Karl Stern in *The Third Revolution* trace a great deal of the present development in our knowledge of man to the work of Freud and his associates. And they do so rightly. But the psychoanalytical breakthrough was .not an unprepared for event. The breakthrough itself calls for explanation. Why was it that only at this particular time, and not before, the human consciousness was able to face up to the facts of depth psychology as it did? Without discounting Freud's genius, we know enough about the communal nature of knowledge and of breakthroughs in knowledge to be sure that some large-scale developments had prepared the ground for Freud's type of discoveries, which were, after all, appropriated by a great many informed persons quite prepared to assimilate them immediately once they were made. (I do not pretend that the informed here, who caught what Freud was saying, at all matched the uninformed in numbers or decibel count.)

We can safely say that the great preparation for our present development in our knowledge of man, the preparation which formed the matrix for the Freudian brain child, was the accumulation of knowledge made possible by writing, particularly alphabetic writing—so recent a discovery of man—and by letterpress typography, and finally further implemented by our new communications devices. The great knowledge build-up began when man was able to recover his past and to become himself as never before. It began with the constitution of history—that is, with the reconstitution of man's past in his present, which is what history is.

With Freud there was signaled a breakthrough into a new interiority which was in history. The Freudian breakthrough was not unique any more than it was perfectly engineered. It was complemented and in part corrected by other breakthroughs into interiority which have marked our day: those of the phenomenologists and of some existentialists, which have often joined with psychoanalytic powers of insight to yield our present concern with intersubjectivity. The result has been the new awareness on the verge of which the present age is trembling: an awareness of history itself not merely as an exterior course of events, nor even as a developing idea in the Hegelian sense, but as an interior reality: history as a process in time which is embodied— literally embodied—in me and you, as a dimension which you and I have, a dimension establishing our consciousness in a different pitch vis-à-vis the actuality around us than was the case with earlier men. Interiorized history is deposited as personality structure. We can begin to sense some of the effects of the interiorization of history quite spectacularly in our day as the personality structures in the developing countries change almost overnight (if not among the entire population thus far, at least among many), as here in the United States the Negro psychic structure, and the white with it, evolves today with dizzying speed to give those of us with dark skins something more like a rightful place in the world, and as in many parts of the world the psychic structures sheltered behind massive national ideologies and images shift—to the utter dismay and terror of the less secure—to realign themselves around international polarities.

To describe how present developments in our knowledge of man have implemented and made inevitable the interiorization of history would take a great deal of time and would lie far beyond our present aims. It suffices here to have made the point, which I hope I have made, that the knowledge explosion of our day reaches far beyond the physical sciences into the areas of anthropological knowledge or "humanities." Whatever the profound intuitions of earlier man, we have available to us today not only those intuitions as recorded and even enriched by subsequent reflection, but also other massive knowledge of man and his works far more exhaustive than was ever available before. We can trace man back, with an accuracy not always complete and sometimes only fitful, but on the whole unimpugnable, through tens of thousands and even hundreds of thousands of years, and in more and more different cultures. We can chart his migrations over the surface of the earth. We have accessible massive records of his literary and artistic achievement, collected and described and analyzed—not completely, to be sure, but in impressive detail. With the help of the physical sciences, we are pinpointing man's relationship to the brute animals, chemically, anatomically, physiologically, and genetically. We are analyzing his cultures in greater and greater depth and establishing their interrelationships, and, more importantly, their connection with man's own various personality structures and various kinds of achievement. Most of this vast knowledge is surprisingly new.

It has, moreover, created many deep rifts in the community of scholars dealing with man as man. There are, first of all, the rifts between specialists such as we find in the physical sciences: just as the expert in population genetics has trouble communicating with the astrophysicist, so the specialist in Koine Greek may have little to say across the dinner table to the specialist in Eskimo artifacts.

On a closer examination, however, this comparison has only a limited validity: failure to establish bridges between disparate specialties is rather less likely in the sciences of man than in the physical sciences. Greek dialects and Eskimo artifacts do offer points of comparison, and experts can turn them up pretty quickly. The more crucial rift in the anthropological knowledges arises from the fact that it is within them that the possibility of integrating knowledge invites attention, and the concurrent fact that with the present complexity of knowledge and the vast fields of time and space in which mankind has now located itself, more than ever those who are able to see some kind of unity in the whole knowledge complex find it difficult to communicate this unity to the specialists. Thus in the anthropological sciences there is not only the problem of communication between specialist and specialist, but also the graver problem of communication between the integrator and the specialist. Integration is not so much the business of the physical sciences, which consequently do not experience quite this same kind of difficulty.

In our enlarged sciences of man what can an integrating vision be? Old clichés are useless. It is beyond naïveté to think of "philosophy" in the way in which this is ordinarily conceived as somehow "integrating" or "synthesizing" all that we know of the universe and of man, although the ability of philosophy to establish and deepen certain strategic and essential insights is real enough and operative. In this universe, inundated with growing knowledge, we find that what we most need is some vision revealing the direction of the growth itself. The immediate appeal of the work of Father Pierre Teilhard de Chardin to serious thinkers across the globe is due in great part to the fact that he sought precisely to provide such a vision, to discover and state where the cosmic processes are tending, especially now that they are concentrated in the mind of man.

Since the knowledge explosion of itself is basically a secular phenomenon, affecting directly man's grasp of the natural world, the Christian can hardly look to revealed religion to provide a specific answer to the present crisis. And yet, precisely as a Christian, he should find himself involved in the knowledge explosion of our time. He has special reasons for interesting himself in the growth of knowledge. One is rather directly theological: the present advances in theology, in the explication of divine revelation itself, have depended in great part upon advances in secular thought— advances, for example, in anthropology, in sociology, in cultural history, and in literary history (the whole field of Scripture studies, particularly in the case of *Formgeschichte*, has been both a cause and a product of a study of literature more sophisticated and elaborate than earlier ages had known).

A second reason for a Christian's attending to the growth of knowledge is that serious efforts at integration of the knowledge explosion are in many places focusing today more and more on areas of intense Christian preoccupation: the study of the human interior consciousness and of human intersubjectivity and the study of comparative religion. This last all-important study has become feasible as a discipline only because of the knowledge explosion itself, with our improved information regarding diverse cultures. Moreover, the study of comparative religion is being accompanied by another phenomenon of intense importance, the lessening of the old tensions between Protestants and Catholics, a lessening which itself is due in great part to increase in knowledges. Historical, psychological, social, anthropological, and other awarenesses have made it possible to articulate issues better than earlier ages were able to do and thus to discover new areas of agreement.

Differences remain, but misunderstanding can now be minimized as never before.

Another reason for a Christian to attend to the meaning of growth in knowledge is more pervasive in its implications. Our intense interest in growth is part of the awarenesses normal in our post-Darwinian world, where significance lodges in process rather than in immobile status. To the mature Christian view such a world has proved more religiously appealing than the world as earlier conceived. We know today that the cosmos is not a perfectly wound clock, not a neat design with everything in its place, a creation demanding only perfunctory concurrence from a nicely rationalized God. The cosmos can be seen today as an event, a happening. It is something "going on."

From the earliest Old Testament times "goings-on," happenings, events, occurrences have been the concern of the God of Hebrew and Christian revelation much more than static patterns have been. If the Christian should be interested in this world for what it is, much more, then, should he be interested in it for what it is becoming. He wishes to see its movement sanctified in Christ. Growth in knowledge, a spiritual actuality, should especially fascinate him, and does.

Like other men, the Christian knows that no full solution to the problems created by the knowledge explosion can be expected. For these problems are intertwined with man himself, are indeed part of the fabric of man, whose nature and destiny have been from the beginning shrouded in the deepest mystery. But the knowledge that a perfect solution is not in sight is no excuse for the Christian to shirk his responsibility, which is the responsibility to enter into the present knowledge explosion as best he can, positively, imaginatively, and creatively. The fact is that the universe cannot be understood except insofar as it is participated in.

Since the knowledge explosion is of itself basically, although not terminally, a secular phenomenon, faith can hardly be thought to provide any special answers to many of the problems the explosion creates. This fact the Christian must accept humbly. But since the explosion is obviously God's will and God's work, faith should urge the Christian on to enter into it and to spend himself both in fostering it and in dealing with its consequences.

4

The Word in Chains

THE CULTURAL LAG in attacks launched against *Webster's New International Dictionary*, Third Edition, by nonprofessional reviewers has been beautifully and circumstantially shown by Karl W. Dykema in a recent article in the *AAUP Bulletin*.[1] Dean Dykema has laid the blame at the door of the right persons. He has indicted first the reviewers themselves for their dated "medieval" linguistic outlook and failure to know what they are talking about, and secondly those of us who should see to it that college and university graduates (including these same reviewers) are properly informed concerning the nature of lexicography and who have not done so. He has suggested possible causes for the heat in the attacks on this monumental lexicographical achievement: the greater anxieties of our present age (this cause he discounts, rightly, I believe, for want of evidence that our anxieties are "greater" than those of earlier man), the uncompromising presentation of "upsetting" information which had been hidden away or muted in editions before this third, the choice of reviewers for nonscholarly journals who could write well or simply entertainingly rather than reviewers who knew the field they were writing about, and the acceleration of linguistic change among "cultivated groups" due to the accelerated upward mobility of persons whose linguistic habits were not formed in the social environment from which earlier "cultivated groups" came.

There appears to be, however, a further reason for the heat in the attacks. This reason deserves mention, for in some ways it is more basic than any of those Dykema lists. It relates to the psychological structures which alphabetic literacy fosters and on which a dictionary builds.

To see what this reason is, we must advert to the relationship of alphabetic writing and alphabetic typography to speech explained in Chapter 1 above here. Writing and print propose to be records of sound. But they are so only in a forced and permanently imperfect sense. Sound is of itself an event in time, one-directional and evanescent as time itself is. Sound exists only when it is passing out of existence. I can stop an object in the field of vision to see it more clearly. If I stop a sound, I get not sound but silence. If I think of sound as quiescent, I am not thinking of sound but of something else.

To reduce sound to the alphabet is to do just this: to think of sound as something else by converting it (and, with it, time itself) into space.

Many and perhaps all languages make possible a certain amount of conversion of time phenomena into spatial analogies—after all, the analogies are there to be exploited by anyone who wishes to avail himself of them. But the kind of conversion which makes the alphabet, and which has been explained in Chapter 1 above here, is radical and weird, setting up strains within the psyche to a degree difficult for us today to grasp, since we are conditioned to the alphabet from infancy. How uncongenial this conversion is can be seen from the fact that the alphabet was invented only once, every alphabet in the world being derived, in one way or another, from the primitive alphabet which arose in the Mediterranean region somewhere in the years around 2000–1500 B.C.[2] If man has been on earth some 500,000 years—a fairly firm working figure—it has taken him almost this entire time to come upon this device, which to us appears so inevitable.

Alphabetic letterpress typography, too, was a nonce invention in the fifteenth century.[3] The invention—or, better, development—consisted essentially of a process of printing from alphabetic types cast from matrices made by being struck with a punch. One first cut a set of punches in hard metal—iron or an alloy of iron—with a raised letter on the head of each, like the letter on a typewriter key. Then one struck these punches into a softer metal, generally brass, to form a mold. To this mold one brought a still softer metal, molten, generally an alloy of lead with antimony (to assure expansion rather than contraction on cooling), casting large numbers of types for each letter of the alphabet. These types were stored in a case or font. To this the compositor came with his composing stick, on which he set up lines of type from copy. This set type was moved to a galley for proof, then, corrected, put into a form, which was locked up and moved on to a press, where it was locked further into position. (These steps, given here more or less as they occur today, were slightly curtailed in the early days of printing.) Then the form was inked, paper brought into contact with it, the platen of the press squeezed into close contact with the paper, removed, and the paper removed. By this time, one is a dozen or more steps away from the spoken word, which has receded into the background so far as to make it unnecessary for those engaged in the typographical operation to know the language they are dealing with or even be able to speak it at all. The reduction of sound to space imitated by the alphabet has reached truly monumental proportions. The voice has been swallowed by something like a huge Rube Goldberg machine. What was once a living operation in sound has become a matter of local motion. Voice, which exists only by moving through time, has been packed away.

Here not only are we far from the spoken word, the free-flowing world of oratory and epic: we are in a new world of pressure and constraint, where exactitude can become on obsession. The analogy, loose at least, between the progression from the oral word to the controlled, constrained, written or printed word and the Freudian succession oral-to-anal is sure to be adverted to here, although what to make of the analogy is not clear since it must be remembered that here the oral is not, as in the Freudian sequence, basically receptive but rather diffusive (it is the ear which receives the word, not the mouth). This is the awesome world out of which the dictionary was born.

The world out of which the dictionary was born has another relevant trait: it is the product of the cultivation of Latin (with some Greek, and a tiny dash of Hebrew) as a basically chirographic language. From the time between the sixth and the ninth century, when Learned Latin was separated from the vernacular dialects of the tongue which became the modern Romance languages, Learned Latin had been the language of all learning in the West—of grammar, rhetoric, logic, physics, medicine, law, theology, and the other academic subjects. By the eighteenth century, the great germinal age for the modern dictionary, Latin was in a curious condition. For roughly a millennium, although it was spoken by millions, it had been spoken by no one who did not know how to write it. The language was far from "dead," for new terms had been formed by the thousands in Latin since antiquity (they still are being formed), but it was subject to total chirographic (and latterly typographic) control. Within Learned Latin there was no properly phonetic development at all. The sound was controlled out of space. What was primary (voice) was being totally controlled by its derivative (writing). The only way to learn a language of this sort is to match everything to written models. Writing and print by definition constitute regularity.

It is a commonplace that the early approaches to the vernaculars were through the Latin and Greek. The efforts of dictionary-makers, like those of earlier devotees of the vernaculars,[4] were powered by a desire to raise the vernaculars to the regularity of the classical tongues—a regularity due to their curious domination by chirography. Dr. Johnson, as Dykema points out, learned to qualify his original desire to see a dictionary as a means of establishing utter regularity in English comparable to that in Latin and classical Greek. He finally owned that his ambition to "fix" the language was one "which neither reason nor experience can justify."[5] But he was unable to forget entirely the regulatory approach.

So were most of his successors before *Webster III*. Even when lexicographers protested that they were registering usage and not prescribing rules, they took as their norm for usage the practice of persons in the community who were, more or less, professional or semiprofessional *writers*. Oral influence was discounted. The new *Webster III* alters this stand. As never before, what falls on the ear is recorded: pronunciation variants, words chiefly heard, seldom written. Most telling about the dictionary's orientation is the fact that persons whose influence on the language is primarily oral, such as Willie Mays, are cited among those whose usage is recorded. (Of course, Willie Mays's oral usage will have to get itself recorded somewhere in print—this much concession to professional writing must always be made by the best-intentioned lexicographers.)

Webster III represents one more instance—a monumental one

—of the breakthrough to a more oral-aural culture which marks our day, characterized by the electronic media of communication, telephone, telegraph, radio, television (more oral-aural than visual—the weather chart is always accompanied by a commentator), and the beep-beep of orbiting spacecraft. The breakthrough manifests itself in language study by the development of linguistics, of which *Webster III* is a product and which approaches language as basically an aural-oral phenomenon, whereas traditional grammar had taken language basically as written (*gramma* is the Greek word for a letter of the alphabet).

It is this breakthrough from quiescent to vibrant, temporally fluid sound[6] which, I believe, constitutes the most deep-seated source of anxiety in reactions to *Webster III*. Space is the great symbol of order, and its primacy is now being compromised. The alphabet and print had made language as never before an instrument of constraint rather than openness, and had thereby reorganized man's life world. To learn the alphabet is to impose on oneself a sense of control which we are only beginning to understand. We have yet to assess the terrible strain on the psyche which the learning of alphabetic writing always entails, although studies of the different psychotic syndromes of literates, as compared to illiterates, have begun to alert us to the state of affairs.[7] Any teacher of a foreign language knows some of the depths which are affected by literacy: how difficult it is, for example, to re-establish among literates an awareness of sounds as sounds —a sense, for example, that the "p" in French is not the "p" in English, and the ability to *hear* a French "p" rather than to *see* an English-sounding "p" when a French word is uttered.

The investment of psychic energy in the mastery of writing (and of typography) is jealously guarded by the psyche, which does not wish to yield an inch of the ground it has so laboriously occupied. Writing has been such an achievement that the psyche feels compelled to overvalue it, to believe that writing, which reduces restless, unpredictable, evanescent sound to the quiescent order of space, *must* control all speech, and, moreover, that speech must normally have the kind of utter regularity which can become an obsessive dream once the threshold has been crossed from the fluid (and real, living) world of sound to the static (and

unreal, dead) world of alphabetic space. The alphabetically
conditioned psyche, in other words, is terrorized by the fact that
Webster III has abandoned the solid world of space for the un-
certainties of time. Wyndham Lewis, who proclaimed himself a
"space" man and hated "time" men, wouldn't have liked it at
all.

This additional reason for the heat in the attacks on *Webster
III* ties in directly with Dykema's analysis at two points. First, it
lends some meaning to a modified version of his first reason,
which has to do with the purported anxieties of our present age
and which he thought no real reason as it stood, since it is not at
all evident how our anxieties as a whole compare with those of
earlier ages. The present account does not contradict Dykema
here, for it does not imply that anxieties today as a whole are
either greater or less than they have been in the past—only that
some of them are different. Just because our anxieties, about
which we have lately become so reflective and so articulate, press
us very hard does not mean that other persons in earlier cultures
were not pressed as hard or harder by other anxieties which to us
now appear only exotic. One can hardly measure with great assurance the over-all anxieties of vanished cultures as one can at
least hope to measure one's own. And, in fact, strangely enough,
a recent study of present-day cultures appears to show that the
society (the United States) most technologically advanced and
thus presumably most unequivocally belonging to the present
world, produces, contrary to expectation, personality structures
with the least anxiety.[8] The phenomena here described, however,
do point to a particular source for some particular anxieties of our
age, identifying them as the result of a sequence of communications developments terminating in our day: the shift from oral-
aural media to chirographic media to typographic media, and now
to a new kind of oral-aural media which electronically transforms
the old kind.

Secondly, the perspectives here suggested give new relevance
to the term "medieval" which Dykema uses as a descriptive label
to cover a state of mind among critics of *Webster III*. He styles
these critics medieval because, like medieval (and Renaissance
and later) grammarians, they opt for the view that the study of

language is basically a normative matter, a quest for and enforcement of "rules." The present account suggests one of the
reasons why medieval man was so beset by the need for rules.
Medieval culture, by contrast with the earlier rhetorical culture
of antiquity, was a manuscript culture, deeply committed to textual commentary and to exactitude—and thus ultimately committed, incidentally, to the quest for verification which helped
form the modern scientific mind. The typical scholar of medieval
times would probably not have liked *Webster III*. The atypical
scholar—of which there were not a few—probably would have.
But even the typical medieval scholar was enough under the influence of a two-sided dialectic not to have given *Webster III* such
short and vengeful shrift as its uninformed reviewers have ac-
corded it.

NOTES

1. Karl W. Dykema, "Cultural Lag and Reviewers of *Webster III*," *AAUP Bulletin* 49 (1963), 364–369.
2. The nonce origin of the alphabet is a fact which, curiously, escapes the notice of a great many scholars, even some in language and literature. It is readily documented from encyclopedia articles and the references they give. A definitive treatment of the subject is found in David Diringer, *Writing* (New York, 1962), pp. 104–184. The Ugaritic alphabet is only a seemingly independent development: it apparently does not model the forms of its letters on previous alphabetic forms, but its inventor or inventors, who lived in the alphabetized Mediterranean area, approached their undertaking with a knowledge of other alphabetic writing. See William Foxwell Albright, *The Archaeology of Palestine* (Harmondsworth, Eng., 1951), pp. 187–88.
3. See Thomas Francis Carter, *The Invention of Printing in China and Its Spread Westward*, rev. by L. Carrington Goodrich (2d ed.: New York, 1955). Carter explains how surprisingly close the Uigur Turks and the Koreans came to movable alphabetic type without being able to cross the threshold: the Uigurs used alphabetic writing and movable type, but the only known Uigur movable type "consists entirely of word-type, in slavish imitation of the Chinese system" (p. 218). The Koreans also had the alphabet and movable type, but their movable type consisted of pieces even more complicated than those of the Uigurs: each type contained not only an alphabetized Korean word but also the Chinese character to which it corresponded (p. 228). There is of course a large literature on the development of letterpress printing in fifteenth-century Europe.
4. See Richard Foster Jones, *The Triumph of the English Language* (Stanford, 1953).
5. Quoted by Dykema, "Cultural Lag . . . ," p. 364, from Johnson's Preface to his dictionary.
6. For further discussion of the role of voice and other media in com-

munication see Walter J. Ong, *The Barbarian Within* (New York, 1962), esp. pp. 49–67, 164–229.

7. See the work reported on in J. C. Carothers, "Culture, Psychiatry, and the Written Word," *Psychiatry*, 22 (1959), 307–320; and Marvin K. Opler, *Culture, Psychiatry, and Human Values* (Springfield, Ill., 1956).

8. Raymond B. Cattell, "The Nature and Measurement of Anxiety," *Scientific American*, Vol. 208, No. 3 (March, 1963), pp. 96–104.

Illusion of Return

5

Evolution and Cyclicism in Our Time

I

THERE CAN BE no doubt that the discovery of the process of evolution, cosmic and organic, has been one of the greatest achievements of the human mind. In a sense, this is the central discovery
in the Western world since Renaissance times, and in a still further sense it is the central corporate discovery of all mankind.

The discovery of cosmic and organic evolution is part of man's
discovery of himself in history. Early man had no effective way of
putting together really extended history. Preliterate man could not
control enough data to enable him to reconstruct a lengthy sequence of events in time. There had been, of course, data gathered and reported by eyewitnesses, but when this information
had been passed on through even a few generations without the
help of writing, fact—provided one had it in the first place—became inextricable from fictional accretion. Instead of a historical
account of their past, preliterate peoples even today have only
myth, related perhaps to fact at certain points but related so
erratically as to make historical reconstruction very difficult.

With the invention and spread of writing, extended records began to create a new and important dimension in human thinking.
As records accumulated, it was only a matter of time until persons would begin to notice that the state of affairs in the past had
been quite different from what it was in the present. In their
hieroglyphic writing the ancient Egyptians accumulated great masses of records. The Hebrews, coeval with the later Egyptians,
and, if in some ways less civilized, still advanced beyond the
Egyptians in possessing the alphabet, had a far-developed his-

torical sense, as the Old Testament shows. Their way of conceiving history is not so developed as ours, yet they have an unmistakable historical instinct and outlook. In Aristotle's day, when alphabetic writing was probably only about fifteen hundred years old, the historical dimension had begun to intrude even in scientific thinking. Near the beginning of his *Metaphysics* Aristotle inserts a quite sketchy and primitive, and yet portentous history of philosophy.

From the ancient Mediterranean civilizations, modern man's sense of history develops in a rather direct line through medieval and Renaissance European civilization into the age of the Enlightenment and thence into the present one world, where it is now in one way or another shared by all men. In this line of development, the sense of a past accessible through circumstantial records grew in the human consciousness as it had never grown at other earlier times or in other civilizations. In the Chinese civilization, perhaps because of the different kind of commitment to time involved in character writing as against alphabetic writing, perhaps because of specialization in other awarenesses made possible by this same remarkable character writing, perhaps because of relative lack of contact with the Hebrew and Christian religious sense of time, or because of all these factors and some others as well, so strong a historical sense did not develop. The Chinese would have to acquire this sense later from the West, most forcefully in its Marxist manifestation. Other civilizations, too, performed more like the Chinese than like the Western segment of mankind. The Hindu, the Central American, the African did not themselves develop the modern sense of a temporal dimension in the cosmos. These and other civilizations have learned this, with modern science, from the West. The margin by which the West outdistanced other civilizations in achieving this sense of history, however, has been in reality slight. If man has been here for some five hundred thousand years, the segment of mankind which first developed this historical sense did not begin to do so until nearly all this five hundred thousand years had elapsed— that is, until roughly some three thousand years ago.

What we mean by this historical sense should be noted carefully. By the eighteenth century in the West, when this sense had pretty well matured, what had happened was not simply that man had become speculatively interested in time. Speculative interest in time he had had for centuries. Nor was it that man had developed a sense of reality as embedded in a flow of time such as Heraclitus had registered six centuries before Christ in his logion, *Panta rhei,* or "All things are in flux." A sense of flux is an old awareness, too. What had happened by the age of the Enlightenment was that man had achieved a sense that the present he knew was growing out of a past with which he was in some kind of verifiable contact and which was different from the present, and that this same present was pointed into a future destined itself to be vastly different from both the present and the past. Today we are taught from elementary school on that earlier ages of the universe differed vastly from later ones, and this notion has become so commonplace that we find it hard to imagine human beings unaware of it. Yet it is safe to say that until quite recent generations most human beings were generally unaware of this fact. Man could become aware of it only when he had methods of probing into the past far enough and accurately enough to be struck by the changes between one period and another, in human culture, learning, and finally in physical and cosmic environment.

By the time of Diderot's *Pensées sur l'interprétation de la nature* in 1754, the sense of a present involved in a past and future vastly different from itself and from one another is manifestly part of the informed Western outlook:

> Could not the philosopher . . . suspect that life had its individual elements scattered and mixed in the mass of matter; that it happened that these elements united because it was possible for this to happen; that the embryo formed of these elements has passed through an infinitude of organization and development; that it has acquired in succession movement, sensation, ideas, thought, reflection, conscience [*conscience* in the original French, which means either consciousness or conscience but seems to signify the latter here], feelings, emotions, signs, gestures, sounds, articulation, language, laws, sciences, and arts; that millions of years have elapsed between each of these developments; that there are perhaps other developments to be undergone and other paths of growth to be followed which are as yet unknown to us.[1]

This passage from Diderot and other passages quoted in H. F. Osborn, *From the Greeks to Darwin,* can serve to remind us that perhaps the ultimate triumph to date of the evolutionary outlook is the knowledge that the evolutionary outlook itself was arrived at by an evolutionary process. Diderot is writing over a century before Charles Darwin's great work *On the Origin of Species,* and yet it is no discredit to Darwin's genius to state that, given the awareness evident in the Diderot passage, the discovery of the principle of natural selection, not only in its primordial Darwinian form but also in its later modifications and refinements was only a matter of time. The insight which Darwin was to crystallize in his work, so brilliantly and scrupulously written and so often painstakingly revised, and to make current with the aid of his remarkable gift for catch phrases—"origin of species," "natural selection," "survival of the fittest,"[2] "struggle for life," to name only a few—was not entirely his own. This insight was itself evolving in the minds of men as they passed on from generation to generation their accumulated records of past experience and their growing reflections on what they knew of the past.

Indeed, by some strange sort of fatality, the very origin of the *Origin of Species* provides evidence of the most explicit and spectacular sort concerning the corporate and gradual origin of human discoveries. For a great many of Darwin's most original insights were on his own humble admission arrived at by at least one other individual at the same time in the same intellectual milieu. The correspondence in 1858 between Darwin and the somewhat younger Alfred Russel Wallace is a commonplace item in the history of ideas. In it we can see the convergence of the two men's individual lights in the theory of natural selection, made explicit in their famous joint communication to the Linnean Society. The case alerts us to a state of affairs which other cases confirm: discoveries are not so much stumbled upon as developed. Knowledge itself is a communal affair and evolves communally. The most an individual can hope to contribute to the process is what we have recently learned to style a "breakthrough" in a front of activity which must be on the whole cooperative rather than purely personal. Because it develops communally, the structure of human knowledge must be explained not only in terms of its various logics. It must also be explained sociologically. The accounts of Henry Ford or Thomas Alva Edison of Max Planck or Albert Einstein working out utterly new inventions all by themselves—normally in cold and ill-lighted attics—belong with Horatio Alger literature or the old Tom Swift books. Reality is something different.

II

When we look back of the Darwin-Wallace correspondence to the discoveries and reflections of men who preceded them, we find even more unmistakably how thoroughly their great discovery or "breakthrough" was dependent on the painstaking work, brilliant intellectual risks, and brilliant insights of others and how much it was dependent also upon obscure and individually uncontrollable, but immensely influential, psychological and sociological forces of which Darwin's own age could hardly be explicitly aware since we are only now learning to identify them.[3]

Evolutionary thinking can be discerned taking dim but real shape in the philosophy and science of the rather remote pre-Darwinian age and in a general build-up of the historical dimension of all thinking. In his *Scienza nuova* Giambattista Vico (1668–1744) focuses attention on development, and this focus is intensified in philosophical thought through Hegel (1770–1831) and Schelling (1775–1854). Auguste Comte (1798–1857) proposed a philosophy built on considerable knowledge of social development as well as on massive theories about the nature of this development. Karl Marx's 1848 *Communist Manifesto* involves still more theories about the nature and inevitability of change, social and other.

Evolutionary thinking was found taking shape at an early date not only in philosophy itself but also in the natural sciences, which even as late as the nineteenth century were regarded, as they were through the Middle Ages and the Renaissance, as part of philosophy, as "natural philosophy." The German philosopher Kant (1724–1804) like the French astronomer Laplace (1749–1827) faced into the problems of the cosmos as it was known to the new astronomy and proposed nebular hypotheses to account for the present state of the universe by a theory of stellar evolution. Descartes and Leibnitz had already bruited abroad the idea that the earth could have gone through a molten stage. Such unfamiliar stages had tended to be explained as aberrations or catastrophes. But in the eighteenth and the nineteenth centuries the English geologists James Hutton (1726–97) and Charles Lyell (1797–1875) discarded the older catastrophic theories in favor of uniformitarian explanations. Catastrophism had viewed the present state of the universe as due to earlier, mysteriously violent deviations from some more pacific "natural" order. These deviations or catastrophes were supposed to be inexplicable in terms of still operating physical processes. Uniformitarianism took for granted that past states of the universe which account for present conditions are themselves explainable in terms of processes subject to the same physical laws as are now operating and verifiable.

Hutton and Lyell did not of course destroy catastrophism. Such a theory still persists in our own day in the minds of many who feel that the only cosmology possible to the devout is one which proceeds by a series of abrupt changes initiated by special interventions of God. To this mind, although the universe was evolving for billions of years toward the point where life, at least on our planet, became possible, nothing short of an abrupt divine intervention breaking sharply with earlier processes can account for the appearance of the first living organisms. In this catastrophic view, although the first human remains in the five or ten billion year history of our universe appear after the patient elaboration over billions of years first of larger and larger molecules out of which organic substances can be synthesized and then of more and more highly developed organisms which finally approximate man in external form, and although these first human remains appear in the very epoch when the organisms approximating man were in full developmental career, one must conceive of the human body as having nothing to do with this stupendous cosmic process. Rather, one must imagine it as being formed quite suddenly from those materials alone—various aluminum salts or other clay-like matter—which had reached their more or less stable forms relatively early in the process of cosmic development and had not passed through any of the later organic transmutations.

The survival of catastrophism in one or another form and the tendency to link catastrophism with a religious view of the universe confused the issues in many religious circles, but it could not stop the development of evolutionary theory in the natural

sciences. By the late eighteenth century Erasmus Darwin (1731–
1802), Charles Darwin's grandfather, was working with the idea
that species are not separated by chasms from one another but
rather connected through intermediate forms in lines of descent,
and Lamarck (1744–1829) had produced his theory of use in-
heritance which Charles Darwin's theory of natural selection su-
perseded. At this time, the term "biology" itself, proposed independently in 1802 by Lamarck and S. T. Treviranus, came into
use, so that the very science of biology, insofar as it can be considered a distinct knowledge, is itself a product of the evolutionary
milieu.

In both philosophy and the natural sciences the interest in evolution was a product of the visions of history which were forming
in men's minds. These visions were not very clear, and yet they
were both fascinating and productive. Although they had to do
with change, these new visions were not quite the same as those
of the older philosophies which had been more interested in becoming in general, with coming into being as contrasted with the
act of existence. The newer visions concerned themselves with
series of individual events which were each unique and yet in some
sense, real but difficult to fix, a part of a pattern.

One can, of course, make a distinction between evolution and
history. Evolution can refer to developments in the cosmos independent of human culture, and history can refer to developments within human culture itself. Of these two concepts, history,
while in a way more constricted, is nevertheless the dominant
notion in the sense that the discovery of evolution is a historical
event, since it takes place in human culture and not outside.
Moreover, since history is closer to him, man has approached
evolution by reflection on history first, so that evolution will
always remain for him something associated with history and
understandable in terms of this association. Here we shall speak
of history in the common intertwined sense in which it refers
primarily to human history but also involves as occasion offers,
the development of the universe itself before men and since.

Determining what the pattern of history is had long disturbed
men and still disturbs us. For, although there are true histories
and false histories, all history is selective, so that one can have
as many histories—and true ones, too—as he wishes, depending

on what items one selects in one's reporting. The number of histories is potentially infinite. The difficulty in finding a pattern which is *the* pattern lodges in the fact that history, whatever else it does, never really repeats itself. Every event is unique. This is what brought Aristotle to state in his *Art of Poetry* that history is less philosophical than poetry itself, which is certainly unphilosophical enough if by philosophical one means, as Aristotle did, capable of treatment in universal terms.

The one way to cast history in these terms is to transmute its singular happenings into universals, and the readiest way to effect this transmutation is to imagine that time is cyclic and as a consequence the history of the universe is, too. That is to say, everything that is now happening has happened before an infinite number of times and will happen an infinite number of times again, so that there is really nothing singular ever possible at all. One can bolster this view by selecting details in history which, put together, form a pattern of rise and fall, waxing and waning, ascent and decline, and so on—spring, summer, autumn, winter. These cyclic patterns are of course really there, provided only that one takes note of the proper details (those which relate to such patterns) and passes by the others (those which do not).

From the time of the most ancient philosphies men have been adept at noting the proper details to discern the cyclic patterns. Cyclic views of history have apparently been the dominant views. They appear in Hindu thought, in the pre-Socratic philosophers and through the ancient Greeks generally, on down through Joachim de Flora (1145–1202) and others to Spengler and Toynbee in our own day. Cyclicism is so pervasive that it obtrudes itself unnoticed in historians, artists, and others who seemingly have never adverted to the fact that their frames of thought have an unmistakably cyclic cast. Thus we have cultural developments explained in terms of a New England spring, summer, Indian summer, and so on—although no winter has been acknowledged as yet. A recent literary historian, Robert E. Spiller, organizes not merely North Atlantic literature but all American literature circularly in his title *The Cycle of American Literature: An Essay in Historical Criticism* (1955), just as E. I. Watkin in his *Catholic Art and Culture* had organized the history of Western art into a classical autumn, Christian spring, medieval summer,

Renaissance Indian summer, baroque autumn, and modern winter, thereby making it rather evident that either art is going to have to go completely out of existence because its possibilities are all exhausted or we are headed directly into a glorious spring. There are many early and detailed precedents for this sort of thing. Between 1720 and 1750 Iohannes Nicolaus Funccius had published in Marburg and Lemgo his five books in Latin entitled respectively (in translation) *The Childhood, Adolescence, Imminent Old Age, Vigorous Old Age,* and *Helpless Broken-Down Old Age of the Latin Language.* This kind of construct is revealing. It works so long as one views Latin and Roman culture as not particularly derivative from anything else and as not destined to feed into anything else. The moment one regards Italian, Provençal, Catalan, French, Spanish, Portuguese, Rhaeto-Romanic and Roumanian as variants of Latin—which they are—the entire picture shifts and the rise-and-fall construct no longer accounts for the facts, since in modern French Latin is still on the rise, unless one detects a cycle in French literature, too.

These cyclic patterns occur not only among historians operating in the field of belles-lettres but in the visions of painters, too. The well-known series of paintings by the English-born American Thomas Cole (1801–1848) entitled "The Course of Empire" is a case in point. It is discussed in the next study here.

In his brilliant book *The Myth of the Eternal Return* Mircea Eliade has exposed the psychological roots of the drive to detect among the details of history a cyclic pattern which will make plausible a totally cyclic view of time itself. Cyclic theories of time accomplish for the learned what the mythological rituals of the seasons accomplish for the intellectually unsophisticated. Both mitigate the terror of history, in which events, and most of all man's personal decisions, are set forever in an irreversible pattern. Cyclic theories tend to cushion or distract from time's impact, dissociating time from unique acts, for in the extreme or pure cyclic view of the universe nothing is unique at all, since even our most personal decisions have been and will be made over and over again. Mythological rituals, more or less seasonal in their celebration and to this extent associated with a cyclic pattern, draw attention from real events to mythological archetypes which are not referable to any real time. To ask a Greek, for example,

when, in what year of the universe, Dionysus was torn to pieces
by the Maenads, is to miss the whole point of the myth. These
things took place somewhere outside time. Their extra-temporal
status gave the myths their psychological value. By referring actual temporal occurrences in one way or another to them, these
temporal occurrences could be disinfected of the curse of time.
Pagan religious views generally register a human aversion to time,
providing at least a subconscious refuge from time's evils.

By contrast the Hebrew and even more the Christian revelation presents time as a good. This point has become a commonplace one in contemporary theology, Protestant as well as Catholic. For the Hebrew, revelation, initially given to an ancestor,
Abraham, who was seen quite definitely as inside history, was
kept alive through a historical people, Abraham's descendants.
For Christians, the Hebrew view was retained and supplemented
by a more momentous historical incident, the Incarnation of the
Son of God, Himself God, together with His subsequent death
and resurrection—all events datable, even today, with greater
surety than all but a few events of secular history. The Christian
view sees Christ as anchored in time in at least three ways. First,
like other men, He is born and dies at one certain time and no
other. But secondly, unlike other men, He appears at the ma-
turing of a special long-term development which calls for His
appearance. He is expected as other men are not. He culminates
the history of the Chosen People by putting an end to an intent
wait of centuries. And thirdly, the centuries-long history of this
Chosen People was itself, according to the common Christian
teaching, not only a wait or watchful preparation but also a pre-
figuration or foreshadowing of His own life and work.

Thus faced squarely into time and at home in it, the Christian
as such has no need for either mythological archetypes or cyclic
theories of the sort studied by Eliade. Yet we do find both these
pagan phenomena widespread among certain Christian populations. Notably, in medieval European culture biography is written
according to these patterns. The medieval saint's life is too frequently fitted to a pre-existent archetypal pattern in which even
the points at which the miracles are supposed to occur are pre-
determined, and the familiar secular biography such as is found
in the *Mirror for Magistrates* or Lydgate's *Fall of Princes* is often

based on a spectacularly cyclic design, the wheel of Fortune. When such pagan patterns occur among Christians, they can be regarded as pagan survivals. Only after the Renaissance did Christians learn to write biography in a more genuinely Christian way by centering attention on the shaping action of the human will and its decisions.

Modern theology has come to speak of the Christian (and Hebrew) sense of time as "linear" rather than cyclic. Oscar Cullmann and many others have made much of this view. The concept of linearity has its disadvantages here, for the Christian and Hebrew sense of time is by no means so spatialized as the term "linear" suggests. It is more interior and psychological, or "human," and, besides, it does involve certain considerations which, when they are handled geometrically, are best handled by analogy not with straight lines but with circles, as Père Gaston Fessard has shown in his brilliant study, *La dialectique des Exercices spirituels de Saint Ignace de Loyola*. Nevertheless, there is a sense in which the Christian and Hebrew sense of time can be said to be linear by contrast with cyclic views. For the Christian the soul's journey through time is a development: the soul starts out in one state and ends in quite a different one in which its career or spiritual evolution has fixed it. In a parallel fashion, the Hebrew and Christian world vision sees the universe in linear time: contrary to the conviction of Aristotle and a host of others, matter is not eternal, but the universe is created in one state and at the end of time will somehow be transfigured, different from what it has been. Christ is incarnate at a certain point in time, and this point is never reached again.

It is true that earlier Christians were ignorant of the full dimensions of cosmic time. As late as St. Robert Bellarmine and even later, we find theologians and others as well quite convinced that from the creation of the world to the expected end of time was a matter of some six thousand years, and the first Christians had done their thinking, it seems, in an even more telescoped temporal world view. It is likewise true that earlier Christians had no idea of the fact that the universe was actually evolving from day to day during their own lives, if on a scale so disproportionate to a single human life that no one person alone could be directly aware of the changes going on. What is important, however, in the Christian tradition is not the statistical errors or observational deficiencies of earlier Christians, but the total frame of mind which Christian teaching fosters. The Church herself has never been specific about the age or life expectancy of the present universe or about its day-to-day stability. Chiliasm in various forms has been recurrent, it is true, but always as an aberration. Hence, despite the defects of the world view in which Christians conceived revelation to be operating, the way for an evolutionary view was as a matter of fact kept open by Christian teaching. For in any view, however otherwise scientifically erroneous, a Christian who followed the teachings of the Catholic Church had to allow for a beginning of the universe and an ending which was different from the beginning. This sense of difference between beginning and end is congenial to evolutionary views. Cyclic views of time and the universe are not.

III

When one reviews in the larger perspective suggested here the developments in thought and in world outlook which precede and accompany the work of Charles Darwin, one is struck by certain relationships between the evolutionary outlook and Christianity. The two seem curiously congenial to each other. The evolutionary outlook has grown up in an intellectual setting prepared by Christianity under the influence of the time sense which Christianity very really if not always with full consciousness encourages. For, like the Christian view, the evolutionary view involves a certain "linear" rather than cyclic sense of time.

The discovery of evolution has opened a vision of the universe which at the beginning is in a condition from which it departs never to return. The progressive changes in the cosmos, moreover, do not consist simply in a running down, as was thought when the second law of thermodynamics, the Carnot-Clausius law, was taken as the ultimate determinant of cosmic activity. According to this law, the universe is tending toward a state of complete equilibrium. The mountains will all eventually wash into the sea, hot things will lose heat to cooler things until all are of a uniform temperature, and so on. We know now that the story is more complicated than this. There is also a winding-up process in the universe, the process according to which life evolves upward in more and more complex, more and more intense forms. For, although there is some regressive organic evolution, the pattern of life on the whole is certainly one of progress.

Life is a struggle upward, a struggle against odds, but on the whole a victorious process. This conviction lies back of Darwinian and other evolutionary views in which the whole of organic evolution is a kind of ascesis, a struggle from worse to better, curiously like the career of the Christian soul. Indeed, it is not difficult to show that Christian asceticism, subtly transmuted, has formed much of the framework for Darwin's thinking. This is all the more interesting when one recalls that this same framework could not be provided by many other religions which regard life as a process in which one relaxes his hold on himself to lose himself finally in some dissolution.

But does what we know of cosmic evolution really accord with Christianity by rigidly excluding the possibility of cyclic time? Is not a throbbing universe possible, and does not such a universe involve cyclic time? That is to say, speaking in a somewhat oversimplified fashion, could it not be that the present expanding universe arose from the explosion of some sort of super-atom and that this universe will ultimately contract into the super-atom only to explode again, and so on indefinitely, so as to give us an infinite series of successive universes? And does not all this suggest cyclic time, with the same events recurring infinitely?

It would seem not. The discovery of evolution has undermined cyclic views even more than would at first blush appear. In the universe as we now know it, there exists no real model or analogue for cyclicism—that is, for identical and inevitable repetition of an event at two (much less at an infinite number of) points in time.

The grossest model for cyclicism is and has been the path of the earth around the sun. The old cyclic myths and cyclic cosmologies had assumed the permanence of the earth-sun relationship, which they commonly conceived in terms of a path of the sun around the earth. But today we know this relationship is not permanent. The path of the earth around the sun is by no means stable. It has come into being by a series of changes, and continues to undergo evolution at a rate which is measurable, although quite disproportionate to the span of human life. No season is, as a matter of fact, quite like any other, and in their succession, although there are so-called cycles of approximate repetitions, the over-all pattern is that of a one-directional change.

Even if the universe is expanding as the result of a primordial explosion of some sort of super-atom (as George Gamow and others conjecture), and if one assumes that it will eventually contract back into the super-atom only to explode and begin evolving again, all the indications we have from the world-in-time-around-us would suggest that, if we face into real particulars and details, the second of these two evolutions would be not the same as the first, but different from it somewhat as year differs from year, or one chain of evolution (European fauna and flora) from another (American fauna and flora). One assumes that two successive cosmic evolutions would be identical on the suspicion that they are like two successive years or eras; but we know now that two successive years or eras are not quite identical. One can set up a mathematical model for cyclic succession, of course, but there remains the problem of finding something in reality which at least hints that reality accords with the mathematical model. Nothing appears to be available. It appears that cyclic theories of cosmic evolution and of history depend upon setting up such a model or construct, for which one can find no exact counterpart anywhere in the universe, and upon using this model, despite everything, as though it applied to reality.

Perhaps it should be added that the highly poetic continuous creation theory put forth by Professor Fred Hoyle seems to leave even less room for exact repetition of events than any of the theories it proposes to replace. It is designed to counteract the Carnot-Clausius law rather than to contradict the view that individual things are different in the end from in the beginning. In this theory, although the universe as a whole does not begin all at once, every assignable item in it most certainly does begin and move through irreversible developmental states. The "background material" continuously created for the formation of clouds of interstellar gas and galaxies is certainly different at the time of its creation from what it is afterward.

Cyclicism is even further disqualified when one considers something further about the evolution of the cosmos which is all too often left out of consideration. That is that the cosmos gives birth to the human person in its utter particularity and uniqueness. In *The Phenomenon of Man* and elsewhere, Pierre Teilhard de Chardin, S.J., has made the point that cosmologies which view the physical universe without regard to the fact that it has given birth to the human person are not only incomplete but impossibly distorted and misleading. Too often a cosmology accounts to some degree of satisfaction for everything except human beings, who appear as some sort of monstrous intrusion on the scene. This is true even when a cosmology does account in some way for the evolution of the human body, explaining its relationship to, and probable line of development from prehuman forms. For, frequently enough, such a cosmology lets the matter go at that, failing even to ask the question as to what the human person, this mysterious self, this interiority, inviolable, known only to me and to God, has to do with the process of cosmic evolution. For it certainly has something to do with this evolution. The universe prepared itself for some five or ten billion years for the advent of just this mysterious self, this interiority, this uniqueness which I am—and which every human being is. How is the process of cosmic evolution related to me?

Both the Christian and the pagan must face this question. And up to the present seldom has either done so. Indeed, it seems that neither knows how to do so as yet. Yet the fact is that the development of the universe to date has had direction and that the direction leads not up to or around or parallel to but into the human consciousness itself. Cosmic evolution has certainly been a process of greater and greater complexification or interiorization of existent things. Without opting for any one of the various theories regarding the initial stages of our universe, we know that there was a time when the matter of which our globe is composed was simply too hot to make it possible for anything more complicated than simple inorganic molecules to exist—probably for a time too hot for even molecules to exist at all, so that everything was retained in a simple atomic structure. Cooling made possible the formation of crystals, organized according to a pattern which is interior in that it is determined by the internal molecular structure of the crystal but which is not very intensely interior in the sense that a crystalline structure is open: it tends to hook on to its borders further molecules without any particular limit. As the earth cools still more and the present continents and seas take shape, the gigantic protein molecules form. Despite their relatively massive sizes, these molecules are more organized in terms of an interior than are the molecules making up inorganic crystals. They do not grow by simple accretion, but have their own peculiar structural equilibrium to maintain without accretion. Their interior exists in a state of tension with the exterior around them. It seems that some of the protein molecules or some of the things very close to them such as viruses, are able to reproduce themselves, not out of their own substance but by generating next to themselves, in certain media with which they may be surrounded, others like themselves. Higher forms of organization, which are generally regarded as properly living, have a still higher interiorizing component. Out of their interior organization, they generate other beings with there own interior organizations. The build-up of interiority reaches its maximum in man, who has the reproducing capacity of lower forms of life plus an interior and transcendent awareness of self which is so peculiarly his own that it cannot be communicated to others. But inside this awareness communication with others can take place. Indeed communication in human society, although it uses external media of all sorts, is basically a transaction between two or more unique and inviolable interiors.

This is a most inadequate sketch of incredibly complex and beautiful stages in cosmic development. But it may help to convey a sense of the way in which the human person is not adventitious but in a very profound sense native to the material universe. Each human soul, it is true, is created by a direct act of God. When I reflect on the interior self which I am, examine this sense of "I" which I alone have, it yields no evidence that it is descended from anything at all. I alone know what it feels like to be myself. Even my father and mother have not known what it feels like to be me. They have no direct consciousness of me such as my own consciousness of myself, nor do I have any direct consciousness of them. To say that my soul, as evidenced to me in my consciousness, is "descended" or derived from these or any other souls has no meaning. This "I" is unique and inaccessible. This isolation of each person, his being on his own, underived from other consciousnesses, is the glory and the terror of human existence. I cannot be duplicated even in the intelligence of another man, as I should have to be were he to know me as immediately as I know myself. Moreover, I know my uniqueness and induplicability in simply knowing myself as I do. With some three billion people in the world, no person in complete possession of his faculties is in the least worried that one of the other three billion will turn out to be a duplication of himself. The present population figure could be doubled or squared without occasioning the slightest alarm on this score. No man is an island, and yet each possesses himself alone. Each of these individual selves is the product of a direct act of God which is truly "special" in the sense that it brings into existence a special soul and consciousness, which will always remain unlike every other, a true person.

And yet these persons are born of the universe in which they live. They do not arise outside it. Matter is prepared for the human soul not merely by the body of a mother and a father; long before any human generation becomes even thinkable, it has to be organized by the evolution of the entire universe over a period of billions of years. For the material things around us, the inorganic matter and even more the organic matter from which we derive our nourishment, are not constitutive of the material universe in its primitive state. Primitive atomic matter must be elaborated by mighty cosmic forces which simultaneously distribute it into the galaxies and solar systems of today and give it the progressively higher and higher interior organization which produces the complex chemical forms with which we are surrounded and inside which we must live. The material in our bodies is billions of years old, and during these billions of years it has not been lying about in a relatively stable condition as had been supposed by Western man up until some few hundred years ago, when the material things around us had been regularly explained in terms of varying combinations of the stable elements earth, water, air, and fire. Built up of these, things were differentiated, it had been thought, without reference to time, by specific natures. Today we know that the very organization of matter is a coefficient of its age. Four billion years ago a protein molecule was not a possibility anywhere in our surroundings. Matter had not sufficiently developed to produce this elaborate structure.

It took much longer for matter to be capable of the incredibly tight organization found in the human body. Nevertheless, over a period beginning with the emergence of life some one billion or more years ago, living beings did develop progressively more and more elaborate organization, more and more "complexifica-tion" or intensity of life. At a point where living organisms ap-proximating the present human body finally were appearing, the first human soul is created by God, infused within a body in the material universe. This is, of course, a special act of God, for the creation of the human soul is always a special act of His, since the soul in its spirituality transcends the merely material. Moreover, God's freedom to create or not to create the universe at the start was of course absolute. But given the created and developing universe, it seems to compromise the divine wisdom to suggest that the creation of the first human soul was not called for at this point in a way analogous to that in which the creation of one's soul was called for when the germ cells from the bodies of his parents united. Is it possible to think that after five or ten billion years of elaboration, God might have simply let the ripe-ness of time go by? might have out of some whim simply failed to bring into being the first soul? To think this would seem to com-promise God's fidelity to Himself. For we know enough of the story of an evolving cosmos to know that cosmic development had been pointing for billions upon billions of years to a certain fullness of time when material being had finally reached a point in which its spiritualization through a rational animal was pos-sible. Because of this gigantic cosmic preparation, of which the preparation of the human ovum and sperm is only a kind of tiny echo, it seems quite proper and necessary to say that the whole cosmos gave birth to man. As a mother, it prepared the material for his body and, while not creating his human soul, presented him to the light of day.

The birth of man in the cosmos is striking evidence against cyclicism if further evidence is really needed. For here we have the cosmic processes terminating not in repetition but in its an-tithesis, the utterly unrepeatable and unique human person.

But the story of the universe is not complete with the appearance of man, or even with the evolution of human society up to the present. As the story of the universe moves on today, man is finding out more and more about his origins in the physical world in which he lives. We are living in an age in which man is identifying himself more and more with the material universe by pinpointing the network of connections between himself and the rest of God's material creation. Darwin's discoveries mark a stage in this movement whereby man finds himself more and more truly by finding the cosmos in which he lives. This movement is the contrary of that of Platonism and other ancient philosophies which drift away from a consideration of this world to a world of separated and supposedly "pure" ideas. The Platonic ideas are visually conceived in the sense that they are conceived by considering intellectual activity as analogous to vision and what we know intellectually by analogy with the objects of sight. *Idea* itself is the Greek cognate of the Latin *video* and of our English "vision." This reliance on vision yields a world of "objects" which are "clear and distinct," and quite directly produces the old Platonic and Aristotelian notion of "species," each cut off from one another, or, to use the more standard word signifying the same thing, "defined" one against the other. Darwin's discoveries represent a direct assault on this visualism, for in his account of the origin of species all distinctness is lost in a blur of variants, potentially infinite in quantity and always at least incipient in the mere differentiation of individual from individual, although how far incipient depends somewhat on how far macroevolution dominates microevolution (if the two are effectively distinct at all).

The complaint has been made that the Darwinian view as against the Platonic focuses on this world and not on the world of spirit. Darwin is preoccupied with the story of the human body rather than of the human soul. Plato is interested in the soul and his "eternal verities." And what is the story of the body compared to my immortal soul? Yet there is something profoundly Christian in the Darwinian conception which is missing in the Platonic. For, although the Christian knows by his faith that the human soul is immortal, insistence upon the survival of the soul after death is not a distinguishing feature of divine revelation. It is not met with in most of the Old Testament, and in the New Testament, while it is supposed, it is enveloped in the more important Christian doctrine of the resurrection of the body. Fascination with the survival of the soul is a mark of certain pagan philosophies. The resurrection of the body—born of this universe—is an article of faith distinctively Christian. Christian writers such as Father Robert W. Gleason in *The World to Come* have made this point, and the point needs making more frequently. The pagan may look forward to getting rid of his body and of this universe. The Christian does not look forward to this at all.

The world view which is opening out before us in our post-Darwinian world is thus one eminently congenial to a follower of Christ. For the universe in which we are finding man to be so profoundly at home—if at the same time so profoundly ill at ease, for we cannot deny this side of his experience although for want of time we must scant it here—is after all God's universe. It is sad that to date Christians are so ill-equipped intellectually to appreciate this universe, much less to elucidate it in a Christian light to others. If one were to ask what is most needed in Catholic intellectual and educational circles today, I should reply without hesitation a real cosmology, and a philosophy and theology which see man in the full time perspectives of the universe we know and which talk about him habitually in these perspectives.

But in the evolutionary picture is not man shrunk to a mere nothing? A conservative low figure for the age of the universe is five billion years. If we imagine that a moving-picture film had been made of the universe from a beginning five billion years ago up to today and that the film is shown in fast motion, speeded up so that the five-billion-year-long run is crowded into two hours, the period from the time when the first aquatic vertebrates evolved to the present day would be just over nine and a half minutes. The period of roughly five hundred thousand years from the time of the earliest known chipped stone tools to the present would be a little more than one-half second—a one-half second which would be the most important era of all. If this one-half second of film were itself slowed down to run two hours, the period from the first domestication of animals and plants to the present would occupy only about the last two minutes, and the period between the life of Christ and the present would take the last twenty-nine seconds.

This seems to make man impossibly small and insignificant. And so it does if we view him as though he were a tiny speck fetched from some realm of separated Platonic ideas and inserted into the vast reaches of time and space which the universe fills, or as a being coming into existence in an Aristotelian-type universe, an eternal datum cyclically organized. And yet if we view man as something which this universe has built up to out of these vast reaches of time and space, he is not insignificant at all. Before him, the prehuman universe is insignificant. For the supposition we have just made about viewing the universe in its early stages is an impossible one. The universe, for most of its early life, was one in which vision, and a fortiori photography, was an impossibility. For vision becomes possible only with living things, and the universe at first is a universe which will not tolerate any life at all. One cannot validly imagine oneself as picking up by sight a universe which would destroy any seeing organ or indeed any living thing, even though at a later time when it has evolved to another state this same universe will produce sight. This would be like trying to imagine what a mass of molten steel in a blast furnace looks like to one sitting inside the molten steel. One can imagine various combinations of bright yellows and reds and blues and whites. But none really represent the actuality, which is simply and totally invisible—try sitting inside a mass of molten steel and see what you see—because it is simply intolerant of the conditions necessary for sight, or indeed for any of the other senses. Hence it is that any attempt to understand the early universe starting from a sensory image can never be fully successful. Any sensory image we can form of it must give us only an analogue of the reality which of its very nature precluded all possibility of its being sensed. However impressive it may be when we reconstruct it now in our imaginations and minds, and however agitated its hyperactivated molecules and masses, this was a dull and helpless universe at its start, intolerant of anything which might register even the fact that it was there. With the advent of man, this fact is registered. And thus the reconstruction of the brute facts of four or five billion—perhaps ten billion—years ago in man's mind today is more wonderful and impressive than the original facts themselves. Against the backdrop of the infrahuman universe which has given him birth, man remains more impressive than the rest of this universe. For he, as nothing before him, really includes it all. It comes to life and fruition in him.

Even if this were not so, it is against this cosmic backdrop that man must be viewed and, indeed, that God's Providence and revelation to man must be conceived. Against this backdrop the Incarnation took place. Any educated man, and much more any Catholic educator, must view himself and all mankind and God's action in this cosmic scene, and must do so not occasionally but habitually. A Christ projected by our imaginations, consciously or subconsciously, into any universe other than this real one is to that extent unreal. Only with as full as possible an understanding of the universe as it actually has been and is can we hope to realize effectively, with His grace, what is the meaning of His Incarnation in this evolving creation and in this always more and more closely knit human society which through Him was brought into being and through Him and with Him and in Him is being brought to its mysterious fruition.

NOTES

1. Diderot, *Pensées sur l'interprétation de la nature*, LVII, 2, in *Oeuvres complètes de Diderot*, ed. J. Assézat and Maurice Tourneux (Paris, 1875–77), II, 57–58. The translation of this passage in H. F. Osborn, *From the Greeks to Darwin* (New York and London: Charles Scribner's Sons, 1929), pp. 171–72, varies at points from the French text which I have translated here, but not significantly in connection with the present issue.
2. Attributed to Spencer as its originator, but certainly used by Darwin at least in later editions of *Origin of Species*.
3. See Robert Scoon, "The Rise and Impact of Evolutionary Ideas," in *Evolutionary Thought in America*, edited by Stow Persons (New York: George Braziller, Inc., 1956), pp. 4–42. Many of the instances which I give of the general diffusion of ideas contributing to or connected with evolutionary thinking before Darwin or in the milieu surrounding Darwin can be found discussed in this collection of studies or in the many specialized monographs referred to in the notes to the various studies.

6

Nationalism and Darwin

I

THE CONCEPTS with which man registers the reality around him
and with which he does his thinking carry within them the record
of their own history. Thus our ordinary ways of conceiving of
the world which lies around and ahead of us, the world of the
postnationalist age, seem inevitably to perpetuate the concept of
nationalism. To get beyond nationalism, we commonly think of
internationalism or postnationalism or transnationalism, conceiving of what is not nationalism in terms of nationalism itself. The
difficulty here is of course unavoidable, for the next age will
have emerged from nationalism, and our concept of it, too, must
perpetuate the realities of history.

Nevertheless, all our difficulties in conceiving of society are
not of this inevitable sort. Sometimes our concepts are entangled
not with the past but with persistent and distracting irrelevances.
Here I wish to explore one of these, namely, the cyclic model,
the image of a circle, which haunts our imagination as we think
about human society and its growth and which interferes
with the development of a large and many-faceted vision such as
present world conditions demand.

What I propose to discuss in the present paper is a cast of
mind which is often as real as it is elusive. It affects our immigration policies and our education, and in the present paper I have
these themes in mind. But, since I am not an expert in demo-
graphic or political or economic problems, and since my interest
in education is somewhat specialized, it has seemed wisest to organize my own thought around larger ideological and psychological realities in the hope that through the interplay of these thoughts
and the more detailed proposals of others we may come to some
sort of serviceable conclusions.

[83]

II

From the English-born American painter Thomas Cole (1801–48) we have a well-known series of allegorical canvases entitled collectively *The Course of Empire*. There are five paintings in this series, named in succession "The Savage State," "The Arcadian or Pastoral State," "Consummation," "Destruction," and "Ruin." One recalls the old wheel of fortune illustrations in medieval and Renaissance works, in which a man is pictured as rising from a low position on the circumference of fortune's wheel to height, eminence, and glory as the wheel turns to bring him to the top of its revolution, and finally returning to his original lowly and humble place as the wheel completes its cycle. The connection of Cole's titles with the old wheel of fortune is obvious, not only in the case of the last three titles—"Consummation," "Destruction," and "Ruin"—but also in the case of "The Savage State" and "The Arcadian State." For in many typical representations of the wheel of fortune, the man (or, as some representations have it, the ape) on the wheel is pictured not only as allegorically moving upward in society to consummation and down again to ruin, but also, while he moves upward, as acquiring more and more clothing in a way corresponding strikingly with the savage-to-pastoral sequence.

The wheel of fortune is only one correlative of the cyclic structure of Cole's allegorical series. Cole himself wrote a detailed commentary on his series which makes explicit its association with the cycle of hours in the day and the cycle of seasons in the year.

The philosophy of my subject is drawn from the history of the past, wherein we see how nations have risen from the savage state to that of power and glory, and then fallen, and become extinct. Natural scenery has also its changes—the hours of the day and the seasons of the year—sunshine and storm: these justly applied will give expression to each picture in the series.[1]

Here we have not only a philosophy of history but—more important for our present subject—a political philosophy and a world outlook. This outlook, moreover, deserves attention, for it is one which haunts all of us.

III

The phrase "rise and fall of nations" has a familiar and even platitudinous ring. Edward Gibbon's *History of the Decline and Fall of the Roman Empire,* Oswald Spengler's *Der Untergang des Abendlands,* and any number of similar titles immediately come to mind. Few readers of such works have to be convinced of the validity of using a diagrammatic up-and-down, rise-and-fall spatial model as a framework on which to organize the events of history. The rise-and-fall pattern seems quite simply natural, representative of the way in which events of themselves typically occur. The reason for this persuasion is not historical but psychological, as has been shown in circumstantial and profound detail by Mircea Eliade in his book *The Myth of the Eternal Return.* This fact is of great importance here because, as I propose to show, when we cast historical events—or, better, when we select historical events—to fit into a cyclic pattern, we are really in great part determining and severely limiting our concept of what a nation is and has been, and in doing so are vitiating our basic attitudes toward international problems.

The disposition to think of national history in terms of rise and fall has a twofold origin: our tendency to represent a nation to ourselves as an individual human being who is born, lives, and dies, and our related tendency to describe human life, and the "life" of a nation thus assimilated to human life, in terms of a cyclic model, as somehow or other reducible to, or like, a mathematical circle.

The tendency to consider the so-called "life" of a nation by analogy with human life is all but overpowering. The reason would appear to be that to reduce other phenomena to items in our own experience makes them understandable by a kind of empathy. Thus, to conceive of a magnet as exercising "force" seems to make its activity intelligible, by enabling us to imagine ourselves in the "place" of the magnet pulling things along the various "lines" of forces, experiencing imaginatively what the exercise of muscular force would feel like to us, and thereby satisfying ourselves with something like an answer to the question, What makes bits of iron in the vicinity of a magnet behave as they do? Of course the relationship of magnetic "force" to what we experience as muscular force is at best tenuous, and when we have said that a magnet works by "exerting force," we have not said much, at least until we have denuded the term "force" of its common meaning and imposed on it the much later, artificially sustained, technical sense of the physicist. Yet such an answer stills the curiosity of many unhampered by a knowledge of scientific physics, for this conversion of magnetic phenomena in terms of human kinesthetic experience is psychologically satisfying. We need no physics to think of the magnet as vaguely like ourselves.

In a somewhat similar fashion, we feel that we "understand" the so-called "life" of a nation if we liken it to the life which we are personally and individually moving through. That a nation is not an individual, much less a person, that it is not generated in a way at all closely comparable to the generation of a living organism, that many of its activities are only with difficulty likened even in the most remote fashion to the processes of life in an individual—what would the keeping of real estate records correspond to? or the election of the members of a house of representatives? or the enforcement of laws against drunken driving?—these are facts seldom adverted to when we talk of a nation's "life" or its "rise and fall."

There is, of course, some rough analogy between a nation and an individual human being, and the analogy is strengthened by the legal fiction that a nation is a kind of moral person—although this fiction has spectacularly weak points, for the responsibility of a person (provided he is mature and in possession of his faculties) is easy to isolate and deal with, whereas the responsibility of an entire nation is not so at all. Moreover, this analogy between nation and individual is further strengthened by the fact that nations are made up of persons and that persons are prominent in the activities of nations, so that it becomes possible to fuzz the edges of our thinking, making it very plausible that a nation is, after all, a person, if only because it contains so many of them. The nation achieves personality by association. Thomas Hobbes's concept of Leviathan, strikingly illustrated in the early editions of his work known by this name, in which the state or Leviathan is pictured in an illustration as nothing more or less than an oversize man made up of an agglomerate of little men, is the classic example of the confusion which can reign here.[2] Hobbes's idea is, of course, a commonplace one. Recent study has shown how widespread the idea of the *corpus civile* was in seventeenth-century Europe,[3] and we know by experience how common it is in our own day.

The tendency to view national phenomena in terms of a cyclic model is connected with the tendency so to view human life. Lived in a one-directional time pattern, made up at its core of decisions, commitments, which are irreversible and in the strict sense unrepeatable, utterly unique so that no one course of conscious life is in its interior reality interchangeable with any other, human life eludes scientific control or description. Science demands repetition, and no event in the life of any one of us really repeats itself. History never repeats itself. Every day is different from every other as I move physically and consciously through time. Nevertheless there exists the almost irresistible drive to find in this flow some pattern, which means some repetition or grouping, or at least some approximation of a pattern. Since no highly particularized pattern can be discerned, such as would for example correlate the details of one man's life and—more important—his personal decisions or commitments with those of another man, one feels driven back to the simplest of generalized patterns. Mathematically, the cyclic group is the simplest group there is. The circle is structure at its barest and most evident. If the flow of life and of consciousness can be thrown into some sort of cyclic representation, one gains assurance because a circle is a symbol of control; it is the closed system at optimum. The openness of history, its unpredictability, and the related openness of the ego and the human consciousness, can be overcome by man only if history or consciousness can be pulled in, turned back on itself, encompassed. The circle is the simplest form of encompassing. Cyclic views stand for the desire to have reality closed in and in this fashion under control.

The drive of the human mind to impose cyclic patterns upon recalcitrant actuality is documented in detail by Eliade in the work mentioned above and is, of course, a commonplace in psychology. The drive registers in the tendency of individuals, reasonably sane as well as neurotic or psychotic, to represent the self diagrammatically in mandala-like figures featuring the circle and the square, which Carl Jung has so thoroughly studied.

There are, of course, assignable bases for applying a circular model to individual organisms. In the case of the human person, the circle, representing a kind of maximum organization of something closed off around a center, readily stands for the isolated and incommunicable self. Moreover, in living material beings, commonly if not always, an original period of infantile helplessness and ineffectiveness is followed by one of maturity and strength, which in turn is followed by another period of senile weakness. The connection of the activities of certain organisms with the movement of the seasons of the year or with the succession of day and night makes cyclicism more plausible, especially when in a pre-evolutionary cosmology one considers the movement of the heavenly bodies to be invariable, as we know today they are not. Commonly, as Eliade shows, the supposed perfect circularity of the hours and seasons affords man a kind of pattern as a refuge from the terrors of time, always yawning open and unpredictable before him. Literature and art are full of visions which resolve both human life and the supposed life of nations in these supposedly invariable and hence reassuring patterns. Thus Thomas Cole aligns his paintings on *The Course of Empire* (or of a nation, for he uses empire and nation indiscriminately) explicitly with the diurnal cycle of dawn, later morning, noonday, afternoon, and sunset, and also with the cycle of the seasons of the year, and by implication aligns man's life, as the analogue for the life of a nation, with the same cyclic successions of events. Long before, Plato had proposed another type of cyclicism for national history, in which there was a more or less regular round of succession in governmental forms, proceeding from the philosopher king successively to a timocracy, an oligarchy, a democracy, anarchy, tyranny, and—although the full details of the means of succession leave something to be desired— back to the philosopher king again.

Preoccupation with these cyclic resolutions of events in time, carried beyond the biological sphere to cover man's social, political, financial, or other careers, produces biographies based frankly on the old wheel-of-fortune motif which dominated medieval writing until the Renaissance biographers gradually devised ways of dealing with human life patterns more in accord with the Christian ethos than medieval ways of dealing with these things had been. In the typical wheel-of-fortune diagram one pictures the individual fixed on the circumference of the wheel rising—in physical prowess, or socially, or economically, or in any way one wishes to think of him—as the wheel turns, from a position at the bottom to the top of the revolution, only to descend, with the wheel's inexorable turning, to the bottom once more. The limitations of this reduction of life to a cyclic pattern are all too obvious. The weakness of old age is comparable to that of youth in many interesting details, of course. But it is by no means the same thing. The organism does not return to a condition exactly like that in which it started. And to describe a complete circle, such an exact return would be requisite. One can make use of the circle model only as the result of a careful selection of details, and the calculated elimination of others.

A special disqualification of the wheel motif applied to biological organisms is the fact that, if we take the totality of organisms in our world, the wheel motif does not really apply even approximately to the majority of them, for most of them never reach maturity to describe even an approximate circle. Furthermore, however well the rise-and-fall or circular pattern may conceivably apply in some approximation to biological life, it hardly works for moral life. A person's moral life would have to be described in terms of all sorts of trajectories—not only up-and-down, but leveling off, skyrocketing, plunging, "bottoming out," or an irregular and unpredictable succession of these and other movements.

Most of all, however, it is the discovery of the fact of evolution which embarrasses cyclic theories. Evolution has dealt what is probably a death blow to the plausibility of all explicit cyclicism, although the projection of cyclic patterns from the subconscious will no doubt continue with man indefinitely.

The remoteness of cyclicism from actuality is particularly evident in terms of studies in population genetics. At this point we can turn our attention from individual to nation, asking whether, even if in some way a cyclic model can be used to describe the course of human life, it can in any effective way apply analogously to the so-called "life" of a nation. If we take a nation in terms of its biological structure we have what biologists call a population. Can populations be considered effectively as individuals? If an individual hamster moves to a kind of maturity or maximum and then declines, will a population of hamsters do the same? It appears not so at all. If a kind of circular pattern can be used to describe in a very, very rough way the individual's life "cycle," has a similar pattern proved serviceable in describing the life or structure of a population? So far as I can find, the geneticists do not use it. Rather, the "career" of a sexually reproducing population as shown in patterns of descent worked out by geneticists shows three characteristic structures; none of them cyclic: (A) a pairing and branching structure (representing the interaction of individual lives); (B) an interlacing structure (representing descent within a single species); and (C) a branching or bushy structure (lineages representing larger evolutionary developments).[4]

It will be noted that these structures are all "open" with reference to the time coordinate, not closed in on themselves as is a circle. They do not turn back or repeat themselves but move ahead through a potentially infinite number of changes. Although one population may die out—and this population may represent an entire species, for, as everyone knows, large numbers of species no longer exist—nevertheless the perishing of a species is not like that of an individual. For a species may perish by being transmuted into another. Individuals do not perish in this way.

Thus, whatever loose sort of relevance a cyclic construct may have to the course of an individual's life, it has much less to the life of a species. In the case of an individual there is at least in many cases a loosely assignable life pattern of rise-and-fall which makes some sort of closed-in view of the individual life at least plausible. Moreover, in the case of man, the individual consciousness has itself a closed-in quality about it. But, since Darwin's and Wallace's discoveries, it has been evident that a closed-in view, such as cyclic patterns commonly symptomize, is not applicable to population groups, which have built-in tendencies to move in open and unprecedented patterns.

IV

Against this roughly sketched background I should like to set the suggestion that we should be much better off if as far as possible we discouraged the tendency to view nations in terms of human persons and life "cycles." The fact that they are neither persons nor cyclic constructs is, on reflection, so obvious that this suggestion risks being somewhat ingenuous. But I believe that it is not so, for the tendency to make a nation into a person and to impose on its development through time a cyclic pattern is deeply rooted in our consciousness and in our subconscious, where it controls more of our thinking than we may readily believe.

We need to replace the cyclic model with some sort of open model more responsive to historical fact. To conceive of the realities of national existence we need perhaps something like the models used by geneticists in thinking of biological populations or by taxonomists in describing the patterns of organic evolution. These models will of course not apply to the totality either, for a nation is more than a biological unit; it is a culture as well. Yet they promise to supplement old analogies which are still much cruder than these models are.

What is more, we need to make these models penetrate our thinking more than they actually do even in those cases where they are present. Perhaps all of us are still too much under the spell of cyclicism in our unguarded moments. Indeed, one of the great tactical advantages which a Marxist society has over our own is undoubtedly its more realistic view of history deriving from the antipathy of its dialectical views to cyclic contortions of reality. I am not hinting that we should proscribe cyclicism by law and impose another ideology by force. Such methods in the end defeat themselves—it would be interesting to find out how the repressed drive to view things cyclically or fatalistically makes itself felt in the Communist consciousness despite its outlawry in explicit Marxist-Leninist theory. But I do believe that we should make every effort to spread the use of noncyclic models where cyclic models ineffectively persist.

Many fields of knowledge have broken drastically with earlier cyclic views which are obsolete not only in biology but also in archaeology, anthropology, and countless other fields. The old discipline of philology, which had encouraged views of Latin as moving through a series of stages from a rise to a decline and fall and which produced works such as those of Funccius described in the immediately preceding study here, is now being encompassed by linguistics, which views languages not in terms of crypto-cyclic patterns, as purportedly tight and perfect economies of expression betrayed by change into renouncing their supposed selfhood, but rather in terms of open models, as moving by infinitesimal changes through history in a way analogous to that of organisms undergoing evolution. For modern linguistics Latin has not "declined": it has simply, with the help of some healthy hybridization, become Italian, Spanish, French, Provençal, Portuguese, Roumanian, Rhaeto-Romanic, and so on. When a linguistics specialist undertakes to describe a language, he starts from the only place one can start from, not from a sociological unit which supposedly uses a completely unified tongue (there is no such thing and never has been), but from the description of idiolects, that is, the individual language which you or I or some other individual speaks, and which only approximate one another, for close analysis of language reveals that every individual uses it in a way which is slightly, but quite really, different from that of every other individual. The situation is like that in the origin of biological species: languages exist always in terms of slight variants in populations where these variants approximate one another, but in such a way that isolation and a change of environment—not to mention cross-breeding—can produce eventually a new language. Languages are oriented not to monolithic permanence but to actively conservative change.

Cyclic views seem to linger chiefly in historical writing and in all sorts of para-sociological literature. It is true that in many ways we do today explicitly remind ourselves in the social sciences that individual societies are all temporary stages in the development of the human world community, that individual societies are not phenomena returning on themselves, rising out of nothing and returning to nothing, but are rather organizations destined to enter into contact with other comparable organizations and to merge their own acquisitions with the acquisitions of other cultures. But at the very time we are doing this, in histories and in para-sociological literature of many sorts there linger the vast cyclic substructures to our thinking which negate or interfere with our more enlightened views.

These substructures manifest themselves not only in the more sweeping views of general cultural history such as those of Spengler or Toynbee, but in all sorts of more particularized views. Writers of literary history, national or regional, project into their accounts the seasonal cycle, spring, summer, and autumn (prefaced where the climate is right, as in New England, by an Indian summer), although to keep up the courage of their readers, these writers are inclined to bring their cycle to a halt before they come to treat winter.

In writings about art the succession of reputed "seasons" is so notorious and so vulnerable upon close inspection that the magazine *Art News* in May of 1956 published an enormous spoof of cyclicism in art history by Ad Reinhardt entitled "A Portend of the Artist as a Yhung Mandala." In a clever maze of symbols and designs, concentric quadripartite circles and sectioned squares are labeled to show cyclic successions of spring, summer, autumn, winter, corresponding with dawn, high noon, dusk, midnight, wherein the "glorious past" and the "glorious future" are contrasted with the "there-now sordid present" and the "now-here sick present," while in a more distant perimeter there roll in neat quadripartite circular succession primitive-constructivist-romanticism, abstract-impressionist-fauvism, naturalist-expressionist-classicism, and social-realist-cubist-futurism. This is only a fraction of the detail in this interesting "portend," which is perhaps one of the most elaborate pictorial jokes recently published, a kind of illustrated *Finnegans Wake*.

Not only in historical writings about literature and art, but in literary works themselves a cyclic view of the human phenomenon is still likely to assert itself—with owlish kindliness in a person such as Yeats, ironically and comically in James Joyce, militantly and ambivalently in Wyndham Lewis's Vorticist movement, furtively and somewhat noncommittally in T. S. Eliot, forthrightly in Ramon Sender. Of course, in poetic imagery itself fascination with cyclic forms does not by any means indicate an explicit commitment to a cyclic view of history. Frequently it has other roots connecting with our tendency to situate ourselves at the psychological center of reality by thinking in terms of mandalas, combinations of circles and squares, with the self at the center and all else deployed about us. But the persons just named go somewhat beyond this in their addiction to cycles, and in any event the *littérateur's* mysterious preoccupation with cycles, per-

haps as marked in contemporary poetry as it has been at any time
in the past, should alert us to the presence of the circle image
deep in our consciousness and to the danger that it may invade
areas of thinking where it is hardly an asset.

V

The considerations which I am offering here are, I am aware,
tentative and diffuse, and I do not propose them as fully worked
out, as definitive. On the other hand, I do propose them as important in realistic thinking and I hope that they prove pregnant
and germinal. For underneath our particular difficulties concerning problems of international ethics there often lurk basic problems
of conceptualization which are tied in with overtly or latently
cyclic views of society and which invest nationalism with an un-
warranted integrity. We seem not to have fully entered into the
vision of an "open" history to which Christianity invites us, in
which Judaism has seen itself at an earlier time, and through
which Darwin's keen mind achieved its own profound insights.
Too often, when at the conscious level the better-informed twentieth-century man is living in an "open," post-Darwinian world,
a great deal of his thinking remains surreptitiously under the spell
of the more primitive cyclic constructs.

We are faced here with an educational problem of international
dimensions, and one which is too seldom approached interna-
tionally. When we think of education on an international basis,
we are likely to think either of promoting understanding by fa-
miliarizing those of one culture with the ways of other cultures,
or of updating science and technology by bringing underdeveloped
areas up to par in these matters and by improving science and
technology generally everywhere. This kind of international educational effort is certainly important. But it is at least of equal importance that the substratum of our thinking keep abreast of
our scientific constructs. As science and technology help make this
more and more one world, we need to put some effort into dealing with the more basic substructures of our thinking. For it is
out of these substructures that human motivations, and international disasters, grow. Persons, springs of action are less likely to
be what they know about the atom than what they feel about a

country, a race, or a language. We need to get into the depths of our thinking, to examine the models and constructs which we have accumulated there, often without much conscious examination, and to provide ourselves and others with new terms for dealing with such basic human phenomena as nation, race, and language. What good does it do to update a nation scientifically if its concepts, and other nations' concepts of what a nation itself is, remain primitive?

I have tried to indicate here some of the ways in which one particularly assertive model of thinking, the circle, can interfere to keep thinking in a primitive mold where it can no longer afford to remain. Cyclic-model thinking encourages a view of all human phenomena in terms of artificial, closed-off units. It promotes a selfishness which does not even have the advantage of being realistic. Cyclicism represents a retreat from the openness of real history and from the interest in process which is a condition of effective thinking today.

To sum up, we can briefly run over some effects of a cyclic outlook in three related areas already mentioned: in the concept of the nation as a person, in racial *apartheid,* and in attitudes toward language.

Viewed as a person, a state or culture is supposed to have a career with a pattern of rise and fall. The supposed threat of the fall deflects attention from others, induces preoccupation with the state-self instead of interest in the international community. If one could more squarely face the fact that the nation is not a person, is not destined to "die" as a person but on the contrary is a construct which has to unite itself to the rest of humanity, a great deal of energy expended on rear-guard action could be saved and a great many neuroses avoided. Only when we view ancient Rome not as a person who was born and died but as a culture which worked itself into a great many other cultures, including our own, where it continued its "life" in a more complex and universal setting, does the story of the rise and fall of the Roman Empire become what it really is—one view of a highly select group of phenomena which certainly meant something entirely different to those who lived through them. To show the grip which the cyclic, rise-and-fall view has on the mind perhaps my own experience is relevant, since it has no doubt been shared by others: I can distinctly recollect how as a young man I only gradually became aware of the obvious fact that the descendants of the ancient Romans and ancient Greeks are still alive and with us. So thoroughly had the idea of the "fall" of the ancient world taken root in my consciousness that I had long supposed that present-day family connections with this world were quite out of the question. Would it be too naïve to suggest that aberrant and fanatic approaches to national history and historical destiny, such as those of Mussolini, were grounded, in part at least, in similar cyclic views, which made it plausible to undertake to return to a supposedly self-contained nationalism rather than to think in terms of international responsibility? Today how far is concern about "surrender of sovereignty" on the part of our nation or other nations based on the assumption that for one nation to identify itself with another is comparable to a person's abdication of his own personality?

This is not to deny that there is something to the analogy between a nation or a culture and a human person. But the analogy is extremely loose and badly misleading. To consider anything as a person which is not a person is always likely to be misleading, even though it may at the same time be helpful. The anachronisms and sometimes impossible legal situations which arise from the British Admiralty's tradition of considering a ship, for legal purposes, as a person are well known. Considering the corporation as a person, if only a "moral" person, entails serious disabilities, for it means that notions of private, personal ownership and property are projected into a situation where they certainly cannot be made to apply.[5] We have to resort to analogies in our thinking, but when they become too hampering to thought and when other analogies offer themselves, we would often do well to let the old ones go.

Secondly, the doctrine of *apartheid,* whatever its manifold social and economic causes, certainly draws support from a view of race which is "closed" and to that extent cyclic. The *mystique* of racism demands that a "race" be considered to be in some way the descendants of one and only one common ancestor or set of ancestors and that it be considered to have its integrity destroyed rather than fulfilled by contact with other men. Openness, symbolized by intermarriage with other groups, purported to be different "races," is regarded as bad and designated as "mongrelizing." It is obvious that realistic views of immigration problems meet with resistance from the "closed" thought model in use in this view of race as well as in the view of a nation or culture just mentioned.

Thirdly, despite the development of linguistics as a science, language still tends to be commonly viewed in terms of closed, cyclic models and thus to reinforce closed nationalisms. The teaching of normative grammar, with its insistence upon "correctness," perpetuates the conviction that a language is a closed system. It is true enough that we have to teach normative grammar in one way or another, and I certainly do not propose to decry its importance or belittle the labors of those who insist on its observance. But we can complement the normative approach with those current in structural grammar and descriptive linguistics, at least to the extent that we become aware of the provisional and shifting character of grammatical "rules." Unless we can do this we cannot face up to the fact that, as idiolects meet in a dialect or language since our own personal way of speaking is a means of communication, faced outside itself, so each language is also faced outside itself, destined to become in some measure another language, at least until all men have achieved satisfactory communication with one another. In the last analysis every language is designed to enable its users to communicate not merely with a select group of persons who here and now share it, but with all men. Only when all men speak the same language or languages will the development of any language be complete—although, to be sure, in the full sense it will not be complete even then.

In an age when the technologically advanced and the technologically underdeveloped countries are coming closer and closer together, it is particularly important that the vestiges of closed, cyclic thinking be exorcized from our thought regarding human society in all its manifestations. The superiority and inferiority complexes which beset us can be dealt with only if we are deeply and profoundly aware of the fact that our cultures are all to grow together, not into a uniform sameness but in a unified and varied richness. National or cultural inferiority and superiority complexes feed on an improper sense of "we" versus "you." We must be aware that our present "we" and "you" are destined to merge in a greater "we." "No man is an island," as John Donne once observed, and much more absolutely no nation or culture is.

An island is something one can draw a circle around. What I am pleading for is that we become less insular by exorcizing the occult influence of cyclic imagery from all those places in our thinking, political, historical, ethical, and other, where it does not have real applicability. In today's world even so appealing a cyclicism as that of Dante is likely to be more a hindrance than a help. It is noteworthy that the circles in Dante's Paradise derive certainly more from the obsolete Aristotelian universe than they do from biblical or Church teaching. They are the weakest, not the strongest, elements in Dante's construct. But they still have a tremendous appeal.

NOTES

1. Quoted in Marshall Davidson, "Whither the Course of Empire," *American Heritage,* VIII (Oct., 1957), 58. Cole's five paintings are also reproduced in this same place, pp. 52–61.
2. For Hobbes's entanglement in metaphor throughout his purportedly non-metaphorical writing, see Louis Francis May, Jr., "Literary Analysis of Thomas Hobbes' *Leviathan"* (unpublished Ph.D. dissertation, Dept. of English, Saint Louis University, 1959).
3. See Otto Gierke, *Natural Law and the Theory of Society, 1500–1800,* trans. Ernest Baker (Cambridge, England, 1950), esp. pp. 252–54, nn. 92–97. The body politic in Roman thought is treated by Alfred Wikenhauser, *"Die Kirche als der Mystische Leib Christi nach dem Apostel Paulus* (Münster, 1937), and in medieval thought by Ernest H. Kantorowicz, *The King's Two Bodies: A Study in Mediaeval Political Theology* (Princeton, 1957).
4. These are here described after George Gaylord Simpson, *The Major Features of Evolution* (New York, 1955), p. 379. The diagram is also reproduced and discussed in John Maynard Smith, *The Theory of Evolution* ("Pelican Books," Harmsworth, Middlesex, England, 1958), p. 255.
5. See Paul P. Harbrecht, *Pension Funds and Economic Power* (New York: Twentieth Century Fund, 1959); also the writings of Adolf Berle, especially his *Power without Property.*

7

Evolution, Myth, and Poetic Vision

> . . . They say
> The solid earth whereon we tread
>
> In tracts of fluent heat began,
>   And grew to seeming-random forms,
>   The seeming prey of cyclic storms,
> Till at the last arose the man.
> . . . .
> . . . Arise and fly
>   The reeling Faun, the sensual feast;
>   Move upward, working out the beast,
> And let the ape and tiger die.
>   —Tennyson, *In Memoriam*, CXVIII

I

THE INFLUENCE of Darwin upon the poetic and artistic imagination has become a commonplace, documented by a large as-
sortment of studies from Lionel Stevenson's *Darwin among the
Poets* (1932) through Georg Roppen's *Evolution and Poetic
Belief* (1956). And yet, surveying the work of the creative human imagination today, one is struck by the slightness of creative
drive connected with an awareness of evolution, cosmic or organic. It is not that the poets refuse to accept evolution. They ren-
der lip service to it. But it does not haunt their poetic imaginations.

One of the great evolutionary philosophers of our day, Father
Pierre Teilhard de Chardin, has been accused of writing often as
a poet. But we are hard put to find poets who make creative
use of evolutionary insights comparable to Teilhard's. Teilhard
faces forward, into the future, as, in its brighter moments, does
the rest of our world, permeated as it is with evolutionary thinking. But the poets and artists tend to exalt the present moment,
when they are not facing the past. There is here certainly some
kind of crisis concerning the relationship of the poet or artist to
time.[1]

The situation is complicated by the fact that today's poets and
artists generally are acutely aware of the ongoing development

of art itself. The existence of a self-conscious avant garde makes this plain enough. Poetry, together with art generally, has a sense of its own domestic time. But cosmic time, as this has been known since the discovery of evolution, is another matter. Most poets and artists are not much interested in it, even when they are most intently concerned with man, who exists in this time. Writers who do deal with larger patterns of development in time tend to slip into thinly veiled sensationalism, as does George Bernard Shaw in *Back to Methuselah,* or sensationalism not so thinly veiled, as in George Orwell's *Nineteen Eighty-Four,* or they handle cosmic time not very successfully, as does Hart Crane, or half-heartedly as does T. S. Eliot. One feels that, in the last analysis, the poet and artist are not very much at home in an evolutionary cosmos.

II

The basic issue between poetry and evolutionism is seemingly the need in poetry, as in all art, for repetition. The drives toward repetition show in poetry in countless ways—in rhythm, in rhyme, in other sound patterns, in thematic management and plotting (Joyce plots *Ulysses*, which for all practical purposes is a poem in the full sense of this term, to match Homer, as Virgil had in a different way plotted the *Aeneid*). Even the key to all plotting, recognition, is a kind of repetition, a return to something already known.

> And the end and the beginning were always there
> Before the beginning and after the end.

writes T. S. Eliot in "Burnt Norton." [2] *Finnegans Wake* is a serpent with its tail in its own mouth, the ouroboros: the last words of the book run back into its first words.

The preoccupation of poetry and of art in general with repetition is shown at its deepest level in the constant resort to the natural cycle of the year: spring, summer, autumn, winter. Indeed, the cosmic myth of the seasons, with its lesser parts, its contractions, expansions and other variations and projections (the succession of day and night, the imaginary Hindu *kalpa* of 4,320,000,000 solar years, Yeats's elaborate hocus-pocus in *A*

Vision), dominates the subconscious so thoroughly that one can speak of it simply as natural symbolism—all nature symbolism comes to focus here—or even as *the* myth, for, in effect, there is no other. Professor Cleanth Brooks, distinguishing interest in history from interest in nature, notes that in modern poets "the celebration of nature is not tied to a cyclic theory."[3] It is my conviction that it need not be. But even in the writers Professor Brooks cites, such as Dylan Thomas, there is a discernible hankering for cyclicism, and in others he cites, such as Wallace Stevens, who shows keen interest in non-cyclic change, one finds less than a wholehearted welcome of a truly historic view. As we shall see, in place of the continuities of history one finds in Stevens rather a discontinuous series of states of chaos, each separately resolved by the imagination, each resolution, in a sense, being a kind of repetition of foregoing resolutions, with no recognizable progress.

In a perceptive study Professor Northrop Frye has recognized this fact, proffering a classification of the archetypes of literature based on the natural cycle of the year because "the crucial importance of this myth has been forced on literary critics by Jung and Frazer."[4] Professor Frye's first phase is the "dawn, spring and birth phase," concerned with the hero, revival and resurrection, creation, and defeat of the powers of darkness, and having as subordinate characters the father and the mother. This, he states, is the "archetype of romance and of most dithyrambic poetry." The second phase is that of "zenith, summer, marriage or triumph." Here we are concerned with apotheosis, the sacred marriage, and entering into Paradise, and with the subordinate characters of the companion and bride. This is the archetype of comedy, pastoral, and idyll. The "sunset, autumn and death" phase is the third, concerned with the dying god, violent death and sacrifice, and the hero in isolation. The traitor and siren are subordinate characters, and this phase is the archetype of tragedy and elegy. The fourth and last phase is the "darkness, winter and dissolution phase," with its floods, return of chaos, defeat of the hero—the *Götterdämmerung,* accompanied by the ogre and witch as subordinate characters. This is the archetype of satire, as instanced in the conclusion of *The Dunciad.*

Waiving questions as to the applicability of the details of this structure to the actuality of poetry and art, we can see that Pro-

fessor Frye here is presenting us with something on the whole
both real and powerful. Moreover, as he himself observes in the
same place, the natural cycle not only touches poetry in terms of
its themes, imagery, and characters, but also in more pervasive
terms, such as that of rhythm itself, which appears essential for
art, verbal or visual: "Rhythm, or recurrent movement, is deeply
founded on the natural cycle, and everything in nature that we
think of as having some analogy with works of art, like the flower
or the bird's song, grows out of a profound synchronization between an organism and the rhythms of its environment, especially
that of the solar year."

Everyone can recognize the actuality of these rhythms, too.
Spring does come back each year. Day succeeds night, and night
day. Men are born and die. There are, however, certain problems
here in establishing rhythmic patterns. The likening of man's life
to a cycle, for example, is based on an all too obvious distortion:
there is *some* likeness between the helplessness of an old man
and an infant, but to mistake one for the other one would have to be
out of one's mind—here the cyclic myth has asserted its com-
pelling power in consciousness and made plausible in our assess-
ment of human life a pattern which is really not there: the life
of an individual actually ends quite differently from the way it
began. One can think otherwise only by blotting out certain facts.

The same is true with regard to groups of men taken as groups.
In the essay immediately preceding, I pointed out in some detail
that the likening of the "life" of a nation or empire or of a culture
or tribe to the life even of an individual man, and a fortiori to a
perfect cycle in which the end is the same as the beginning, is
quite indefensible and utterly contrary to fact, although by leaving
out of consideration certain obvious facts, by proper selectivity, a
certain analogy, very loose, between a nation and an individual,
and a much feebler analogy between the history of a social group
and circular movement can be made out. But, on the whole,
these analogies probably deceive more than they inform. The
Roman Empire "fell" (returned to its starting point from which
it had presumably "risen") only in a very loose sense. It "died"
only in a very loose sense, too, for it was never really conceived
and born as a human being is. The institutions of the Roman
Empire are still all around us and in us, more widespread today

than ever before, the descendants of its citizens are extraordinarily active over a greater expanse of the world than ever before as mankind becomes more and more unified. Much as a circular area, say a foot in circumference, can be discerned on an absolutely blank blackboard simply by disregarding the rest of the blackboard, so rise-and-fall or birth-and-death patterns can of course be discerned in events in the stream of time by proper selectivity. But what do such patterns explain? We like the rise-and-fall pattern probably less because it informs us about what is actually going on in the world than because it is, after all, a pattern, and the simplest pattern of all, imposed on the field of history, noteworthy for its lack of pattern. The attraction of periodicity operates largely from within the human psyche.

What sort of actuality do the cycles of nature have when we view them in terms of what we know of the universe since the discovery of cosmic and organic evolution? In the last analysis, they do not have much. Rhythms are approximations. Perfect cycles, exact repetitions, recurrences of identical starting points, are not really to be found. Although each winter is succeeded by spring, every year is actually different from every other if we look to details. What lengthier rhythms there may be—several years of drought and several of floods—themselves are not really exact cycles, but approximations of cycles which gradually alter. On the whole, the global climate is changing in some kind of linear-style pattern, for the evolution of the earth is progressing toward an end-point quite different from its beginning. In the cosmos as we now know it, there is no real repetition anywhere, for all is in active evolution. One sees repetition only in the rough, where one does not examine more closely. But the universe is being examined more closely all the time. Weather patterns, to stay with our example, are being fed into computers to give us the remarkably accurate forecasting which has developed over the past decade or so. Climatic changes are being studied as they really occur over telling expanses of time, not as impressionistic constructions fabricated out of the limited experiences in one man's lifetime, inaccurately recalled.

Of course, there is a human dimension to the universe, and in the dimensions of one life, rhythms of repetition humanly identifiable and humanly satisfying are to be found. But the human dimension today also includes a great deal of abstract, scientific knowledge—for science is nothing if not a human creation, since it exists only within the human mind. Our abstract, scientific knowledge, which is now entering so thoroughly into planning as to be eminently real as well as abstract, includes a knowledge of the evolution of the cosmos and of life. This means that, in conjunction with an immediate experience of approximate recurrence we experience also, if we are alert to the world in a twentieth-century way, an awareness of the fact that recurrence does not stand up *in detail*. Quite literally, in the modern physical universe, nothing ever repeats itself. Least of all does history.

The classic model for cyclic repetition, when it was rationalized, had been the supposedly immutable path of the sun around the earth. Now we know not merely that the earth moves around the sun, but also that it moves in a path, not circular but elliptical which is gradually changing its form, in ways which are measurable. The stars are not changeless, but in full evolutionary career. So is our solar system. And the elements themselves are dismembered and reconstituted in the process of cosmic evolution.

One can still project a cyclic model of perpetual repetition upon actuality, pretending that everything now happening happened before an infinite number of times and will happen again an infinite number of times. But study fails to reveal any warrant within actuality itself even for the model. Even if we are living in a so-called "throbbing universe," which expands to a maximum and then over billions of years reverses and contracts to a single, unimaginably hot super-atom only to explode and expand again, all the evidence we have from the universe itself around us suggests that the pattern of events in the second explosion will be different from that in the first. To cap all this antirepetitiveness is the appearance of human life itself in the cosmic process. For each man is a unique individual, utterly different from his fellows, all of them, no matter how many they are. The difference is not merely genetic. It is conscious, as can be seen in identical twins, who have the same genetic structures but quite different consciousnesses, the one "I" utterly distinct from the other. Each of us knows he is unique—that no one else experiences this taste of myself which I know directly, a taste, as Gerard Manley Hopkins put it, "more distinctive than ale or alum." No one in possession of his wits is concerned that one of the other three billion or so persons in the universe today is identical with himself. For each man knows his own induplicability and interior inaccessibilty. In simply knowing himself, each knows that his interior landscape is unique, and open only to his own mind. With man at the term of the cosmic and organic evolutionary process, we thus are aware of the universe in its entirety as building up to maximum unrepeatability, self-conscious uniqueness, singularity folded back on itself.

III

With this kind of awareness, what remains of recurrence as a foundation for poetry and art? We are, of course, as we have seen, still acutely conscious of approximate recurrence to a degree: there is, after all, the evident succession of spring, summer, autumn, winter, repeating year after year. But this basic repetition, and all that goes with it, is no longer at the heart of life in the way in which it used to be. It has been displaced. It is now eccentric. A somewhat sentimental account explains the displacement by urbanization and industrialization: large numbers of men now live far from the wilds of nature or the domesticated life close to nature on the farm. But, more radically, the displacement has come about by the intellectual discovery of the cosmic facts, which are known to persons in rural areas as well as in the cities: we live not in a cyclic, perpetually recurring, but in a linear-type time. I say "linear-type" rather than "linear," because time, being nonspatial, is not entirely like a straight line, either. But it is like a straight line rather than a circle in the sense that events in time end at a different point from that at which they begin. (Whether they are really "strung out" like points on a line is another question: in fact, they are not.) My life at its end is different from what it was at its beginning. The universe, even now, is different from what it was five billion years ago and gives evidence of continued progressive differentiation from its initial stage and all subsequent stages.

The displacement of the sense of recurrence as the dominant human awareness is, I believe, a major crisis, and probably the major crisis, in the arts today. The displacement does not of course affect everyone in society equally. The sensibility of millions of persons even in highly technologized societies is doubtless still dominated by a feeling for recurrence which is functionally little different from that of their ancestors two hundred years ago, at least in many areas of life. They do feel the spring, summer, autumn, and winter as a real part of themselves. But even they are undoubtedly affected more radically than they are consciously aware by the psychological structures of society today, particularly by the stress on planning, whether economic or social or industrial or international or interplanetary. Planning means the conscious control of mind over the elements in nature and spells the end of the dominance of quasi-cyclic experience. With planning, matters end up differently from the way in which they had begun. Moreover, with modern technology, the effect of the seasons—basic to sustaining a sense of recurrence—has been blunted in ways which cannot but be telling, if only subconsciously, for all. A heated and air-conditioned building is pretty much the same in summer and winter, and more and more persons, educated and uneducated, are spending more and more time in such buildings. Transportation, formerly so much affected by the movement of the seasons, is more and more independent of this movement. In technologized societies, menus are increasingly the same year round, or can be. On television, one can see skiing in the middle of one's own summer and aquaplaning in midwinter. The difference between night and day, for practical working purposes, has long disappeared from major areas of human existence. One has to gloss the text, "The night cometh when no man can work," to make it comprehensible to a swing-shift worker in an assembly plant. Even the most unreflective are affected by this detachment of life from the rhythms of nature.

A fortiori, the poets and artists are affected. And they know it. In accord with their deeply felt desire for up-to-dateness, which is the desire to speak for man in our time and is itself an anti-cyclic or post-cyclic phenomenon, contemporary poets generally will give at least lip service to the eclipse of recurrence as a central human experience. But how far is poetry affected by this lip service? Poets in English and some other languages continue to use rhyme—although it is significant that they no longer use it so often as they once did. They continue to use lines of more or less matching lengths—although again they do so less than they used to. Occasionally, in fits of desperation, they may resort to bongo drums. But here again, although jazz is indeed relevant to modern living precisely because of its apotheosis of rhythm, resort to jazz is regarded more and more as an escape, if a necessary one. Primitive man banged his drums to attune himself to cosmic harmonies. Modern man resorts to jazz to get away from it all.

The real crisis, however, for modern poets occurs in the images of which they can avail themselves, and of course in stylistic and structural devices of repetition where these intersect with or otherwise engage the imagery of a poem. The old reliable cosmological imagery of recurrence appears less and less serviceable. What sort of enthusiasm could be brought today, for example, to the creation of a work such as Edmund Spenser's *Epithalamion*, where, if we can believe Professor Kent Hieatt's fantastic calculations,[5] the day and year are represented by the twenty-four stanzas and 365 long lines of the poem, the apparent daily movement of the sun relative to the fixed stars is figured in other line totals, and at one point the ratio of light to darkness at the time of the summer solstice, when the action of the poem takes place, is properly signaled to the reader? One can, of course, cite Joyce's *Ulysses*—but here the relevance of cosmic imagery is indirect. It is maintained by literary allusion rather than by direct feeling for nature. Joyce builds out of Homer, and countless others, not out of "nature" directly. Of course, Spenser builds out of other poets, too, for he is filled with literary allusion. But with him cosmology itself is also more directly operative. Milton, here, is a key figure. *Paradise Lost* was built on a cosmology no longer viable in Milton's day, but clung to deliberately by Milton for poetic reasons. My point is that poets and artists generally today are faced with a crisis similar to Milton's, and even deeper than his was. The polarization of literary dispute around the figures of Milton and Joyce in the mid-twentieth century is perhaps symptomatic: both Milton and Joyce face cosmological problems, and both retreat from them.

IV

Awareness of the modern cosmological crisis in poetry has seldom come to the surface of the contemporary sensibility, and a
case for modern "cosmic poetry," with some of the marks of the
older recurrence-based patterns has in fact been made in the
book *Start with the Sun* by James E. Miller, Jr., Karl Shapiro,
and Bernice Slote.[6] The authors of this book also show how,
more or less in association with the drift to old cosmic themes,
another emphasis is capital in many modern poets: the stress on
the aesthetic moment, on "creativity," on the instant of "epiphany."
This emphasis, which has an obvious Coleridgean as well as
Symbolist and Imagist background, deserves attention here, for
it throws great light on the poets' relationship to the sense of
cosmic time itself. Mircea Eliade has shown that the primitive
sense of time, particularly of sacred time, involves a psychological
need to recover the beginning of things.[7] Early man—and we can
assimilate to early man all mankind generally, more or less, until
the psychological effect of typography had entered deep into the
subconscious and established a new relationship toward records,
the past, and time—felt time and change as somehow involving
degeneration, a moving away from a perfect "time" at the beginning, a time which was really not a time but an extratemporal condition, the so-called "time" of mythological existence. The events
of mythology—for example, Athena's springing from the head of
Zeus, Dionysus's dismemberment by the Maenads—were not the
sort of things for which one could supply dates. (As has frequently
been noted by scholars, the Biblical accounts of origins involve
a different, contrasting sense of time, even when the Biblical accounts are obviously influenced by extra-Biblical mythology.)

Time poses many problems for man, not the least of which is
that of irresistibility and irreversibility: man in time is moved
ahead willy-nilly, and cannot actually recover a moment of the
past. He is caught, carried on despite himself, and hence not a
little terrified. Resort to mythologies, which associate temporal
events with the atemporal in effect disarms time, affording relief
from its threat. This mythological flight from the ravages of time
may, at a later date, be rationalized by various cyclic theories,

which have haunted man's philosophizing from antiquity to the present. In the wake of romanticism, however, we find a new refuge from the pressure of time in the cult of the here-and-now aesthetic experience, the aesthetically achieved moment which gives a sense of expanded existence and of a quasi-eternity. Georges Poulet, in *Studies in Human Time*, Frank Kermode in *Romantic Image*, and others elsewhere have elaborated various ways in which this sense of escape from time is managed, from the French writers leading up to Proust on through various American writers—Emerson, Poe, Emily Dickinson, T. S. Eliot, and others. Post-Romantic aestheticism depends in great part on the sense of this aesthetic moment, different from and more valuable than experiences in ordinary time. We find this sense particularly acute in the Bloomsbury aesthetic growing out of and around G. E. Moore's *Principia Ethica*, which influenced so typical a modern writer as Virginia Woolf. James Joyce's doctrine of "epiphany" of course belongs in this same setting. And the influence on the New Criticism is evident: the poem as "object" is assimilated to a world of vision, which is a timeless world by comparison with that of words and sound. An aesthetic of "objective correlatives," whatever its great merits, to a degree insulates poetry from time. Up to a point, all poetry provides an aesthetic refuge from "real" time, but earlier poetic theory, even that expounding poetry as divinely inspired and thus different from ordinary talk, generally lacks this exaltation of a moment of "realization" which is so commonplace today.

The stress on the moment of realization, on epiphany, under one of its aspects, can thus actually be a dodge to avoid the consequences inherent in the knowledge we have that we live in an evolving universe. It can provide a means of escaping from the real—that is, from cosmic on-goingness, a latter-day time-shelter, replacing the primitive's mythological refuge. This is not to say that the older attempts to escape from time have been entirely abandoned. The quest for a lost Eden, the "radical innocence," which Professors R. W. B. Lewis, Ihab Hassan, and others have discerned in American writers particularly, revives some of the old mythological routines. But this quest for a lost Eden, although real enough, must today be looked for closely to be found. Writers do not openly advertise that their creative drives are being powered by a quest for a lost Eden. They often do talk openly about the value of the aesthetic moment.

V

Once we are aware of the psychological issues here, it is possible to discern some fascinating perspectives in modern poetry. Those which we shall here employ are related to Professor Cleanth Brooks's division, already adverted to, between poets preoccupied with history (related to evolutionism) and those preoccupied with nature (related, as we have seen, to cyclicism). But they refine this division further, as I believe. We can view poets in three groupings, not always too neatly distinct, but, given the proper reservations, highly informative concerning the poet's problem of relating to the known universe.

There are, first of all, those poets who are consumed with the imagery of the old cosmic mythology to such an extent that it rather effectively dominates their entire outlook. Such would be, for example, D. H. Lawrence, Dylan Thomas, Lawrence Durrell, and Robert Graves. The suggestion of cyclicism takes various forms here, but common to them all is at least preoccupation with fertility (or its opposite, sterility). Indeed, the present cult of sex (often clearly an obsession) in literature appears from the point of vantage we occupy here to be a flight from time comparable to the fertility ceremonials of primitives, but more desperate because our sense of the evolutionary nature of actuality makes time more insistent today than ever before. Radical innocence is sought more frenetically because we are more aware of its inaccessibility.

In the case of Lawrence, the cult of sex and death—which yields such beauties as "Bavarian Gentians"—is linked with a nostalgia for the past and conscious revivals of old chthonic images, such as the serpent, which were supposed to restore modern man to his lost Eden. Dylan Thomas immerses himself more spectacularly in nature imagery. "Fern Hill" runs on in a riot of time and fertility symbols: apple boughs, the night, time, barley, "all the sun long," grass, sleep, owls, the dew, the cock, "Adam and the maiden," the new-made clouds, "In the sun born over

and over," sky blue trades, morning songs, "the moon that is always rising," "time held me green and dying." This stirring poem
is a litany of life and death, in its cosmology still of a piece with
Lucretius. Lawrence Durrell celebrates the mysteries of sex with
a sophisticated neopagan fervor, having little to do with a sense
of man's present position in the cosmos he is taking over more
and more, although Durrell does have some sense of temporal
progression in the evolution of social groupings. Graves protracts what he takes to be ancient continuities into the present.

> Is it of trees you tell, ...
> . . . .
> Or of the Zodiac and how slow it turns
> Below the Boreal Crown,
> . . . .?
> Water to water, ark again to ark,
> From woman back to woman:
> So each new victim treads unfalteringly
> The never altered circuit of his fate,
> Bringing twelve peers as witness
> Both to his starry rise and starry fall.[8]

Here one notes strong, and doubtless deliberate, suggestions of
the old wheel of fortune, so well known to students of the Middle
Ages and so revealing of the pagan cyclicism which haunted the
medieval mind. Other poets deeply involved in various ways in
chthonic, cyclic themes are Edgar Lee Masters and, most of all,
Yeats. Indeed, Yeats is so spectacularly and desperately anti-evolutionary that there is little point in discussing him here. But it is
worth noting that in *A Vision*, "Byzantium," and elsewhere his
cyclicism comes patently and directly from his poetic needs.

The work of poets such as these, deeply involved in sex, fertility rituals, and, by the same token, death, could perhaps be described as Dionysian, and, by contrast, an evolutionary view
which takes full cognizance that history and time do not fold
back on themselves but move resolutely forward with the mysterious upthrust evident in the ascent from protozoans to man,
could be described as Apollonian. Perhaps all poetry must be
in some way Dionysian because of its sources in the subconscious.
But one hesitates to make this judgment if only because one
suspects that the Nietzschean division into Dionysian and Apol

lonian is itself the result of a flight from time. Nietzsche's own cyclicism suggests that his thought, whatever its other brilliances, was not relating itself to the full facts of an evolutionary cosmos.

A second group of poets is related to time in another way. These are the poets adverted to above, who attempt to solve the problem of time by greater concentration on the pure aesthetic moment. In his *Studies in Human Time*, Georges Poulet beautifully describes the way in which Emily Dickinson presents in her poetry moments without past and without future except insofar as the future threatens the loss of the moment.[9] Each poem is a moment of experience which releases us from time.

> Safe in their alabaster chambers,
> Untouched by morning and untouched by noon,
> Sleep the meek members of the resurrection,
> Rafter of satin, and roof of stone.[10]

Miss Dickinson does not flee evolutionary time by resort to the seeming endless recurrences associated with a cult of the Earth Mother. She simply dwells in the instant, and attempts to protract it. In this, her work is an early example of what would become a regular style, particularly from the Imagists on, a style revived by many poets at the present moment. The cult of the aesthetic moment (or epiphany) marks to a greater or lesser degree the poetic performance and beliefs of James Joyce, Edith Sitwell, Conrad Aiken, Wallace Stevens, E. E. Cummings, William Carlos Williams in his more Imagist phases, and countless others. To a greater or lesser degree it permeates the contemporary consciousness from the heights of the New Criticism down to the level of the most unimaginative beatnik writers. Ezra Pound, with his own complicated sense of history, shows its influence, most evidently in his constant cry to "make it new"— although this exhortation has other implications also. In his poetry and poetic theory, Wallace Stevens, despite his predilection for change, bypasses the development of the universe as such and views existence—poetically conveyed—as a series of disconnected aesthetic mergings of imagination and chaos. And the newer generation of poets—James Wright, Robert Bly, Donald Hall, Howard Nemerov, John Knoepfle, and others—may repudiate their predecessors on other scores, but they show, if anything, an even more intense devotion to the aesthetic moment, often very intimately conceived.

The drift toward the old chthonic fertility cycles (more noteworthy in the Old World poets, at least until very recently) and the retreat into the aesthetic moment (discernible on both sides of the Atlantic) are complemented by a third tendency in modern poetry, a disposition actually to accept linear-type change and even to demand it as a condition of poetic activity. This disposition is more marked among American poets than among the British and Irish, a fact which is of course related to the nature of the American experience. Whitman is obviously a striking expositor of this experience, with his attitude of total acceptance toward being and his sense of a dynamic present, diverging toward past and future and uniting and equalizing them. Probably more than the somewhat doctrinaire and clinical acceptance of evolutionism which one meets with in early British writers such as Tennyson, George Bernard Shaw, and H. G. Wells, or even Swinburne, Whitman's sense of participation in the ongoing work of the universe appears to acclimate evolutionism to the poetic world. But does it really succeed? Poulet is quite right in noting that Whitman's is "an enunciation, at once successive and cumulative, of all that has been, and of all that will be." [11] "The universe is a procession with measured and perfect motion," Whitman announces.[12] But, unlike Péguy's comparable procession, which as Poulet again explains, has a termination, Whitman's procession simply advances, occupying worlds and times, but never changing anything, never getting anywhere. In fact, in Whitman we find little if any attention to the inner dynamism of evolution itself; what Teilhard has called the "inwardness" of things, the drive within the evolutionary process which moves from the externally organized original cosmos to the cosmos known and more and more controlled from the interior of man's person,[13] is missing from Whitman.

This is not to say that there is no historicism at all in Whitman. Whitman comes off one of the best in his awareness of the one-directional process of history, for his sense of a dynamic present, diverging toward the past and future and uniting and equalizing them, as well as his sense of the uniqueness of the individual imply a sense of the evolutionary, essentially nonrepetitive movement of time.[14] And yet, Whitman, too, is trapped by the old cyclicism, as, for example in "Song of the Answerer":

> They bring none to his or her terminus or to be content and full,
> Whom they take they take into space to behold the birth of the
>   stars, to learn one of the meanings,
> To launch off with absolute faith, to sweep through the ceaseless
>   rings and never be quiet again.[15]

In the last analysis, there is little or nothing in Whitman to differentiate past and future. Whitman's is still a cult of the present moment, temporally expanded, with little real anguish. For him the present does not grow out of the past nor the future out of the present. Past, present, and future simply coexist—and all too peacefully. The universe and Whitman's appetite, as Poulet notes, exactly equal one another. How can anything happen when so much bland approbation reigns? Whitman has little of the dissatisfactions of the reformer or the future-oriented man.

But if he is not especially concerned about improving things, other American poets more typically are—William Carlos Williams, for example, who insists, dramatically in his *In the American Grain* and by explicit assertion in many other places, that it is the business of the present in America to reconstitute its past and to improve its poetic language and hence its poetic realization of actuality.[16] It is interesting that Williams does not think much in terms of degeneration or decadence (which often reveal a cyclic model in the subconscious): the plight of Americans is not that they have defected from their past but rather that they are only now in a position to lay hold of it reflectively and effectively for the first time, since it now is old enough really to be a past to them. Williams dedicates *Paterson* to this enterprise of recovery, which in a way does look ahead. Yet the time which Williams deals with does not unfold, nor thrust forward. The present is authenticated by the past and the future lies as a potential in past and present, but there is little adventure in facing what is to come, little sense of unattained horizons ahead. Such a sense, or course, is not necessary for the writing of poetry but it would seem to be something which could be included in poetic awareness.

One discerns comparable attitudes in Hart Crane. Crane's

vision, conceived in *The Bridge*, is born of his sense of his own moment in history, in time, at the dawn of the machinge age. His reactions are not querulous, but positive, like those of Whitman, whom he eulogizes. Crane's confident assertion of faith in the future of industrial America hints at a feeling for linear, evolutionary time. But his compulsion to create the "American myth" drives him toward more cyclic views to fulfill his need for a pattern, and we find in the "Ave Maria," for example, a fascination with the old cosmic movements and with cyclic patterns in a variety of forms:

> Of all the amplitude that time explores,
> . . . . :
> This disposition that thy night relates
> From Moon to Saturn in one sapphire wheel:
> The orbic wake of thy once whirling feet,
> Elohim, still I hear thy sounding heel!
>
> White toils of heaven's cordons, mustering
> In holy rings all sails charged to the far
> Hushed gleaming fields and pendant seething wheat
> Of knowledge,—round thy brows unhooded now
> —The kindled Crown! acceded of the poles
> And biassed by full sails, meridians reel
> Thy purpose—still one shore beyond desire![17]

The fascination with cyclic patterns echoes in the last line of "To Brooklyn Bridge": "And of the curveship lend a myth to God."

Crane's representation of history is more interiorized than Whitman's expansive canvases, but his quest for a stabilizing myth, a symbolic structure which will somehow catch the historical process in poetic toils, draws him back at time into something like primitive cyclicism. Crane had read Oswald Spengler. At other times, perhaps under the influence of P. D. Ouspensky, he retreats from the flow of time into a mythical eternal present which alone exists but is parceled out to man piecemeal.

Crane is typically American in his determination to try to make poetic sense of history. Other Americans show a similar concern. Allen Tate, Robert Penn Warren, William Carlos Williams, Archibald MacLeish, and Robert Lowell, for example, have felt compelled at least from time to time to build poetry around historical events which have felt to them as part of their own life world—the Civil War for Tate and Warren, the New Jersey city of Paterson for Williams, for MacLeish American miscellanea, New England for Robert Lowell. All these poets evince a distinctly open-end or linear-type view of time. They are helped by the fact that the American past they turn to is a recorded, truly historical past, free of prehistory and of prehistory's cyclic tow to all intents and purposes. (The exception which must be made for the native American Indian prehistory is relatively minor.) Another American, Robert Frost, shows the same open-endedness in his own less explicitly historical, more anecdotal concerns. There is little if any mythical reconstruction in Frost. No cyclic nostalgia shows, for example, in the typically courageous, forward-looking poem *An Old Man's Winter Night*. Nevertheless, in the particular perspectives we are considering here, it appears that the achievements of these poets are often limited. Their historical mood is predominantly retrospective. It may seem strange to suggest that history can be anything other than retrospective, and yet we know so much history now that we rightly feel the knowledge of the past driving us into the future. I am not saying that these or other poets should be obliged to treat history otherwise than as they have, for they have done exceedingly well in following each his own genius. Nor do I intend to suggest that anyone should opt for a fatuous view of pure progress as man's destiny in his earthly future. I am only saying that these poets cannot be cited as having caught up in their poetry the entirety of present-day man's real time sense.

Even Pound and Eliot, whose personal and poetic journey from the United States back into Europe was a quite conscious reentry into history, have not provided a point of view in which one can assimilate a full historical and evolutionary vision to a poetic one. Pound piles historical incident on historical incident. His *Cantos* read as a vast pastiche of eyewitness accounts, overheard conversations, and reflections from everywhere out of the past, with Ecbatana and the ancient Near East jostling what Pound in *Canto XXVIII* styles "solid Kansas." But the impression one gets is not of the development of history so much as it is the impression of a present in which all this history is caught up and somehow moved out of time. "Time is the evil. Evil," *Canto XXX* cries. Eliot's great essay on "Tradition and the Individual

Talent," with its sensitive description of the relationship of past, present, and future, provides one of the purest examples of truly historical thinking in our century, and the line from "Burnt Norton" which states, "Only through time time is conquered," is a gnomic expression of the condition of both history and transcendence. And yet, the same "Burnt Norton" opens with a quotation from Heraclitus which states, "The way up and the way down are one and the same," focuses, especially in its Part II, on the image of whirling movement ("There is only the dance") and concludes with the lament, "Ridiculous the waste sad time/ Stretching before and after." It is noteworthy that the Heraclitean fragment, "The way up and the way down are one and the same" strongly suggests cyclic fatalism (return to point of departure, or inability to leave it) and by no means says the same thing as does Eliot's much advertised other source, St. John of the Cross, or the Gospel source on which St. John relies, "He who exalts himself will be humbled, and he who humbles himself will be exalted." The words of Jesus incorporate a dialectical movement missing in this somewhat paralyzing quotation from the Greek sage. All in all, in his poems and plays (for example, *Murder in the Cathedral*, Acts I and II) Eliot interlaces references to historical, evolutionary time with references to cyclic patterns so frequent and intense as virtually to immobilize the historical. Geoffrey Bullough has pointed out Eliot's preference for "formal patterns" over Bergson's open-ended *élan vital*.[18]

In a sense, the point thus far made in this study might be seen as predictable. The poetic theorists, from Aristotle through Sir Philip Sidney and beyond, have always known that poetry and history are at root incompatible—despite the fact that, as we are well aware today, the poetic imagination has in fact often been stimulated by historical events, proximate or remote. But the point here is precisely that such theory is no longer adequate. Incompatibility of poetry and history is today a more desperate matter than it used to be. A sense of history, seen as evolutionary development, has now become an inevitable dimension of all reflective human existence, and if the very feel for evolutionary development is unassimilable by poetry, then poetry cannot compass one of the most profound and intimate of modern experiences.

A sense of history, which is of a piece with a sense of an evolutionary cosmos, is a sense of the present as growing out of a past with which we are in some kind of verifiable contact and a sense that the present differs from this past with which it connects and that the future will differ from both present and past. It is a sense of continuity and difference, each reflecting the other, such as Eliot so well expounds in "Tradition and the Individual Talent." We have seen the basic reason why such a sense poses a problem for poets: it undercuts structures dear to them, first by downgrading recurrence as such, making what repetition there is only approximate and somewhat incidental, and secondly by making the present not only a present but also a sequel and prelude. The problem may not appear pressing when we experience only a single poem, but when one looks at the entire body of work of a poet, either in its larger themes or images or in the theory which it at times consciously—perhaps often too consciously—shows forth, the problem, as we have seen, is urgent indeed. A significant drift toward either cyclicism or the isolated moment is unmistakable in modern poetry.

VI

The poet has always been ill at ease, to some degree, in the world of actuality. Poetry is imitation, as the ancients well knew. Admittedly, poetry as such cannot be history. But it must be human, and the urgent question today is whether it must write off the modern experience of evolutionary historicity, whether it can even talk about this experience without betraying itself as poetry. This unresolved question, I believe, is what, deep in the subconscious, in great part underlies the malaise of poets and their friends today, occasioning the unrealistic complaint that poets are outsiders more than they used to be, discarded by "modern society," a complaint which flies in the face of the fact that probably never were poets more read and more courted than in our present technological United States. The basic question is, Can poetry face into continuous nonrecurrence as such and assimilate it without distorting it? Can it be that the poet (and the artist generally) feels himself an outsider today less because he has been actively expelled from modern society than because he has failed to make his own one of its deepest insights, its sense of historical time and its drive into fulfillment in the future?

We have noted above the American poets' share in the American sense of drive into the future. This sense holds some promise of change. Further promise of change is to be found in the Christian world view itself, which calls for specific attention here because it has been the source of so much of modern man's sense of history. For the Christian, both the universe and the life of the individual man end in quite different states from those in which they began. Time makes a difference. Time tells. Christian teaching urges no one to try to recover a lost Eden. Salvation lies ahead, at the end of time. And Adam's sin, which drove man from the Garden of Eden, is even hailed in the Holy Saturday liturgy of the Roman Catholic Church as *felix culpa*, "happy fault," because it gave God occasion to send His Son Jesus Christ to redeem man. The promise of the future is thus greater than that of the past. Christian (and Hebrew) teaching underlines the nonrepetitiveness of actuality and by the same token the importance of the unique, unrepeatable, human self, the human person. Christianity, like evolutionary thinking, is anti-cyclic.

Many of the modern poets who espouse an open-end view of time also give evidence of more or less explicit Christian influence —Allen Tate, Robert Lowell, Richard Wilbur, and W. H. Auden would be examples in point, although I do not believe that any of them have fully solved the problem of assimilating our modern sense of time to the artistic medium. There is also another poet generally classified as modern who is especially worth looking into here for the directness—and precocity—with which he has faced into the problem of time, historicity, and the human person living in time. The grounds on which he faces the problem may be too explicitly Christian to solve the problem for some. Yet there is, I believe, something to learn from him. This poet is Gerard Manley Hopkins, an artist who, although he apparently had read little if any Darwin, is still, I believe, more at home in history and in an evolutionary cosmos than most other modern or near-modern poets, although he is not quite aware of his own entire at-homeness here. His Catholic dogmatic background simply fitted him for an evolutionary time-sense despite the fact that the initial steps toward evolutionary thinking caused no little consternation in Catholic and other religious circles.

The key passages in Hopkins for our present purposes are in

The Wreck of the Deutschland. In this poem Hopkins is dealing with the significance of a horrifying event, a wreck when the German ship, the *Deutschland*, outward bound from Bremen, foundered on shoals in the North Sea during a storm, and was stranded for thirty hours without help, with great loss of life in the most horrible suffering and distress. In one rescue incident, a seaman, lowered on a rope from the rigging to help a woman or child drowning on the deck, was dashed by a wave against the bulwarks and decapitated. The next morning, according to the *Times* report, "when daylight dawned, his headless body, detained by the rope, was swaying to and fro with the waves." [19] Among the details which he picked up from the *Times* accounts, Hopkins focuses on one particularly: "Five German nuns, whose bodies are now in the dead-house here, clasped hands and were drowned together, the chief sister, a gaunt woman 6 ft. high, calling out loudly and often, 'O Christ, come quickly!' till the end came." [20] The central movement in Hopkins's thought in his poem turns on his inquiry into what this nun meant in her cry, "O Christ, come quickly!" He explores many possibilities—Was she asking for rescue? For death as a relief for herself and all those around?—and finally settles for the cry as one of recognition and acceptance. This horrible visitation, this agonizing, not even private but involved with the agonizing of all those around her, was the real advent of Christ himself in this nun's life: here she would meet him in her death, and she called out for him to come and take her "in the storm of his strides." She sees Christ not as an avenger, but as God, her Lover, and in his love as "the Master/ *Ipse*, the only one, Christ, King, Head:/ He was to cure the extremity where he had cast her;/ Do, deal, lord it with living and dead." This was the point—unknown until now—to which her life had been building up, and she was ready, for she had known that God's coming need not be gentle, that he is present not only in "the stars, lovely-asunder" or in "the dappled-with-damson west," but in all the events in history, even the most horrible, out of which he can bring joy. Hers was a faith which could see God in everything—in disaster as well as joy, indeed most of all in her own death—and never waiver in its confidence in Him. Had not St. Paul asked in the Epistle to the Romans (8:35, 37), "Who shall separate us from the love of Christ? Shall tribulation, or distress, or persecution, or hunger, or nakedness, or danger, or the sword? . . . But in all these things we overcome, because of him who has loved us."

What we note here is a sense of history at perhaps its highest possible pitch. Hopkins, as we find in his theoretical observations was devoted to the "instress" of things, to uniqueness itself, to what made each thing itself only, other, different from all else. His poetry everywhere testifies to the intensity of his love for variety, for "All things counter, original, spare, strange," as he puts it in his poem "Pied Beauty." Hopkins connected his interest in the uniqueness of things with the thought of his thirteenth-century predecessor at Oxford, Duns Scotus, but interest in the unique was beyond a doubt far more intense and explicit in the post-Romantic Englishman than in his medieval compatriot, who was necessarily far less sensitized to history by his age than Hopkins by his. Hopkins, in fact, is clearly a proto-existentialist in his preoccupation with the singular and the singularity of existence, with "my selfbeing, my consciousness and feeling of myself, that taste of myself, of *I* and *me* above all and in all things, which is more distinctive than the taste of ale or alum."[21] His sonnet "As kingfishers catch fire, dragonflies draw flame" announces a kind of self-definition in action: "Whát I dó is me." But his fascination with the unique and his sense of historicity is shown perhaps most strikingly by the way in which in the *Deutschland* he has fixed on the consciously accepted death of a human being—the utterly unique culmination of an utterly unique existence—as the very focus of existence and meaning.

He relates this death to the action of God's grace—the free gift of God which establishes the unique relationship between each unique individual and God. But grace itself, Hopkins insists, is a historical event. It does not come from heaven, direct from God's existence beyond time. Hopkins knows this will shock but presents it as a central Catholic teaching:

> Not out of his bliss
> Springs the stress felt
> Nor first from heaven (and few know this)
> Swings the stroke dealt—

> Stroke and a stress that stars and storms deliver,
> That guilt is hushed by, hearts are flushed by and melt—
>   But it rides time like riding a river
> (And here the faithful waiver, the faithless fable and miss).[22]

It is clear from the preceding stanzas of the poem that the "stress" is God's grace, the pressure he exerts on man's life (firm, delicate, mysterious, in Hopkins's image like the pressure of the streams trickling down from the surrounding hills which hold the head of water in a well up to its level). This grace, "delivered" through the universe in the violence of storms as well as in the interior movements of consciousness which bring the sinner to repentance and hope, does not come directly from God in eternity ("his bliss") but only in history through Jesus Christ, who was and is both God and man, and as man a real material figure identifiable in actual cosmic time. Hopkins goes on about grace:

>   It dates from day
>   Of his going in Galilee;
>   Warm-laid grave of a womb-life grey;
>   Manger, maiden's knee;
> The dense and the driven Passion, and frightful sweat;
> Thence the discharge of it, there its swelling to be,
>   Though felt before, though in high flood yet.

The grace at work in the world today comes into the present through the historical life of Jesus Christ—His Incarnation, birth, and, most of all, His passion and death. Even the grace given fallen man antecedent to Christ was given in view of Christ's coming into historical time.

"It dates." This is the scandal. Hopkins' uncanny appreciation of the drives in the human psyche which make it want to dissociate itself and what it values from time is evident in the fact that he recognizes the scandal of time, which creates difficulties even for believers. "Here the faithful waiver." For it seems indecent that an Almighty God would tie Himself so firmly into the flux of things, focusing His definitive visitation of man at one single brief period, the lifetime of Jesus Christ, and spreading all out from there. Equally uncanny is Hopkins' deep appreciation of the psychological mechanism of the old cosmic mythologies. Far ahead of his time, writing as though he had read

Professor Eliade, he states with precocious insight that myths are nothing less than an attempt to escape from time, to make significance dateless. "The faithless fable and miss." They do not see the religious factor in life as something that "rides time like riding a river." They try to find meaning by escaping from time.

Written in 1875, only sixteen years after the appearance of *The Origin of Species* and without any discernible direct Darwinian influence, *The Wreck of the Deutschland* actually makes use of a theme assimilable to an evolutionary sense of time, an "open-end," developmental structuring of events more explictly and downrightly than any other poem of comparable size or importance which I know of since. The presence of grace has proved, in the Christian sense of history, to be a presence curiously of a piece with the presence which man himself feels in the universe since knowledge of cosmic and organic evolution has shaped his deeper attitudes toward his life-world. Hopkins' open-end view of time is focused in the world of the human person and of grace, which lives in persons, rather than in the more material world of cosmic and organic evolution. To this degree, his view remains underdeveloped. Hopkins was not greatly taken with Darwin's discoveries, although perhaps he would have been had he lived longer. But his world is open to them; indeed, it would welcome them, with the sense of the uniqueness of things to which these discoveries can give and have given rise.

Hopkins is certainly not the only poet who is influenced by a Christian sense of God's grace operating in real historical time on persons each of whom is unique. Many other poets, most of them far less consciously, are influenced by the same open-ended historicism, as Professor Cleanth Brooks has pointed out in *The Hidden God*. Such open-ended historicism is part of the Hebraeo-Christian heritage, which in fact was perhaps a necessary condition for Darwin's seeing what he saw: it appears unlikely that a sensibility overconditioned by cyclic views would have been gripped, as Darwin was, by evolutionary patterns.

But to say that open-ended historicism and the related evolutionary outlook are at home in the Christian world view is not to say that earlier poets, even the most Christian, had entirely succeeded in accommodating a truly Christian sense of time to their poetic sensibilities. Professor Brooks has suggested that "with the breakup of the Christian synthesis, nature and history have tended to fall apart."[23] We have to be careful about imputing to past ages a Christian synthesis. If such a synthesis should include a sense of man's real place in the real physical universe of time and space, as apparently it should, there has been not only no valid Christian synthesis in the past but not even a moderately good synthesis. You cannot have a valid Christian synthesis based on a false cosmology or even on a notably defective one. We must face the fact that earlier cosmologies were both defective and, in many crucial points, false. Nature was never until recent times effectively conjoined with history. The problem today is not to restore an old union but to implement a new one.

This problem, the present study suggests, is not particularly distressing to the Christian who understands his heritage in the depths at which it can now be understood. But it is a grievously distressing problem for the poet and artist of our time as poet or artist—whether he be Christian or not—and one from which most poets and artists, consciously or subconsciously, retreat. In other words, despite some initial clashes between evolutionary science and Christian thought, it has proved far easier for the Christian as such than for the poet or artist as such to subscribe in the depths of his being to an evolutionary universe. It is also easier, *mutatis mutandis*, for the Jew, since the Old Testament sense of time and the New Testament sense of time are of a piece, although the entry of God into time and history is less intense without the New Testament doctrine of the Incarnation.

The plight of the modern poet and artist is truly extreme. The poet or artist is acutely ill at ease in our present life-world. The earlier life-world belonged to the poets in great part because it was so largely constructed out of the archetypal images which poetry and art tend to favor. If to a degree the modern world has rejected the poet, the poet also often has rejected the modern world because it demands a reorganization of his sensibility which is utterly terrifying. If the poet speaks for his age, he tends to speak for those who turn away from the characteristic awarenesses of modern man concerned with history and time.

With some exceptions, in his sense of time and history and of the succession of events the poet thus has tended to be an aborigine, a primitive. Some maintain that the poet or artist must continue always to be such. I do not believe that he can afford to do so. Of course, no one can prescribe how a poet must speak. If, however, the poet is going to speak for modern man, he is going to have to take into account somehow man's total consciousness, even though this entails a reorganization of his own psyche and of the entire tradition of poetry so drastic as to fill us with utter terror. Very possibly, the archetypes in the psyche are themselves in process of being reorganized under pressure of present discoveries. How subconsciously archetypal can archetypes be when they are the objects of knowledge as conscious as that which we bring to them today? Let us be honest in facing the future of poetry and art and man. What will poetry be like ten thousand or one hundred thousand years from now? Will man be able still to live with his once fascinating little dreams of recurrence?

NOTES

1. In another context, but using some of the material used here, I have treated this subject in the study, "Myth or Evolution? Crisis of the Creative Imagination," *McCormick Quarterly*, XVIII, Special Supplement (Jan., 1965), 37–56. This previous study had been read as a paper at a Colloquium on Myth and Modern Man sponsored by McCormick Theological Seminary in Chicago, October 22, 1964, with other papers by Paul W. Pruyser, Mircea Eliade, and Schubert M. Ogden. The present study is a revised and enlarged version of a lecture given May 11, 1964, for the Thirty-First Peters Rushton Seminar in Contemporary Prose and Poetry at the University of Virginia. For material in both these studies I wish to acknowledge help from papers and discussion by members of a 1964 Saint Louis University graduate seminar on modern poetry and evolutionism: John K. Crane, Sister Mary Ruth Gehres, O.S.U., Elaine K. Halbert, Judith Hoemeke (Mrs. Gerald A.), Leah Jansky (Mrs. Radko K.), Barbara Lawrence, Lannie LeGear, Young Gul Lee, Catherine Manore, John A. Marino, Sister Mary Joan Peters, O.S.F., Barbara Quinn, Mary Slackford, Sister Dorothy Marie Sommer, C.PP.S., Norman J. Stafford, Doris Stolberg, and Alice Zucker.
2. T. S. Eliot, *Collected Poems 1909–1962* (New York: Harcourt, Brace, and World, Inc., 1963), p. 180.
3. Cleanth Brooks, *The Hidden God: Studies in Hemingway, Faulkner, Yeats, Eliot and Warren* (New Haven: Yale University Press, 1963), p. 130.
4. Northrop Frye, "The Archetypes of Literature," in *Myth and Method,* ed. by James E. Miller, Jr. ("Bison Books," BB105; Lincoln, Nebraska: University of Nebraska Press, 1960), pp. 154–156.
5. *Short Time's Endless Monument: The Symbolism of Numbers in Spenser's "Epithalamion"* (New York: Columbia University Press, 1960).

See also Alastair Fowler, "Numerical Composition in *The Faerie Queene*," *Journal of the Warburg and Courtauld Institutes*, XXV (1962), 199–239, and the same author's *Spenser and the Numbers of Time* (New York: Barnes and Noble, 1964).

6. *Start with the Sun: Studies in Cosmic Poetry* (Lincoln, Nebraska: University of Nebraska Press, 1960).

7. Mircea Eliade, *The Myth of the Eternal Return* (New York: Pantheon Books, 1954), *passim*; cf. the same author's *The Sacred and the Profane* (New York: Harcourt, Brace, and Co., 1957), and *Patterns in Comparative Religion* (New York: Sheed and Ward, 1958).

8. Robert Graves, "To Juan at the Winter Solstice" (1946), *Collected Poems 1959* (London: Cassell, 1959), p. 212.

9. George Poulet, *Studies in Human Time*, translated by Elliott Coleman [with an Appendix, "Time and American Writers" written for the translated edition] (Baltimore, Maryland: The Johns Hopkins Press, 1956), pp. 345–350.

10. *The Poems of Emily Dickinson*, ed. by Thomas J. Johnson (Cambridge, Mass.: Belknap Press of Harvard University Press, 1955), p. 151 (No. 216).

11. *Studies in Human Time*, p. 344.

12. *The Complete Poetry and Prose*, ed. Malcolm Cowley (New York: Pellegrini, 1948), I, 120.

13. Pierre Teilhard de Chardin, *The Phenomenon of Man* (New York: Harper, 1959), *The Divine Milieu* (New York: Harper, 1960), *passim*.

14. See Poulet, *Studies in Human Time*, pp. 342–345.

15. Quoted by Bernice Slote, "Start with the Sun," in Miller, Shapiro, and Slote, *Start with the Sun*, p. 238.

16. See, for example, his "Author's Note" contributed to Kimon Friar and Malcolm Brinnin (eds.), *Modern Poetry: American and British* (New York: Appleton–Century–Crofts, 1951), p. 545.

17. Hart Crane, *Collected Poems*, ed. by Waldo Frank (New York: Liveright, Inc., 1946), p. 8.

18. Geoffrey Bullough, *Changing Psychological Beliefs in English Poetry* (Toronto: University of Toronto Press, 1962), p. 226–227.

19. "The Historical Basis of *The Wreck of the Deutschland* and *The Loss of the Euridice*," Appendix [giving the text of the *Times* reports] in Norman Weyand, S.J., ed., *Immortal Diamond: Studies in Gerard Manley Hopkins* (New York: Sheed and Ward, 1949), p. 368.

20. *Ibid.*, pp. 367–68.

21. I have pointed out this existentialist strain in Hopkins in a review in *Victorian Studies*, III (1960), 305–308.

22. *The Wreck of the Deutschland*, in *Poems of Gerard Manley Hopkins*, ed. W. H. Gardner (3rd ed.; New York: Oxford University Press, 1948), p. 57.

23. Cleanth Brooks, *The Hidden God*, p. 129.

Faith in Our Age

8

Religion, Scholarship, and the Resituation of Man

IN TODAY'S TECHNOLOGICAL society, what does religion expect of scholarship, in particular, of humanistic scholarship? The grounds of the question and of any acceptable answer are not what they would have been a few generations ago. The operations and range of humanistic scholarship have shifted, and the relationship of religion to human society has changed.

The vagaries of the concept of the humanities through the course of history are interesting and informative. Cicero, Aulus Gellius, and others use *humanitas* in the sense of liberal education, mental cultivation fitting a man, good breeding, elegance of manners or language, refinement—more or less synonymously with *doctrina, litterae, eruditio*. The concept was opposed to what belonged to mere brute animals, the infrahuman, and, by extension, to what was servile. By the fifteenth century the English cognate "humanity" is used somewhat in the sense of secular as opposed to sacred, as when William Caxton's edition of the *Golden Legend* speaks of a person as having "floured in double science . . . that is to say dyunyte and humanyte." The Renaissance, manuscript-oriented as the Middle Ages had been and further influenced by the invention of printing, tended to associate *humanitas* with reading and writing, giving particular play to the concept *litterae humaniores*. But this association of the humanities with letters helped dissociate the concept from philosophy. The subjects beyond grammar and rhetoric which were grouped under the generic name of "philosophy" were taught in the Mid-

dle Ages and much of the Renaissance by lecture and disputation
without the use of written exercises. Under these conditions hu-
mane letters came to mean the study of grammar and of a rhetoric
which was in practice, if not in theory, controlled far more by
written expression than ancient rhetoric had been.[1] Since the
study of literature as a formal discipline ended generally with
rhetoric, to which poetry was more or less assimilated, the humanities were rather generally restricted to elementary and sec-
ondary schools until rather recent times, despite the plans of the
great early humanists.

Today we vacillate in our use of the term; by the humanities
we sometimes understand the study of literature and sometimes
all the subjects covered by the term liberal education, that is, the
broad or general fund of consciously cultivated knowledge which
forms the core of our educational tradition and with which all
educated members of society must be given at least some elemental familiarity. In a brilliant study, Alphonse de Waelhens
describes the problem of humanism in phenomenological terms
as that of "man facing his future and his past in his present situation,"[2] and explains that this problem is quite centrally one of
expression, although, since all works of culture are modes of
expression, humanism extends itself far beyond the arts of communication. The problem of facing the future and the past in the
present, Professor de Waelhens points out, appears less acute at
some periods than at others, but in our own time, with our high
degree of self-consciousness, it is acute in the extreme. Here, although I cannot undertake to repeat Professor de Waelhens's
brilliant and circumstantial analysis, I shall understand humanism in something of his sweeping sense, since this is certainly in accord with current usage as well as with his telling insights. Here,
then, except when the context indicates otherwise, the terms humanism, humanities, and humanistic refer in this large sense to
disciplines or activities centered in some manner around language
and literature but including also the study of philosophy, history,
religion in its historical and theoretical aspects, sociology, anthropology, mathematics, the fine arts, and related subjects.

When we take the term humanities in its large sense, we tend,
somewhat hesitatingly, to oppose it to the physical sciences, or
at least to technological subjects however intellectually demanding

such subjects may be. But we are not quite sure of our ground here, and our hesitancy hints at the existence of a problem, which is perhaps the great secular problem of our age: What is the relationship of man to things, particularly now that he is so much in control of them? Antiquity tended to oppose *humanitas* to the brutal. The ancient *humanitas* implied primarily a contrast between man and animal and, by extension, between an upper social class and a brutalized, servile social class. Today our concept of humanistic suggests more overtly a contrariety between man and a world of inanimate things (where work is not necessarily physically brutal at all). Our tendency to contrast the humanistic with the overspecialized reinforces this suggestion, for, in a society where details are becoming more and more the business of computers, specialization strongly suggests some sort of mechanization of intellectual function.

The changed relations between man and the physical world around him impart a nuance not only to the concept of the humanities but also to the way in which religion affects man's life. The central shift of religious interest here is that which has changed the relation between man and natural or cosmic religion. This shift, which began to be manifest at the time of the Enlightenment and has become spectacularly evident in our technological age, has affected those who profess a supernatural, revealed religion as well as those who profess a natural religion or no religion at all.

Man has never been entirely immersed in nature, for he has from the beginning adulterated it with his own fabrications. Nevertheless, in earlier times man had closely aligned his religiosity with the mysteries of nature around him, exploiting for religious purposes the sun and moon, waters, vegetation, and the whole panoply of natural objects which Mircea Eliade has discussed in his *Patterns in Comparative Religion* and which he, Jung, Daniélou, Beirnaert, and others have shown to have a kind of objective symbolic content accounting for and warranting their world-wide acceptance in quite diverse human cultures.[3] Religious attention to nature may be more or less pantheistic, but it is not necessarily so, and natural symbolism is built into the monotheistic religions and even into those religions (Judaism and Christianity) which, in the terms of Eliade and others, inculcate a respect for history and time, rather than a flight from their terrors. Nevertheless, although the waters of baptism or the bread for the Eucharist and other such symbols have a permanent place in Christian life, this place is assured primarily by the fact of their connection with historical events of some two millennia ago when they were instituted, and with the symbolic sense which then reigned not only in Israel but through the world generally. If the symbolism in Christian rites were unsupported today by association with the realities of man's past, if this symbolism were launched for the first time in our abstract twentieth-century glare, it would hardly be convincing.

When pretechnological man addressed himself to nature and in or through it to God, he was addressing himself to something in which he felt himself deeply involved, from which he could not stand off in objective contemplation. Hans Urs von Balthasar distinguishes in man a threefold relation to truth: a relationship to the "coordinated being that meets him, usually and misleadingly called object of knowledge" (the relationship which engenders abstract science), a relation to the cosmos "based on his own bodily being and the immanence of the human spirit in the world," and "a relation of assent to the absolute and to the 'light' and the 'word' that flow into him from there because of his 'openness.' "[4]

Earlier religion, like much early philosophy of practical cast, such as Stoicism, drew heavily on the second of these relations, that based on man's bodily being and spiritual immanence. Confronting the universe in terms of his continuity with it and immanence in it, supported by traditionalist institutions which he had little ability or desire to explain abstractly, early man felt strangely at home in the cosmos, even when it was doing him the utmost violence. By the same token, he had little occasion to encounter himself as distinct and alienated from his surroundings, alone. It was I-and-my-context or man-and-context which preoccupied the mind—a form of thought which Dorothy Lee finds persisting today in the concept of the self among "primitives" such as the Wintu.[5] In this pretechnological culture the concept of man is poetically rich because it has so broad a support, suggesting as it does so much else with which man is in contact.

It was through this same world with which he felt himself continuous that early man's religiosity expressed itself.

From this world of nature man has pulled further and further away. He no longer feels much at home in it—although the relations with it, hinted at by known evolutionary processes and structures, are now opening the possibility of renewed acquaintance. Man's present changed relation to the cosmos has come about as the result of a long series of shifts, the basic sequence of which Auguste Comte tried to catch in his three-stage pattern of social development: the magic stage, the philosophical stage, and the scientific stage. Whatever the ultimate validity of this proposed description, we are now living in a different world from that of earlier man, one in which two principal termini of development can be conveniently located for our present purposes. These are mechanization and man's encounter with himself.

The mechanization effected by technology has a long history, running back to such distant sources as the quantification of thought in the Middle Ages.[6] It stands as one terminus of a great effort at abstraction, which has enabled man to hold things at a distance from himself, to extricate himself from his context and to deal with it as something in which he is purportedly for the moment not involved.

What I mean by man's encounter with himself is in a way a correlative of mechanization. For mechanization is an operation which affects not only man's efficiency but his very sense of his place in the universe and even his self-possession. To gain control over the material world, we have had to move away from it, in the sense that we have had to operate on it more and more indirectly. The old agricultural activities, for example, rich with folklore which emphasized man's continuity with nature, have been in great part replaced by activities still agricultural in aim but carried on in distant factories, in botanical laboratories, and in cost accountants' books. As man's presence becomes more and more effective and his responsibility for the world more and more actual, his individual operations become more and more remote from the end result. Gadgetry intervenes between us and the universe at the very time when the universe appears within our grasp. The plight of the spaceman becomes symbolic. How will he ever be genuinely present to outer space, when he is so thoroughly insulated from it in his pressurized suit? And how will he be present to other men, and other men to him? The problem of survival in physical, personal isolation is one of the major problems of the space projects, which are in so many ways the most typical endeavors of our age. Man needs a sense of community to keep his own self-possession. Deprived of this sense, he is more than isolated or lonely; he is alienated or estranged from himself.[7] Technology works against the communal sense on several fronts at once, both openly and insidiously. It is not surprising that the themes of isolation and alienation have become a commonplace of literature and the arts today.

And yet this is no adequate view of technological society. Technological society has indeed created certain special conditions favoring isolation or alienation, but it has not invented these states, which have been long known to man, although they have been brought about by diverse causes in diverse cultures. We must not forget Lear and Hamlet and the bitter human experience which made these *isolés* plausible to their own ages, as well as to ours. As a matter of fact, moreover, mechanized, technological society has placed the conditions for the encounter of man on a basis more intimate than ever before. Society has not, of course, created this encounter, and it can even be perverted so as to prevent it. Only love can create a genuine encounter between man and man. But there can be no doubt that technology has made possible an enlargement of the range of love.

Technology has made possible the total exploration of the earth's surface. It has brought the separate human colonies scattered across this surface, unknown to one another for certainly hundreds of thousands of years, into contact with one another, and it maintains this contact daily and hourly. The resulting sense of the solidarity of the human race is new, and it has immediate religious relevance. A Christian in the West today can live with a sense of involvement with his non-Christian brothers in Asia such as could hardly be acquired by medieval Christians, hampered as they were by the quasi-militarist concept of Christendom which was rooted in a lack of contact. Society has become more and more self-conscious about its responsibility for its individual members. Our development of communication, our study of personality structure, of intergroup relations, of depth psychology, of sociology, of the fuller significance of literary and art forms— all have made person-to-person relations accessible to explication as never before. To explicate relations between man and man is of course not to create them. For this, love is necessary. But I see no indication that love is less active today than it has been in the past, provided that we view the past as it was in actuality and not in some romantic transformation.

The preoccupation with isolation and alienation in our literature is itself an encouraging sign, for to know one's disease is to increase the possibility of a cure. The present trend toward isolation and estrangement, with its special roots in technological society, has paradoxically called attention to man himself and his own human problems more explictly than was ever the case before.

This does not, however, restore man to his context in nature. His estrangement continues insofar as his relation with nature is concerned. And this presents a special problem in man's encounter with his fellow men. His encounter with them is now relatively stark, naked, direct, rather than cushioned in the living forces of nature, real or imaginary. If man today feels that next year's corn crop may be threatened, he does not organize the community for a rain dance which, however meteorologically ineffective, at least in the past established a bond between man and man based on their common dependence upon natural forces. The farmer concerned about his crop nowadays consults an agricultural expert to find what sort of hybrid seed corn is available, produced especially to fit the rain patterns of his particular area. He and the agricultural expert are not linked to nature as to something on which both depend to the extent that obtained in the past. The two are managers of nature, meeting not in nature but above it, looking down on it.

Under these conditions, human encounter takes on a new importance because of its starkness. Outside nature, men are all alone —but they are all alone together. They are more obviously than ever one another's context. One can describe the situation in the terms which Ludwig Binswanger has made current in phenomenological and existential psychology, the *Umwelt*, the *Mitwelt*, and the *Eigenwelt*, which represent three modalities of man's world.[8]

By the *Umwelt*, Binswanger refers to the world of objects about man, the natural world, the world which man shares with other animals, in short, approximately what we mean by environment. The *Mitwelt*, on the other hand, belongs to man alone: it is the world of interrelationships with human beings. This world differs drastically from the environmental world, for action within it is personally reciprocal. It is the world of personal relationships, of encounter between man and man. Here one individual does not influence another in the way in which environment influences us, for in encounter one man influences another insofar as he himself is influenced by the other. For me to become acquainted with you does something not only to me but also to you—one can only hope that it is not too disastrous. The *Umwelt* by contrast is inert: environment is not expecting us in the way another person is. Binswanger's third world, the *Eigenwelt,* one's "self-world," is the one in which one encounters, faces up to, lives with oneself. It, too, is a world known only to man.

These three worlds, or "three modes of world," are interrelated, and the disruption of one necessarily disrupts the others. Within the past few centuries, and more intensively within the past few generations, as the *Umwelt* has become more subject to him, man has consequently had to turn his attention in some ways more to the *Mitwelt* and to the *Eigenwelt*, to make special adjustments.

As he looks out on the world today, man's chief problem is thus himself. We do not genuinely worry any longer about technological advance—perhaps we never did, for advance thrives not on worry but on enthusiasm. Although one or another technological problem may enter deeply into the concern of one or another individual whose work is technological, collectively we are not troubled about technological development. Given time, it will come, somewhere or other. We even state in advance and in public how many years it will take to be able to shoot a dog or a man or a space ship into orbit. But we *are* concerned about ourselves. From the university professor's lectures to the Sunday supplements, we find the same theme harped on: Can man survive his own responsibility? Accidents still happen, and they always will in individual lives. But more and more, when things go wrong, it is likely to be not nature but man who is account-able. He has failed in properly running through the count-down.

This situation of man has profound religious implications. Heretofore the religious matrix was I-and-my-universe (includ-ing other men) open to God. Now, with the physical world more and more at our command, the religious matrix is becoming more and more I-alone or we-alone open to God. In the per-spectives suggested here, one can see some reason for the puzzling fact that, as technology has become more and more dominant, personalist philosophies, philosophies of "presence," of encoun-ter, and of dialogue come more and more to the fore. It is not merely that the depersonalization enforced by technology gen-erates a personalist approach to existence by way of compensa-tion, although this is a partial explanation. At least equally cogent is the fact that man's control of things has made objects or anything treated as an object less fascinating in many philosophical circles than formerly. One turns from objectivity to intersubjectivity, not simply because one is overwhelmed and surfeited with objects but because one finds the more central problems really are the intersubjective ones.

In the shift from a world in which man finds himself embedded in nature to one in which he finds himself more and more ex-ternally managing nature lies the core of the problem concerning the relation of religion and the humanities today, if by the hu-manities we mean those disciplines which are of special concern to man as man and to his place in the scheme of things. For this place itself is undergoing a profound change. One still comes across explanations of the state of humanistic studies and of re-ligion which querulously imply that the secularization of life and the increased prestige of technology are due to some kind of *trahison des clercs*. This is a provincial explanation which fails to get to the bottom of the problem, for what has been at work is not a greater and greater willingness of humanistic scholars or religious men, first Western and now Eastern, to compromise with the mechanics in the pits, but a major development having to do with man's gradual discovery of himself in the universe, a discovery connected with much larger movements, such as the growing together of isolated cultures, the development of mass languages, of exploration, of communications, and the extrusion of the mechanistic, technological armor which was the price man had to pay for freeing himself more fully from a contingent environment.

The occurrences of the past few centuries which are relevant to the present discussion can be summed up as follows. After a very slow start and an initial diffusion in tiny pockets across the surface of the globe, man has gained more and more mastery over the physical world. The knowledge and techniques developed by one or another group of people have been communicated to others as the scattered human colonies grew in size and finally established permanent contact with one another. The concomitant processes of populating the earth to an efficient density, gaining control over natural processes, and improving communication are by no means complete, and doubtless never will be, but the general pattern of consolidation and subjugation is unmistakable. At the present time man tends to find himself less embedded in nature, in the sense that he is less able to turn to it for psychological refuge, for nature is less his mother now than heretofore and is rather something over which he has assumed responsibility. As man looks out on the globe today, he more than ever finds that he is face to face with himself. This is the age of man's encounter with man. Such a fact cannot fail to affect the meaning of humanism. And it cannot fail to affect man's encounter with God.

Under the present circumstances, when man is plunged into a stark encounter with himself because of his new dominance over physical forces, there is one answer which immediately suggests itself to the religiously committed person when we ask what religion can expect from the humanities. One may simply respond that religion expects more and more attention to man as a religious being. But this answer is trite and unilluminating. Religiously committed institutions and persons presumably know of the need to be aware of man's religious activities, and, for religiously uncommitted or partially committed scholars and institutions, detailed suggestions concerning possible lines of thought and action which throughout the curriculum would call more attention to man as a religious being have already been spelled out in a number of volumes—for example in *Liberal Learning and Religion* or in *Religious Perspectives in College Teaching.*[9]

I shall pass over what these and similar books have treated and consider the question on a more fundamental level. Under the present circumstances, what religion would most welcome from humanistic scholarship, I believe, is the resituation of man within the natural universe, from which his quite unavoidable development of technology has removed him. When I answer the question this way I am of course speaking from the viewpoint congenial to the Judaeo-Christian tradition—at least, to the extent that I am supposing that man's situation within the material universe is a matter of positive religious interest, that his viatorial status is not something of itself evil, and that, while it is the business of religion to keep man from making too much of purely material things, it is not on the other hand the business of religion to insulate man from time, history, and materiality, but rather to orient him within the temporal and material universe in which he comes into being. Other religious traditions may regard the situation differently and consider time and matter as evils or illusions from which it is necessary to free man. Certain religious traditions which espouse such views have much to contribute to the Judaeo-Christian understanding of the universe, and I believe that a Christian such as myself has much to learn from them. Yet in the cosmos as we know it now, especially since the discovery of evolution, it appears that this negative or fearful or hostile attitude toward time and matter is no longer a viable one, although individual insights associated with it may prove to be of great, and even unique, worth.

The resituation of man within the physical universe is called for because, in trying to express and handle man's present problems, we have overspecialized of late in helping him to know himself as an interior consciousness, and neglected relating him to the cosmos in its sweeping evolutionary structures. Never has man been more articulate about his own interior. He is to some extent prepared by literary and artistic productions and by humanistic studies for the new situation in which he finds himself, that of encountering himself as man has never quite encountered man before. Poetry, fiction, and drama—not only in Rilke, Kafka, Bernanos, Marcel, or Sartre but also in protoexistentialists such

as Henry James or Conrad—have presented us with a literature
of alienation and encounter; and phenomenonological and personalist philosophies have developed many of the tools for
analyzing the person-to-person relationship or its absence. Specifically religious thinkers such as Martin Buber, Eugen Rosenstock-Huessy, Hans Urs von Balthasar, and others have gone into
the religious implications and the dynamics of the dealings between man and man in dimensions far beyond those ordinarily
considered in a treatment of "social" life. In the United States the
interaction of self and other, including the "generalized other,"
has preoccupied George Herbert Mead and his followers, and
John Dewey and his school have seen communication as paramount in mental life. Since Wittgenstein, linguistic and logical
analysis has taken a definite social turn opening into interpersonal
relations. Psychology, anthropology, and semantics are all deeply
concerned with intersubjectivity and the problems of personal
identity.

Yet this kind of thinking, which provides such fine and real
insights into the isolation of each individual human soul and the
encounter between self and self, is not enough. Man does encounter himself in the universe today more starkly than ever before, so that he needs this kind of thinking; but he still encounters
more than man. He still finds "things," the *Umwelt*, his physical
environment. Indeed, although he is less intimate with nature, he is nevertheless related to it in greater detail than ever
before. Especially since Darwin, one of the major intellectual en-
terprises of man has been that of pinpointing his connections
with the physical universe in which he has put in his appearance.
As the evolutionary universe has opened itself to us in the past
few generations, the pinpointing has run back now, at least in
sketchy fashion, over billions of years of past history. Man no
longer has to rely on guesses to know fairly well where he came
in.

This knowledge of man's physical place in the cosmos, in
space and time, has, however, been assimilated hardly at all to
his knowledge of his own interior. The *Angst* of the existentialist
hero or anti-hero appears to have nothing whatsoever to do with
what paleontology tells us of man's past. Space novels, even those
of C. S. Lewis, are of little help. The more we situate man in

space, the less we situate him in his own interior, and vice versa. When the phenomenologists probe his interior, they lose sight of the stars. Man seemingly cannot be relocated in nature any longer.

The difficulty lodges in part in the fact that man's connection with the cosmos today is established abstractly and intellectually, whereas earlier it was established emotionally and infra-intellectually. The primitive felt his world as the reality around him. With the rest of things he was in no physical contact and virtually no intellectual contact. Today we are intellectually in contact with the most distant places and times. We calculate the precise period and location at which civilizations emerged. Thus oneness with nature in terms of a felt internal experience means less and less, whereas continuity with nature as a documented fact means more and more.

What is needed in this situation is to unite the interior and exterior, to restore man to his home in the cosmos. It is obvious that in this mortal life man will not find his permanent home here. And yet the material universe is in some sense his home: his material body is a part of his person, and in Christian teaching it becomes again a living part of each individual in the resurrection. In the Preface in the Mass for the Dead (echoing 2 Corinthians 5:1) we read:

Thus for Your faithful, O Lord, life is changed, not taken away, and when the house of this earthly stay has crumbled, an eternal dwelling is made ready for us on high.

Tuis enim fidelibus, Domine, vita mutatur, non tollitur, et dissoluta terrestris huius incolatus domo, aeterna in coelis habitatio comparatur.

Even in this context of death and decay, the body is spoken of as a house or home (*domus*), with an ease which today is enviable. Advocates of both religion and the humanities commonly decry the materialism of contemporary man. But we must not forget that the remedy for materialism—making too much of merely material things—is not to be sought in getting away from material things, for this is quite impossible. Even the most high-flown varieties of Platonism will not help us here. Materialism is not cured by flight from this world but by establishing our bearings within it, by impregnating it with intelligence and love.

Because of their concern with the human center of the cosmos in one way or another, the humanities seem particularly qualified to help man resituate himself in the universe by relating his interior and exterior points of reference. Are there any salient developments in contemporary scholarship which particularly indicate that within this scholarship such a resituation may be under way? Those that exist, I believe, may be conveniently grouped under two headings: the growing tendency of historically oriented studies to focus in the present, and the growing tendency of a great many disciplines to group themselves around anthropology.

For some time humanistic scholarship has been historical and evolutionary in outlook and method. This point is obvious and commonplace. But within the historical outlook there is a growing tendency to give explicit attention to the present, bringing knowledge of the past to rest there. This tendency is evident, for example, in the sensitive area occupied by linguistic studies. Here, while it is true that research on ancient languages continues to make progress, a whole new area of interest in contemporary usage (from English to Hopi and beyond) has come into being. In the teaching of English literature, the center of activity has moved, in the United States at least, from Old and Middle English, past the Elizabethans and Jacobeans, into the contemporary period. Work on contemporary literature can easily be superficial; but even after the necessary culling, the bulk of truly serious work on contemporary writers is overwhelming and without a real counterpart in earlier ages.

At its best, the trend to an interest in the present is not at the expense of an interest in the past. On the contrary, the latter has grown. We are faced with a paradox: as modern scholarship penetrates farther and farther into past ages and cultures—for the farther we get from the beginning of things the more our common store of knowledge about the beginnings accumulates—our interest in the present proportionately grows. Of course, an active and detailed knowledge of both past and present is not held in one and the same mind or minds; but it is possessed by society as a whole, and it is accessible to those who wish it.

Often enough, therefore, serious literary scholarship brings a circumstantial and detailed knowledge of the past to bear on the interpretation of the present—as it is indeed forced to do in interpreting the works of a T. S. Eliot or a James Joyce. The conscious exploitation of the past for the illumination of the present which we find in creative writers such as Joyce and Eliot is itself significant. But the trend to a present-focused historicism is not due merely to the existence of such writers or artists. Rather, their work and that of scholarship itself follows a common trend, observable also in other fields. In sociology, for example, the study of primitive cultures has enriched, and profited from, elaborate studies of the societies in which the sociologists earn their livings. In political science, the study of contemporary institutions has become a major undertaking. In history itself, a deeper and deeper penetration of the past continues; but the historical documentation of the present (as, for example, with the Roosevelt, Truman, and Eisenhower collections) proceeds along an even wider front. And this is true of many other disciplines.

This present-focused historicism undoubtedly manifests a growing interest in bringing our contacts with all reality to bear more immediately on man's present and future situation and thus to help him situate himself in the universe as a whole.

In *The Myth of the Eternal Return,* Mircea Eliade has shown how the concept of a Golden Age to which one dreams of returning represents a certain flight from time and the responsibilities of life in time. The present state of scholarship is such that a nostalgia for a Golden Age, which haunted even the learned in antiquity, no longer troubles us. Most nostalgic attitudes toward the humanities (certainly in learned circles) must be at least partly concealed to persist at all. The special kind of scholarly antiquarianism which marked the Renaissance and lingered on through subsequent centuries has now fairly disappeared. What antiquarianism we have appears not so much in scholarship as in Frontier Days' celebrations and other commercially stimulated folk activities, which scholars find it hard to take seriously, except (and this is highly significant) as manifestations of contemporary culture.[10] Yeats's "Byzantium" makes good poetry, but it does not tempt paleontologists or tease city planners out of the twentieth century.

Closely allied with the present-focused historicism of scholarship is its tendency to orient itself around an anthropological center. The older focus of attention on nature (in all the many senses

of that word) in our day has yielded to a new focus on man and
to a detailed study of man's relation to his environment quite unknown in earlier days. This anthropological shift has thus registered within the humanities themselves the changed status of man
in the cosmos, his relative independence of nature and his growing success in subjugating nature to his own interests. Earlier
philosophies talked of the dominance of the microcosm within
the macrocosm, but this dominance was realized in a quite limited
way.

The cultivation of anthropology as a field of inquiry had to
wait until mankind had built up a certain population density
around the earth, and then, by expanding travel and communication, had become conscious of itself as a whole and of the di-
versity and unity of the social structure. Anthropology is thus the
product of the present stage of human self-consciousness. By
now, anthropology has become a point on which a great many
scholarly and scientific operations (perhaps in a sense all of
them) more and more converge. This alliance with anthropology
was noteworthy in philosophy from the nineteenth century on,[11]
not only in those Continental currents which were to move into
contemporary phenomenology and existentialism but also in Anglo-Saxon linguistic and logical analysis, in which an interest in
the sociology of knowledge and the role of communication has
been especially manifest since Wittgenstein. The alliance with
anthropology was doubtless to be expected in paleontology, archaeology, history, and psychology, but the anthropologizing which
linguistics and semantics now entail—for example in work of the
sort done by Bronislaw Malinowski and Benjamin Whorf—was
hardly foreseen a few generations ago. Sociologists such as Johan
Huizinga and Eugen Rosenstock-Huessy have entered into sociology and anthropology through the door of philology or even
textual criticism—"grammar," in the large, classical sense of that
term. Depth psychology, linguistics, and the weight of the sociological element in today's thinking have generally drawn literary criticism into the anthropological orbit. Northrop Frye's
The Anatomy of Criticism is a good case in point: it is virtually
impossible to decide whether this work is a literary or an anthropological study, for it is both, and very likely, in some sense,
inevitably both. And even fields not commonly associated with

the humanities, such as architecture, are quite explicitly caught up into anthropology, with the present developments in the sociology of city planning.

The present-focused historicism and the anthropological drift which mark scholarship in the humanities at this hour, even at their very center, where the humanities are concerned with human expression, language, and literature, represent trends which are religiously promising today. It is not easy to gauge trends so pervasive as these. Yet they appear to indicate that, as our scholarly knowledge of ourselves and the world around us grows, it is becoming more feasible to join a knowledge of intimate interior states to a knowledge of the exterior structure of the universe in time and space. A historicism focused on the present does something to the human consciousness that is different from what the more antiquarian variety does. Relating events from history and prehistory (which are always relatively external in their reported form) to man's sense of the here-and-now, it relates the exterior structure of the universe to a state of mind. For the present, in which alone man enjoys the interior sense of the *presence* of another (there is no *presence* in the *past*), is more directly personal and immediately interior than the past-as-past can ever be. The greater focus on the present in historical treatment thus represents not merely a shift from one "point" in time to another "point" (time really has no "points") but an altered state of mind affecting the exterior-interior relationship. The situation can be seen in *Finnegans Wake*, where past external events are transformed in a newly realized interior consciousness. Joyce's work is not, of course, precisely the same as that of a professional historian. Yet, more than the work of a professional historian ordinarily can be, it is directly representative of the contemporary historical state of mind. Ezra Pound's *Cantos*, shouting their author's defiance of the artificial order achieved by the selectivity of history and favoring more personal recollections, are representative in another but related way.

What we have styled the anthropological drift has similarly pulled the interior and exterior into a more explicit relationship with one another. Anthropology roots man in external environment, in time and space, descriptively and scientifically. Yet in doing so it in turn invites the relating of this external environment to man—which is to say, to an interiority, for it is in his possession of an inviolable interior, a personal conscious center, that man differs from other phenomena in the universe. When anthropological studies become involved with man's interior (as they are more and more), they develop their present keen interest in communication, which relates them not only to linguistic and literary studies, to psychology, sociology and philosophy, but also to something more directly religious—love itself. Informed work in communications today proceeds with an awareness of the human consciousness as a realm in which the interior and exterior meet, where interpenetration takes place between person and person. Fully informed studies of communication show an intimate awareness that communication and human knowledge, which is inevitably communication, cannot exist at all except in a context of love. At this point, scholarly interest abuts on what is specifically and centrally religious.

I do not mean to suggest that anthropology has fully succeeded in linking man's interior with the external world, but only that it gives promise of some more unitary vision. In the remarkable efforts of the late Pierre Teilhard de Chardin, we certainly encounter some kind of major anthropological and religious breakthrough. It would seem that the fascination which *The Phenomenon of Man* has for alert thinkers through the entire world today lies in the fact that it seeks to formulate, perhaps for the first time fully and consciously, the work which lies ahead of synthesizing our awareness of the person with our knowledge of the evolutionary universe. Father Teilhard was an anthropologist (more specifically, a paleontologist), who had, moreover, besides a Catholic priest's concern with the spiritual, a keen interest in depth psychology and in his own strain of phenomenology. He was not much taken with "humanism" as an ideal. I recall talking with him on one particular afternoon in the garden of the Jesuit house in Paris where we were living in 1951 and feeling him bridle a little, in his gentle and smiling way, at the term *humanisme*. "Ça, c'est fini," he protested with emphasis. To him, humanism signaled a harking back, an attempt to catch the world vision of fifteenth- and sixteenth-century man, possibly an educational system in which training (in literature at least) is an attempt to integrate today's knowledge around such a pole. Nothing, he thought, could be so futile. And I agree. If humanism can mean only this, we must have done with the term. We must indeed know the past intimately to know ourselves; but any synthesis must be a creation of our own time.

Religion, centered on God, is a unifying force; and from humanistic scholarship it demands as far as possible an integral view of man. Man's personal salvation, we can assume, is the business of religion itself. But religious man needs a knowledge of the whole background, as far as this can be ascertained, against which his personal salvation is being worked out. In the Judaeo-Christian tradition, the entire universe, no matter how far extended in space or time and no matter how deeply hidden in some of its aspects within man's consciousness, is seen as God's universe, despite its imperfections and despite sin. Alfred North Whitehead once noted that the scientific mind, which is traceable back to medieval Europe, has its roots in the Hebraeo-Christian tradition even more than in the Greek, because by believing in one God who created all things without exception and who was infinitely intelligent and wise, medieval Christians approached the universe with a conviction far beyond that of the pagan Greeks that everything in it ultimately admitted of explanation, no matter how difficult it might be to find what the explanation was.[12] Scholarship needs this kind of conviction to serve religion today—and very likely even to survive. Its maximum service to religion, as to itself, will be realized by continued dedicated work, specialized and generalizing, carried on under the persuasion that there is a unity to be found in the relations, however complex and however changing, between the human interior and the universe in which man has appeared.

NOTES

1. See Walter J. Ong, "Latin and the Social Fabric," *The Barbarian Within* (New York: Macmillan, 1962), pp. 206–219.

2. "Le problème de l'humanisme, dont on nous parle tant aujourd'hui, s'est posé à toutes les époques, car il n'est autre que celui de l'homme confrontant son avenir et son héritage dans sa situation présente" (Alphonse de Waelhens, *Existence et Signification* [Louvain: Editions E. Nauwelaerts, 1958], p. 143).

3. Mircea Eliade, *Patterns in Comparative Religion*, translated from *Traité d'Histoire des Religions* by Rosemary Sheed (New York: Sheed and

Ward, 1958); Jean Daniélou, "The Problem of Symbolism," *Thought*, 1950, *25*: 423–440; Louis Beirnaert, "La Dimension Mystique de Sacramentalisme Chrétien," *Eranos Jarhbuch*, 1950, *18*: 225–286; Jung's voluminous work is well known.

4. Hans Urs von Balthasar, *Science, Religion and Christianity*, translated from *Die Gottesfrage des heutigen Menschen* by Hilda Graef (Westminster, Md.: The Newman Press, 1958), p. 29.

5. See Dorothy Lee, "Notes on the Conception of the Self among the Wintu," *Explorations* (University of Toronto), 1954, No. 3, pp. 49–58, a revision of an article which appeared earlier in *The Journal of Abnormal and Social Psychology*, 1950, *14*: 538–543.

6. See Walter J. Ong, *Ramus, Method, and the Decay of Dialogue* (Cambridge: Harvard University Press, 1958), pp. 53–91, 306–318; cf. R. Hooykaas, *Humanisme, Science et Réforme* (Leiden: E. J. Brill, 1958), and John U. Nef, *Cultural Foundations of Industrial Civilization* (Cambridge: Cambridge University Press, 1958).

7. The term alienation and its cognates perhaps warrant a special note. From the ordinary dictionary sources, we learn the following: The English term "alienist" was first used largely as a legal term for a physician skilled in handling mental diseases; but the association of alienation with mental aberration goes back to ancient Latin. We find *alienatio* in Celsus and Pliny in the sense of an aberration of mind, a loss of reason, delirium. The term originally meant the transfer of property from one to another (*alius*), but then it came to signify also a casting off or aversion, in the sense of a withdrawal of warm, friendly feeling from another person (cf. the English "alienation of affection"). It is remarkable that out of this concept grew that of mental illness, loss of sanity, which is obviously conceived of by the early Latin-speaking world as an "othering," a separation from oneself (cf. the English "I am beside myself"). The key perceptions of contemporary existentialism thus seem to have obvious roots in the Latin past.

8. See Rollo May, "Contributions of Existential Psychotherapy," in Rollo May, Ernest Angel, and Henri F. Ellenberger (eds.), *Existence: A New Dimension in Psychiatry and Psychology* (New York: Basic Books, 1958), pp. 61–65; see also Ludwig Binswanger's contributions in this same volume.

9. Amos N. Wilder (ed.), *Liberal Learning and Religion* (New York: Harper and Brothers, 1951); Hoxie N. Fairchild and others, *Religious Perspectives in College Teaching* (New York: The Ronald Press, 1952).

10. For an excellent study of such celebrations as contemporary culture, see W. Lloyd Warner, *The Living and the Dead: A Study of the Symbolic Life of Americans* (Yankee City Series, Vol. 5; New Haven: Yale University Press, 1959).

11. See Balthasar, *op. cit.*, pp. 28–61. The anthropoligizing of philosophy can be observed also in neoscholastic circles with the appearance of books such as George P. Klubertanz's textbook, *The Philosophy of Human Nature* (New York: Appleton-Century-Crofts, 1953), which represents a focus of attention unknown in medieval scholasticism.

12. Alfred North Whitehead, *Science and the Modern World* (Cambridge: Cambridge University Press, 1926), p. 17.

9

Post-Christian or Not?

THE TERM "post-Christian age," with its correlative "post-Christian man," has been with us for some time. Like many other catch phrases, these terms perhaps say more about the mental state of those who use them than about the referents to which they supposedly apply. They conceal more than they say. It is tempting to propose that they be abandoned. But such a proposal is futile, for they will not be, for a long time at any rate. Since this is so, we can perhaps be excused if we inspect the terms briefly so that we can at least see what we have to live with. And, since the terms are so much used in an offhand way, it may be well to note some of their more immediate, less recondite implications.

Speaking of "a post-Christian age" or "the post-Christian age" (generally "the," because it is supposed to be permanent, final) suggests quite evidently that there is something about Christianity which is finished. What could this mean? Certainly it cannot mean the most obvious thing it might be taken to mean, namely, that there are no Christians around any more. There are millions of them—more, in fact, than ever before.

Neither can it mean that those who are around now are not "real" Christians, whereas those of former ages were. Such a view is not seriously held by those familiar with former ages in any first-hand way. Circumstantial investigation of history shows that men professing to be followers of Christ were, in earlier ages as now, pretty weak vessels, falling mostly far short of what they were called upon as Christians to be.

Could "post-Christian man," then, perhaps refer to a state of affairs in which, while there are more Christians around than ever before, "man" in some generic sense has abandoned Christ and Christianity? Could it refer to an abandonment of Christianity by mankind as a whole with the exception of the several hundred millions who are now Christians? This is closer to the meaning which more sophisticated users attach to the term. But at this point the implications of the term become queasy in the extreme.

The first implication here is that at some time in the past mankind as a whole received the Christian message. For how could all mankind abandon Christianity without having been in contact with it? This implication is of course totally contrary to fact. For the fact is that, although from the beginning it has been apparent that in its deepest interior Christianity is driven to spread the Gospel, the Good News, to all men without exception, this drive has not yet at all realized its full potential.

By far the greater part of mankind has never heard the Gospel preached at all. Most of Asia and much of Africa have not yet heard the Gospel. Until quite recent centuries, the entire Western Hemisphere knew nothing of it. The Europeans who knew Christianity did not always spread it to the American Indians rapidly not simply because they were not all enflamed with the Gospel (many of them were, many of them were not) but because their contacts with the Indians were not always immediate or intimate. The Franciscan Missions in California, for example, often thought of by Americans and others as quite ancient, date only from the late eighteenth century, although there had been some earlier evangelization of the Indians by pioneer missionaries such as Father Kino. In many parts of Latin America, the Indians have still not been reached by the Church effectively, and in some parts not at all. Large indigenous populations are not always very accessible.

It is easy to point to this situation censoriously, deciding that it shows what hypocrites or at least dastardly shirkers most Christians have been. Should they not have moved with more alacrity? Doubtless they should. We all should. But such judgments, although they are tremendously satisfying to the ego of those who level them, fail to take cognizance of certain psychological and social facts. Mankind, old as it is (somewhere between 500,000 and 1,000,000 years, it would seem), has been aware of itself as a whole for only a few centuries. Man has had to get used to the feeling of global unity. Although he is drawn into contact with all his kind (Teilhard's "convergence" tendency), he also at first resists having his parochial views of himself enlarged. The sixteenth-century Europeans who wished to argue that the rational creatures in the areas of the world opening to Europeans were not men may have been motivated by snobbery or venality (if they were not men, you could dispossess them without qualm). But there was more to it than this. It just did not seem right that there would be all those millions of people whom one had never even thought about or known of. One had to get used to thinking of them before one could plunge into anything like evangelization. The missionaries who did plunge ahead were far ahead of their times. The new situation which followed on the age of discovery took a long time to sink into the minds of most men. Some few could imaginatively assimilate the entire globe almost immediately—missionaries such as St. Francis Xavier or those who dispatched them such as Loyola, or the explorers and adventurers who moved out into the new lands. But most could not. They listened to the returning adventurers and missionaries and returned to their own workbenches in amazement. Eventually expertly organized corporations such as the Massachusetts Bay Company lured more and more into new lands. But this took time. It took time to develop the emigration mentality. And it took still more time to develop a feel for the family of man, a feel which has a sociological and psychological substructure as well as a religious superstructure.

Once man knew that the globe was fairly well covered with his fellows, to varying degrees of density, he still did not experience their presence quite in the way which today we take for granted. For centuries, it took months and even years for the most technologically advanced cultures to know what was going on in some of the regions with which they had newly come into contact. Man has been able to communicate rapidly with his fellows across the entire globe for only a few decades.

If we look at human history (including prehistory) in full perspective, it is plain that the possibility of Christianity's spreading over the face of the globe has not only not been realized thus far but thus far has hardly been psychologically possible. Still, those who speak of a "post-Christian age" appear to assume that the good news of the coming of Jesus Christ did somehow reach everyone everywhere. The "world" was once Christian, we are often told. And it is at this point that the snobbishness of the term "post-Christian age" makes itself evident. For those who refer to the "post-Christian age" are in one way or another identifying the entire human race with European culture. This is Belloc's well-meant but horrible "the faith is Europe and Europe is the faith" all over again. It is not any defection at all from the faith that produces a "post-Christian age" or "post-Christian man" but the defection (if this is what it is) of Europe. To test this provincialism of the term, we only need imagine how unreal it would sound on the lips of an African or Indian bishop.

Defections from the Christian faith are not new. There were sizable defections in apostolic times, duly noted in the Epistle of St. James, for example, and there were large-scale defections during the persecutions under the Roman emperors, when martyrdom was not always the typical response to repression. Later, the whole of North Africa, once solidly Christian, turned Mohammedan after the military conquest by Islam.

One does not speak of these earlier phenomena in terms of "post-Christian man." Why? Because they seem regional, and "post-Christian man" is used with some kind of universalist implication. And at this point the ugly supposition back of this concept reveals itself: the supposition is that the only part of mankind that really counts, so that one can speak of "man" or "mankind" when one means only this part, is the European or European-oriented sector. If notable numbers of this sector have turned away from Christianity, all mankind has done the same.

This is not only a provincial view of mankind; it is also unchristian and quite intolerable. The bases for such a view, unfortunately, are still drilled into us in the West from infancy. Textbooks employ expressions such as "the then known world" to refer to the world known to Europeans, or to those around the Mediterranean basin, as though the rest of mankind did not know that it was even on the scene, or the hardly less offensive expression "*the* discovery of America"—instead of the *Europeans*' discovery of America. After all, most of the ancestors of most Latin Americans knew about America long before Christopher

Columbus hove into view. It was only ignorant Europeans who did not know that the Americas were here—the men living on them had for thousands of years been quite intimately aware of the fact.

The expression "post-Christian age" snubs the non-European world not merely by smugly identifying the cause of all mankind with the fate of Europe but also by subtly congratulating European civilization on an achievement it had never realized. For almost inevitably the expression "post-Christian man" gives a quite false impression of past actuality. It implies that at some time or other in the past Western man was as a matter of fact adequately Christian, that he had a thoroughly Christian view of actuality. Such an understanding of the past only a cavalier interpretation of history can suggest.

The Middle Ages are often singled out as the time when in Europe Christianity was in the ascendancy, as it certainly was. But whether Christianity was then at its maximum is at best open to question. The Middle Ages hardly give us a picture of mankind as adequately Christian. Not only did vice abound, as it has in all ages, and massive pagan superstition with it, but the ability of the age to generate or assimilate a Christian world view was extremely limited. Central to any Christian view is a sense of the value of personal decision, of the will acting with deliberation under the influence of grace. The Middle Ages had a sadly deficient view of the role of decision in the Christian's life. However speculation on the subject ran among philosophers and theologians about freedom of the will, the medieval world view retained basically a pagan fatalism even in—or especially in—its legends of saints themselves. Instead of a real person making difficult choices under God's grace, the medieval saint is portrayed typically as a kind of symbolic automaton, his life shored up by marvelous happenings at the time of his birth (or often his gestation), through his life, and at his death, an individual sure to be a saint in spite of himself. The typical saint's life perpetuates the heroic tradition, which makes over the individual into a type and which Kierkegaard has quite rightly contrasted with the tradition of the Christian "knight" (this term of Kierkegaard's could be bettered). It was, of course, inevitable that this heroic

tradition be perpetuated, given the social and psychological structures of medieval man, but the result was at best equivocally
Christian.

Medieval European culture is sometimes authenticated as Christian in terms of "Christendom," itself a medieval concept. But the
concept of "Christendom," though it arose among Christians is,
paradoxically, hardly a Christian concept at all insofar as it implies that "we," the Christians, are in "here," identified by alle-
giance to some special political realm, and that "they," the
"others" or non-Christians, are out "there," viewed with hostility
or suspicion, the enemy against whom we undertake even military
action. Again, such an enclave mentality was inevitable in medieval
society, not only in Europe but all over the world. Psychological
and social structures connected with man's limited control of his
material environment still favored a kind of permanent siege
mentality and thus a life-world pitting in-groups against out-
groups to a degree growing more and more intolerable today.
But the fact that this mentality could not for the most part be
helped did not make it less a handicap to a full realization of the
Christian ethos.

For a true Christian, there are no "others" in the sense of persons "out there" for whom his religion equips him with feelings
of hostility, whom he does not wish to win to Christ or has de-
spaired of winning to Christ. Insofar as a Christian feels himself
within an enclave, geographical or political, he feels his work as
a Christian radically defective; he is unquiet and ill-at-ease. He
knows that the Christian era has most emphatically not matured,
for the message of the Gospel has not yet been carried with full
effectiveness to all nations.

In part, the concept of Christendom was supported by an inability to distinguish what in one's life-world is properly Christian and what is due to one's own particular culture. Without this
ability one risks joining to the preaching of the Gospel the im-
position of one's own cultural peculiarities on other peoples, and
thus running directly counter to what is truly catholic in Christianity—the adaptability and presence-to-all which is signaled by
the Greek word *katholikos*, "throughout-the-whole." Christ's
presence is a presence suited not to merely one or two or three,
but to all cultures, as much at home in one civilization as in an-

other. To use the New Testament figure, the Kingdom of God is like yeast which, no matter where it starts, works its way into every part of the dough in which it is planted. In the Middle Ages, Christianity became too closely identified with specific social institutions for its own good, and this identification has remained a handicap up to the present time. The Second Vatican Council has publicly signaled (although it did not initiate) the great breakthrough to a more open state of mind in the Roman Catholic Church.

Medieval European man still had only limited access to other cultures, and on the whole did remarkably well under the circumstances. Still, again, his circumstances impoverished his vision as a Christian. We have no warrant today to think of ourselves individually as better Christians than our medieval or other forebears. Nevertheless, we are as a group far better situated to realize the true catholicity of the Church than was earlier man, who did not know what we do today about history and anthropology, which make possible intercultural penetration and understanding in ways hitherto unknown.

European Catholicity—not to mention European Protestantism, for which I do not speak here—has made serious mistakes in the past, mistakes such as that of introducing Gothic church architecture into cultures to which it was completely exotic, or of giving European names to new Christians in cultures where such names have latterly proved a serious liability, since they suggest that to be a Christian one has to remove oneself from one's native civilization. (In parts of India now, at long last, lists of names are available for candidates for baptism which qualify both as Christian names and as distinctively Indian in meaning and tone.) Earlier Western Christians were actually prevented by the very vigor and ascendancy of European political and military institutions and scientific discoveries from having as Catholic an outlook as they might have had. Their own natural history limited their assimilation of the catholicity of Catholic truth.

In our day Christians can readily enjoy a more open vision since the enclaves which in past ages have sealed off one part of mankind from another and thus tended to seal off Christianity, too, are breaking up with the growth of global consciousness. Seen in terms of global history rather than in terms of European or Western provincialism, the Christian era is thus in some sort opening up today more than ever before. Christianity suffers in many places today from bitter and cunning persecution. But in the twentieth century it has also been arriving faster in many non-European areas than it ever has since apostolic times. Today nearly one-third of the world population is Christian. Christians in Africa number over 38,000,000 (this figure includes among Catholics some 15,000 priests and over 37,000 members of religious orders). Asia has over 50,000,000 Christians. The growing geographical range of Christianity showed clearly in the Second Vatican Council, where the hierarchy was patently more international and interracial than it had ever been in the past, although on this score the hierarchy lags behind the Church as a whole. All this provides a curious background indeed for talk about the present as a post-Christian era.

In urging these strictures against the concept of a "post-Christian world," I do not mean to deny that something has happened to society in the West which is recorded in the talk of Nietzsche and others about the "death of God," though Martin Buber in his *Eclipse of God* has styled such expressions "sensational and incompetent" and their sensationalism is evident enough by the way they fall into newspaper headlines as into a kind of natural habitat.

Much has been said and written about the changed condition of modern man which has brought to the fore such sayings, evidently of a cut with the expression "post-Christian age." It is evident that man's religious stance in the world is different from what it was in the past, although just what is meant by the "past" (the line of demarcation between it and the "present") is not too clear, nor is there very general agreement at all on just how different the present religious stance is from what went before it or on what the basic difference is. One of the troubles with discussions of this matter is that, while the present situation is often described with some knowledge and insight, the "past" situation of man is not infrequently pictured in terms of some symbolic transformation of the past rather than a report on it. The Golden Age syndrome is a permanent part of human psychology. We are all too prone to consider man's religious condition in the past as more integral, consistent, and satisfying than in fact it was. If we read St. John of the Cross, we find that social conditions were pretty distressing and the night of faith terribly dark in sixteenth-century Europe, and if we read St. Paul with some knowledge of history and with empathy, we find that man's life-world in the Mediterranean area at the time of Christ was hardly integrated by religion to the extent that some would have us believe.

This is not to deny differences between past and present or to minimize them. There are differences, and some of them can be spelled out, even though they do not translate into slogans. One fruitful way to discuss the differences is in terms of man's changed relationship to the physical world around him, for this relationship has radically changed in ways of which we now know a great deal.

Early man stood in awe before the world around him—"nature," that is—which he understood intellectually or abstractly hardly at all. Modern man, in contrast, looks at nature as something to be understood and controlled—not entirely, to be sure, but with steadily increasing sweep, already wide enough to give him great confidence. Man has grown in knowledge and technological prowess, which abet one another in a myriad of ways. As knowledge is accumulated with the help of writing, particularly of the alphabet, which has a most intimate relationship to technology, the areas of awareness where growth is greatest and most obvious command more and more attention. These are largely those areas having to do with the natural world, understood in the large sense of this term as including man's intellectual activities themselves as well as the workings of the sensible world around man.

Because he understood nature intellectually or abstractly hardly at all, early man was awe-struck by it—not, however, by nature thought of as a neutral thing but by nature felt as somehow redolent of more than things, that is, of life and some sort of intelligence, which is to say of person. But when early man invested nature with sacral qualities, he did not always do so in a happy way. Instead of moving from the reality of nature to the reality of God, as the Hebrew and Christian and some other religious traditions advocated, early man could all too easily mistake nature for God, in one way or another falling into the worship of sun, moon, or stars, or of forces felt to be operative in the changes of seasons.

This attitude of mind which gave plausibility to nature religions formed the background of all man's thinking. Its presence meant that when an individual or groups fell away from Christianity, they tended automatically to revert at least to some form of nature worship, express or implied. This tendency still obscurely persists even in advanced cultures and has broken out in our time in Nazism, which manifested even the ultimate horror of nature religions when these run wild: ritual murder.

But for the most part the tendency toward nature worship is now attenuated, and is so insofar as the technological view of the universe has gained ground. When individuals or groups turn away from Christianity today, they do not so inevitably revert to a primitive nature religion.

An awareness that this older pattern has changed underlies not a little of the talk about "post-Christian man" or the "death of God." Since Christianity, and its antecedent, Judaism, grew up against a background of nature religion, from which the Hebraeo-Christian tradition cut loose, the disappearance of the background is taken for the disappearance of Christianity. Thus, although individuals or groups in earlier ages fell away from Christianity back into some form of nature religion, they are not thought of as "post-Christians," for they reentered the background out of which the Hebraeo-Christian tradition emerged. When individuals or groups fall away from Christianity today without returning to a nature religion, they are taken to be "post-Christian" simply because they tend to step into something of itself younger than Christianity, a secularized mentality made possible, but not inevitable, by our technologized culture.

It is highly informative in this connection to read the famous passage in Nietzsche, section 125 in *The Joyful Wisdom* (*La Gaya Scienza*), which makes the by now well-publicized announcement that God is dead. "We have killed him—you and I," Nietzsche's madman shouts. But, strangely enough, the passage makes no mention of any human action which could be construed as "killing" God except for the statement that he "bled to death under our knife," which does little more than reiterate that we have killed him. What the passage does do is exclaim with great anguish about the death of the old semi-animistic pre-Copernican universe, and the advent of the mechanistically conceived, "silent" world of Newton and modern science.

Have you ever heard of the madman who on a bright morning lighted a lantern and ran to the market-place calling out unceasingly: "I seek God! I seek God!"—As there were many people standing about who did not believe in God, he caused a great deal of amusement. Why! is he lost? said one. Has he strayed away like a child? said another. Or does he keep himself hidden? Is he afraid of us? Has he taken a sea voyage? Has he emigrated?—the people cried out laughingly, all in a hubbub. The insane man jumped into their midst and transfixed them with his glances. "Where is God gone?" he called out. "I mean to tell you! *We have killed him*—you and I. We are all his murderers! But how have we done it? How were we able to drink up the sea? Who gave us the sponge to wipe away the whole horizon? What did we do when we loosened this earth from its sun? Whither does it now move? Whither do we move? Away from all suns? Do we not dash on unceasingly? Backwards, sideways, forwards, in all directions? Is there still an above and below? Do we not stray, as through infinite nothingness? Does not empty space breathe upon us? Has it not become colder? Does not night come on continually, darker and darker? Shall we not have to light lanterns in the morning? Do we not hear the noise of grave-diggers who are burying God? Do we not smell the divine putrefaction?—for even Gods putrefy! God is dead! God remains dead! And we have killed him! How shall we console ourselves, the most murderous of all murderers? The holiest and the mightiest that the world has hitherto possessed has bled to death under our knife—who will wipe the blood from us? With what water could we cleanse ourselves? What lustrums, what sacred games shall we have to devise? Is not the magnitude of this deed too great for us? Shall we not ourselves have to become Gods, merely to seem worthy of it? There never was a greater event—and on account of it, all who are born after us belong to a higher history than any history hitherto!"—Translation by Thomas Common, *Complete Works*, Vol. X (London, 1910).

A fascinating passage, especially when we cut through the rhetorical questions and ask ourselves what events Nietzsche has in fact described. Of course, we should not really expect him to describe a physical action of killing God. If God is conceived of in the Hebrew and Christian tradition, and Nietzsche thus conceives of him or thinks he thus conceives of him, a detailed description of a physical attack on him, as on a human being, becomes impossible apart from such an event as the crucifixion of Jesus Christ, who is God and man, and Nietzsche is clearly not concerned with this. If not a description of a physical attack, we might possibly expect some mention of actions of overt hostility of one sort or another against God—impiety, flouting of prayer, blasphemy, eversion of Christian teaching, atheism in one or another of its varieties, casual or programmatic, personal or political. There is none of this, and for good reason. Nietzsche is concerned that man has in a sense "killed God" without knowing it. How has man done this? What are the events which, though man has not been aware of the fact, have overthrown and done away with God?

They are, it becomes apparent on close attention to the imagery here, in actuality those which did away with the old cosmology and established the new. The old Aristotelian sense of an absolute "up" and "down," the madman shouts, has yielded to mathematical cosmology, which knows no absolute up or down—there is not a fixed "top" or "bottom" or our globe or to the whole universe. Everything is "backwards, sideways, forwards" simultaneously. The earth is no longer the center of the universe. The earth is actually in motion, as are all bodies. The physical universe is no longer something homelike, womblike, human, but rather a mass of "things" in cold, empty, dark space—space mathematically conceived, deficient in all sensory qualities but extension. And all this is supposed somehow to stand for the "death of God."

There are other passages in Nietzsche's writings which bear on this one and give it fuller meaning. Our concern here, however, is not the fuller meaning but the simple fact that when he delves into the grave of God, this is what we find Nietzsche coming up with here—a disqualified Aristotelian-Ptolemaic cosmology. Whatever he meant by the death of God, the disappearance of the more primitive, "human" universe was a great part of it. Whether Nietzsche falls into this account consciously or subconsciously we may not be able to say. If he does so consciously, it is highly interesting. If subconsciously, it is even more interesting.

We are left in either event with a significant question. Why should the disqualification of the Aristotelian-Ptolemaic cosmology (and with it, the death of all more primitive cosmologies) —consciously or subconsciously—somehow stand for the "death of God"? What this disqualification actually has to do with this presumed "death," we are not told, although we are told that the world which results from the new cosmology is a great achievement, as indeed it is: "There never was a greater event,—and on account of it, all who are born after us belong to a higher history than any history hitherto!"

Nietzsche's thought is intriguingly presented by his anguished madman, but on close inspection of the supposition back of it, the thought appears, in all fairness, obtuse and annoying here in its cavalier, and quite naïve, identification of Christianity and of theism with the cosmology, or one of the cosmologies, with which Christians in the past managed to live. Once this identification is assumed, the passing of the old cosmology is of course the passing of Christianity and, in the context of Nietzsche's thought, of theism, and the "death of God." But this identification simply cannot be reconciled with the brute facts. There exist today hundreds of millions of Christians who thrive and rejoice in the world of modern science. Indeed, they even thrive and rejoice in the world of technology itself, the child of science, toward which, for all his drive into the future, Nietzsche exhibits not a little uncontrollable hostility.

The scientific, technological mentality is indeed younger than Christianity, but this is not to say that it supersedes Christianity. What is new does not by any means always supersede what is older. Christianity is a part of the technological world, too, which in fact grew out of a culture dominated by Christianity and only out of such a culture, spreading from there to the rest of the world. The Christian can as a matter of fact find much in technological culture which is religiously superior to earlier cultures. It is true that with the predisposition to nature religions found among earlier man (and still persistent in groups of mankind not yet in effective touch with technological civilization) there goes a propensity to invest with a sacred character many phenomena or objects which technological man habitually considers in a secular frame of reference. But, although such a propensity keeps religion always at the surface of life, it is religiously by no means entirely a boon.

The sacral and the secular are different moments or casts within reality, and both must be honored. If it is a fault in contemporary technological civilizations to tend to press secularization too far, it has been a fault of nature religions to look for religious explanation where secular explanation is in order. The particular natural events which affect me as a unique person—the death of a father or mother or wife or child, the achievement of a particular success—have a distinct religious meaning in the unique shape which they give my own life. But this is not all there is to such events. They are also events within nature, to be explained as such naturally, and, where possible, naturally controlled. To see them as only religious events is a mistake which can be detrimental and degrading to religion. Religious explanation supplements scientific explanation. It does not supply for it.

To be aware of this fact, to admit that there are aspects of the world which should be desacralized in the sense that they should be subject to scientific investigation is not to make ourselves post-Christian. Christianity is not a nature religion. It has not, it is true, in the Catholic Church at least, exhibited any great hostility toward pre-technological cultures favoring nature religions, even when it was gradually remodeling the cultures in which such religions flourish. But Christianity has, if anything, even less hostility to modern technological culture. Developments in the United States provide a case in point. Here, at the present height of technological accomplishment, there are far more Protestants with active church affiliation than there were at any time in the American past from colonial times on, and that not only in absolute numbers but in proportion to the entire population deriving from Protestant background, as Franklin H. Littell has shown in *From State Church to Pluralism*, and the Catholic Church is flourishing as she seldom has in any other type of civilization.

Talk about a "post-Christian age" is likely to imply that even if Christianity can adapt itself to technological culture, at least it operated at maximum efficacy in pre-technological cultures favoring the old nature religions. The implication is founded again on the Golden Age syndrome (things were perfect, or at least much better, in the past, and Christianity must have been so, too). However, even moderately close scrutiny of Christian practice in cultures favoring the old nature religions does not show this practice as always deep-rooted or very conscientious.

In such cultures a typical and widespread phenomenon is "folk Christianity" or "folk Catholicism"—the religious practice which one finds still among some peasant populations in Europe and in much of Latin America, where pre-Christian beliefs and practices are accommodated to Christian teaching and practices, sometimes in a successful and Christianly meaningful way, sometimes in ways full of superstition. But folk Christianity is not a notably inspiring form of Christianity. Christians reared in its practices are not particularly strong Christians at all once they are removed from their peculiar cultural envelope. And often even within it, their practice of Christian virtues—and of rather essential ones, such as fidelity to the marriage bond—is not noteworthy. The disappearance of such cultures or their diminution can hardly appear as necessarily a weakening of Christianity. Today Christianity calls frankly for more positive individual commitment, and in this calls for strength.

When we turn from the Christianity of peasants to that of the intellectual sophisticates, we find even less warrant for seeing earlier ages as more thoroughly Christian than the present. If this is an age when many persons in Western culture devoted to intellectual activity have fallen away from Christianity, it is also an age when in the very cultures where these have fallen away, Christianity has achieved new kinds of intellectual vigor unknown in earlier ages.

There is no doubt, for example, that the intellectual vigor of Christianity in France and Germany today is far ahead of what it had been for the past two or three hundred years. In these countries and in the United States and elsewhere, the intellectual (and social) force of Christianity is going up rather than down. Unless some untoward accident reverses the trend, Catholic thought generally will soon be once again in its entirety, and not just in various individuals (often numerous enough) completely at home in the world of scientific and historical fact from which it had been, unfortunately, more or less estranged corporately from the time of Galileo through the nineteenth and early twentieth centuries.

The Christian image of man is something of which we catch fitful glimpses in various cultures, but not something which anyone can seize intellectually in its totality. Our feeble attemps to represent it are always seen to be deficient in following ages, for in its completeness the image lives only in the entire Church herself, not in statements or gestures which individual men and women make here and there.

Talk about "post-Christian man" or a "post-Christian age" presumes a grasp of the total meaning of Christianity which those who habitually rely on such terms seldom if ever enjoy. A favorite of those addicted to "post-Christianizing" has been William Butler Yeats, who, seemingly out of a desire to create poetry rather than to explain anything, treats of a post-Christian age in *A Vision* and his later poems. But Yeats gives no evidence of an adequate grasp of Christianity such as would pass muster in an assembly of devoted Christians today, although he was indeed a great poet and the immediate descendant of Christians. He had no real contact, for example, with the kind of Christian phenomenon represented by Newman's extraordinarily vital thinking in his own time or with the interior life of the Catholic Church of which Newman was such a live part. Like Nietzsche, whom he often echoes, Yeats could make statements about "Christianity" only if you allowed him to be selective enough to mean by Christianity just what he wanted to mean, or could mean, and no more.

Indeed, whole areas of Christianity simply elude Yeatsian or Nietzschean analysis because neither is big enough for them—for example, the present liturgical revival (more adequately handled in terms of depth psychology and phenomenological analysis, although by no means entirely adequately even in such terms), or the specific individual reactions of Christianity to technological forms of civilization, which nobody yet understands adequately at all. What would Yeats have to say if confronted with the theology of Henri de Lubac or M.-D. Chenu or Yves Congar or Karl Rahner? Certainly nothing worthwhile, and most likely nothing at all. He would hardly even be interested in knowing what such persons were talking about, although they write from the depths of the Christian tradition. What would he have had to say faced with the writing of Pierre Teilhard de Chardin? He would have been utterly nonplussed, for the Yeatsian cosmology, like the Nietzschean, although it can produce some marvelous poetry, is committed to a retrograde cyclic view of reality which is quite unable to digest the fact of an evolutionary cosmos such as science knows and Teilhard seeks to interpret.

Our age is indeed different, and religiously different. But whatever it is, it should not be styled post-Christian. It is as much a pre-Christian age as a post-Christian age. Vast developments in Christian thought and action lie ahead. Until recent times, for example, theology has been severely handicapped in its exploration of the Incarnation of the Son because it has had to set this Incarnation against the backdrop of a universe very inadequately and even falsely conceived. The Aristotelian and Ptolemaic cosmology against which for hundreds of years Christianity, like natural physical phenomena, was interpreted we have long known to be defective and untrue. The truer natural picture of our evolutionary universe is, however, only now being opened up. It is far from completely opened yet, but the astrophysicists and geologists and paleontologists and biologists are getting at it more and more. It was in this real universe—not four thousand years old but some five to ten billion years old—that the Second Person of the Blessed Trinity, the Son of God and Himself God, became incarnate.

We shall not penetrate adequately the full message of the Incarnation until we have achieved a greater understanding of the natural universe as it really is in its totality and have seen God's work and Christ's in its relationship to the real whole. The Christian has to bring his theology to bear on a universe not only as reaching back five to ten billion years, but as reaching ahead in time in comparable measure.

Far from having had time to assimilate such perspectives, Christianity has not even had time as yet to make its way effectively all across the surface of the globe. For this is painstaking work, and the geographical frontiers have been open only a few generations, while many of them have recently been closed down again artificially by political action. Many of the by-products of the Western civilization long identified with, and certainly in complex ways dependent upon, Christianity have by now affected men everywhere on this surface, to be sure—analytic science, technology, the idea of revolution, democratic ambitions. But the spread of Christianity is not the same as the spread of such things. Christianity cannot be a mass import. It has to engage the person as a person.

Christians who are Christian enough not to identify Christianity with the West nor with obsolete cosmologies see the past as something they are glad to get away from, despite all its many fine contributions for which we must always remain permanently grateful. The age which is dawning presents the challenge and the thrill.

A Christology of an evolving cosmos lies ahead today as one of the greatest challenges which Christian theological speculation has ever had to meet. And the Christianizing of a technological society will tax all the ingenuity we can muster under God's grace. Christianity may even have to do its work in a state of siege. Certainly faith will have to assert itself against indifference and unbelief with greater energy and courage than ever before. The tasks for the future make the tremendous achievements of the past look picayune. But this is the way it should be. Christianity has always been a religion of the future, although perhaps no Christians have been so intensely aware of this fact as alert Christians today. No age in the past is worth recalling. They were all less than satisfactory. Fulfillment lies ahead, where God's will is realized at the end of time.

10

American Culture and Morality

1. Some axioms

A DISCUSSION OF culture and morality in today's United States can well begin with some axioms. First, it appears that original sin cannot be considered as a quantitative variable: some persons do not have more of it and some less, nor do some ages have more of it and some less. Secondly, although culture is undergoing vast changes, in the technologically advanced societies as well as in the newly developing ones, unless we can produce documented evidence one way or another, we should not assume that morality is clearly changing on the whole for better or for worse.

The fields in which moral choices are made have altered. The immediate consequences of certain moral choices are often more vast, and perhaps the agony of decision is more excruciating at times. One decision may have as its immediate consequence the death of hundreds of thousands or millions of innocent persons. Some avenues of moral influence are more unified—for example, in the mass communication media. But to say that of the moral decisions made in the world today a greater proportion are evil decisions—either subjectively or objectively considered—than was the case a hundred or five hundred or a thousand years ago goes totally beyond the evidence on hand and probably beyond any evidence which will ever be naturally available. To know the full state of affairs, statistical studies as well as evaluatory studies would have to be made, and such studies comparing the whole field of moral choices through successive ages appear impossible. We must face the truth that when vast cultures are said to be morally "corrupt" as wholes, it is difficult to assign a satisfactory meaning to "whole." It is not evident that such a state of affairs is due to the fact that there are more morally bad decisions being made, for it may well be that a relatively few decisions in sensitive places are the factors really being considered, so that "corruption" refers to culturally crucial decisions rather than to total moral behavior. The "meaning" of a culture is frequently defined by minorities. The most "corrupt" cultures produce a surprising number of saints, and—what is more interesting—followers of saints. An astonishing number of heroic moral decisions were made by Christian martyrs in the purportedly all-corrupt Roman Empire.

Of course divine revelation in Old Testament times and with the coming of Christ had certainly a strengthening effect on moral behavior, associated with a vaster supernatural effect on man. But circumstantial measurement of total moral rectitude or deviation in sizable groups of persons after divine revelation remains as difficult as ever. God's visitations on his people often punish their sins, but the case of Job stands as a reminder that there is no way of proving an exact correlation between magnitude of sin and the rigor of temporal suffering. Often God makes his sun shine upon the just and the unjust. To get at the total morality of a large group of Christians constituting a whole culture in every single facet of their very fluid lives appears ordinarily impossible, especially when one recalls that, according to his own teaching, Jesus Christ does not merely resolve moral crises for individuals but also creates them, that the commitment of individuals to Christianity even in a purportedly Christian culture varies greatly, that grace acts unpredictably, and that often, as St. Paul is at pains to point out, grace more abounds precisely where sin abounds.

It is well to state flatly that we have no cogent evidence that we, the vast population of the United States, are on the whole morally better or worse than earlier ages generally, because much discussion often implies the contrary. Individuals who are unfamiliar with the past, as even individuals who have lived through a good deal of the past sometimes manage to be, know the past chiefly as a vacuum devoid of all circumstantiality. They tend to fill it with their own projections. If they are under some compulsion to think that man in the present is getting better and better morally, they think of the past as a brutal wasteland from which man has escaped. If they feel that the present age must be admonished—as most people at one time or another tend to do—their ignorance of the past offers them a cheap formula: the present is measured against an imagined past when men, society, and culture are assumed to have been not only different but clearly better. This assumption is, at best, difficult to prove. One familiar form it has taken has been the conviction that in the early Christian community everything was sweetness and light. I have often wondered what those obsessed by this assumption could make of the Epistles of St. Paul to the Corinthians.

Much moralizing, it appears, is based on Murphy's Law. Murphy's Law, I am told, is a simple one: if things can get worse, they will get worse. It usually comes equipped with two corollaries. First, they can. Second, they will. Much popular writing—

and, I am afraid, preaching—superficially critical of our age simply applies Murphy's Law retrospectively. Things have got worse and worse and worse. This view, which has of course assignable psychological roots, has also very curious implications: if we are still alive at all, a few hundred years ago everything must have been almost perfect. And the future is going to be unbearable— if not in 1984 certainly not long after.

2. *Some comparisons*

Having thus maintained that the present is on the whole not demonstrably worse or better than the past, and having suggested that our present paper is not a jeremiad but rather a reflective investigation, we have not maintained that moral conditions in the present are good or that they are all the same as in the past. They are never very good. Countless individuals, today as earlier, find the moral situation desperate. Indeed, it is desperate for us all. We are all capable of the worst, even if our past performance has been good, as it very likely has not been. Each must work out his salvation in fear and trembling to his last gasp. Each of us, alone. The situation is worse than bad: fundamentally, it really is desperate—save for God's love and mercy (the Christian will mean here in Christ).

Furthermore, the situation today is in many ways morally different from what it has been in the past. Ages and cultures vary in the emphases they put on one or another aspect of morality, and they also vary in the kinds of temptation they may specialize in. Shifts in attitudes, and sometimes even in standards, are observable between past and present. But these shifts are not at all clearly in one direction. Some are for the worse, and some are for the better. There is both retrogression and advance.

The example of retrogression which perhaps most readily leaps to the eye has to do with marriage. Most early Americans considered that only the most utterly grievous circumstances could justify the permanent breaking up of a family by the separation of husband and wife, and that the husband-wife relationship was so profound and sacred that in those rare cases where separation was invoked to secure against worse disaster, the parties to the marriage were not free to give themselves to others. Today it is quite acceptable socially, and, in the opinion of many, morally, for an individual to have whole cascades of successive marriage partners, or for groups to interchange their partners in bewildering patterns which, if the persons are prominent enough, are duly recounted in the daily press. The changed attitude toward marriage has been accompanied by a changed attitude on the part of many Americans regarding sexual behavior and chastity generally. Personal control of sexual activity on moral grounds in the view of many—although by no means of all—is not so much urged or even considered desirable as it used to be.

As a Catholic, I believe in the sacredness of sexual powers and of marriage, and consequently regard this shift in principle concerning divorce and sexual activity as regrettable, although I do not by any means believe that all who do not totally share Catholic views regarding the indissolubility of marriage and regarding sexual morality are in bad faith. One does not, however, have to share the Catholic view regarding divorce to see the present situation in the United States as alarming. Roughly, one out of every four marriages in the United States ends in divorce, one out of every three in either divorce or separation, and in many urban areas one out of every two in divorce (some of these being divorces of persons already previously divorced once or oftener). This instability in the social institution most intimately involved in enabling the individual to find himself and others is sure to be reflected in curtailed ability of the individual to perform successfully his role as an individual and member of society. Informed persons of any religious persuasion or of no religious persuasion at all are almost all inclined to feel that this situation is not a desirable one.

If we look for areas where moral standards in the United States have on the whole improved, perhaps the most obvious is that of social justice in most of its aspects. Exploitation of the individual laborer by a relative few in privileged positions such as was tolerated or even regarded as inevitable or good in the past would not be tolerated today. Slavery is gone, although its consequences still haunt us. Race relations are far from ideal, but are vastly improved and improving. There has been a clear shift in standards here, as it has become clear to more and more that many of the standards earlier applied were not in fact in accord with justice or Christian teaching, although Christians earlier had managed by elaborate rationalization to think they were. If an ultimate moral standard such as the brotherhood of all men under God has not been changed, the proximate moral standards, which articulate such lofty-sounding principles with actuality, certainly have been.

The case of race relations reminds us that confusion resulting from a shift in moral standards can be a sign that the standards are going up quite as well as a sign that they are going down. In many areas in the United States white persons have been commonly conditioned from infancy against ever allowing themselves to relate to a dark-skinned person on terms of full human equality. They are, in other words, reared in a caste system of behavior. Sociologists point out that in caste systems it is usually obligatory for an individual of the supposed superior caste to insult the individual of the inferior caste at every contact. Such obligatory insult has been effected in our culture by strict taboos to which whites in certain subcultures have trained themselves, such as that forbidding the use of the titles "Mr." or "Mrs." in addressing dark-skinned persons, and, much more, in thinking about them. When individuals reared in this caste system are forced to change, the trauma is extreme because the whole system is structured not on accessible reasons but on irrational superstitions and inaccessible fears deep within the subconscious.

Here the real roots of behavior have been so far submerged that moral teaching has in the past largely disregarded them. They belonged to the things one was inhibited against talking about. Now that the roots of old interracial behavior patterns are becoming exposed and the issues are being cleared, the implications of religious and moral teachings concerning them are being spelt out as never before. The result is, of course, consternation and confusion for those who have been from infancy rigorously conditioned to a behavior which, they are now told, is immoral and unchristian. The confusion certainly demands to be eliminated. But meanwhile, its existence is here a good sign. It is one of the many signs that social justice is a greater reality today than two or three generations ago. And it is not merely that we have stumbled into greater social justice. People actually care about social justice more.

Improvement in social justice has been associated with a general diminution of overt public hostilities in American society today as compared with American society of some generations ago or with earlier society generally. Religion is seemingly much less contaminated by hatred. Understanding is in the air.

Some of our hatreds have, of course, been merely repressed and left to express themselves deviously. In many contemporary novels, as in our contemporary society which these novels portray, sexual activity, normally associated with love, is in fact an instrument of hate between marriage partners as well as between others—for example, in William Styron's *Lie Down in Darkness*, a work which is not by reason of this use of the sexual theme at all a bad or immoral book, but rather a course in morals for our time.

But not all our hatreds have been handled so unsuccessfully. Some have seemingly disappeared as suspicions have disappeared —for example, again, those between some religious groups. The mass media, with their enforcement of a certain openness in the exchange of information and understanding, have undoubtedly diminished intergroup suspicions, whatever else for good or evil they may have accomplished. The commercial base of American society also performs some role here, thus far little understood: it is perhaps significant that in an age when hostilities between nations are shouted over the world communication systems, displays of open hostility between manufacturers or merchandizers are simply not tolerated at all on the mass media or, for that matter, anywhere publicly. Whatever private antagonisms there may be between General Motors people and Ford people and however murderous the sales competition may be, Chevrolet advertisements do not openly attack Ford, or vice versa. The reason may be the danger of legal reprisals. No matter. The result is a kind of public equanimity enforced within and around commerce and industry despite actual conditions of stress.

Diminution of hostilities appears to have some root in our newer family structures. The current pattern in the American family, that of the "nuclear family" of parents and children, uncomplicated by close and continued obligatory contact with other members of the family is not an unmitigated blessing. Still, there appears to be evidence that this family structure generates fewer intrafamilial tensions and correlative interfamilial feuds than the more massive structures of the past. The intense hatreds between not merely individuals but also family factions generated in the past and memorialized in ancient Greek literature and subsequent literature have been greatly reduced in range, if by no means completely eliminated. Albee's *Who's Afraid of Virginia Woolf?* memorializes hatred, but between individuals, not whole dynasties.

Other tensions in society, which are often enough projections of tensions first experienced within a family structure, appear also to be somewhat abated today. Most notable is the decrease, already noted, in tension and unedifying hatreds between religious groups in this country and some others. There are those who ascribe this simply to an increased religious indifference, to a diminution in commitment. Such explanation does not, it appears, stand up against the fact of what religious commitment was in the past or what it is today. (Of this commitment more will be said later.)

One might argue that within the nuclear family if there is less occasion for ramified hatreds, here is also less opportunity for love. But how much love should be focused into the family rather than outside it? One recalls here St. Thomas Aquinas's reflections upon incest: one of the reasons for the incest taboo is to prevent the concentration of love within the same group of persons and to turn it outward toward other family groups from which marriage partners must be chosen.

3. The problem of divergent traditions

The differences between the moral outlook in the United States today and that in the past are complicated by differences within the moral traditions of the present itself. In the United States we have known three main traditions, which are closely related and yet not the same: Protestant, Catholic, and Jewish.

As interpreted by Protestants generally, Christian morality incorporates a variety of trends. The characteristic Protestant reliance on the Scriptures as privately interpreted exists in a fixed historical setting. First, there is the Augustinian heritage deriving through the Middle Ages from St. Augustine of Hippo with a strong emphasis on the hereafter and abiding distrust of the material world and even of secular government, a strong sense of sin, and of man's incapacity to do anything about his sinfulness himself. Connected in various ways with the Augustinian tradition is the general Protestant distrust of natural law, an outgrowth of the classic Protestant teaching that human nature was totally corrupted by Adam's Fall. Contending, however, with this distrust of human nature and of natural law there exists also a strong rationalist strain in the Protestant mind, historically mingled with the humanitarianism of Benjamin Franklin and Thomas Jefferson, and having as one of its sequels Unitarianism and even secularism.

Another mark of much American Protestantism from the beginning has been a strong attraction to the Old Testament, which at times almost takes precedence over the New. The early New Englanders in particular had a deep feeling for the Old Testament Covenant between God and his Chosen People. In many ways Protestant devotion to this Covenant, extended into Puritan times, was an equivalent of Catholic interest in the natural law.

Covenant theology also encouraged a kind of socialized personalism. Religious conviction in this tradition is still likely to implement itself through political action ideally undertaken by the community as a whole, as in the "Blue Laws" against gambling and other diversions terminating in the quondam American constitutional amendment prohibiting intoxicating liquors. The strong socialized bent in Protestantism resulted by the end of the nineteenth and the beginning of the twentieth century in the social gospel which concentrated religious activity on work for the social betterment of the neighbor under the leadership of persons such as Walter Rauschenbusch.

Of late an important development in the Protestant moral tradition has been the speculation concerned with situation ethics, which are related to certain existentialist trends and which tend in their pure form—probably never realized—to solve a moral problem as an absolutely unique affair without reference to so-called principles.

Christianity in the Roman Catholic Church is also strongly Augustinian, but Catholic Augustinianism is tempered by a scholasticism whose leading, if not most typical, figure is St. Thomas

Aquinas. This scholasticism makes free use of the rational, validating the natural law as still operative, if subordinate to Divine Revelation. Of recent years the scholastic tradition among Catholics has itself been tempered by a personalist and theistic existentialism which favors in many ways a re-emphasized Augustinian outlook. The new emphasis has insisted on the limits of the rational, but it has not for the most part taken a disparaging view of natural institutions. The discovery of evolutionary patterns, particularly in human thought and social institutions, has even encouraged a greater, if still reserved, hopefulness regarding these institutions.

Surprisingly, in a tradition which validates the natural law, there has been and is still at the moment among American Catholics relatively little interest in political action for social or political reform. Catholics have been interested in social work, and many individual Catholics have campaigned and campaigned hard for social betterment, but in its tendency to be scornful of "do-gooders" and in its reservations regarding the sincerity or efficaciousness of social reform movements, the Catholic community as a whole might be styled Augustinian rather than Thomist.

Catholic moral teaching is highly unified because of the possibility of securing authoritative decisions from the Church as a whole through those on whom she confers orders and thereby (to varying degrees) a definitive role in the teaching office which she believes she holds from God. Her moral teachings, while not insensitive, have often been carefully and explicitly articulated. The profundity of the Catholic respect for the natural law when conjoined with divine revelation is shown in the strong and carefully developed tradition of casuistry which exists in the American Catholic community as among Catholics generally, particularly since the Renaissance. Catholics are likely to think of a concrete moral problem as complex but also as amenable to rational solution, under grace, if the proper skills and patience are employed.

The Jewish tradition of course furnishes much of the background for Christian morality as interpreted by Protestants and Catholics. This tradition can be characterized in itself as marked by reverence for the Torah with its prescriptions, and by a varying set of attitudes toward the Talmud. Moral problems are often interpreted through stories, pointed and sometimes enigmatic, such as in the Haggadah, but individual interpretations vary enormously among Orthodox, Reform, and Conservative Jews.

Jewish Messianism has worked itself out in our day, as earlier, in a tradition of benevolence and social justice. This of late in the United States has taken the form of concerted political action which often aims not directly at the betterment of the Jewish community, but at the betterment of man in general, particularly in areas where man's freedom is compromised.

The Jewish tradition is marked also by a strong family and in-group feeling. Its morality is tinged with both mysticism and rationalism, sometimes competing and sometimes joined.

4. *Secularism: the distancing of God*

These three principal moral traditions in the United States are basically religious, relating morality in one way or another to obedience to God. Of late, however, a new morality is making itself more and more heard: secularism, in one or another of its many forms. Its confrontation of the three existing traditions of which we have spoken is in many ways the most striking moral phenomenon of our time.

Secularism comprises, as a matter of fact, a broad spectrum of attitudes. At one end, where it is tangent to a definite religious heritage, secularism may mean simply a disposition to "let religion take care of itself" as one sets about enjoying, or coping with, the immediacy of the present life without specific attention to any religious resonance. With this disposition to minimize religion, there may go commitment to a more or less articulate moral code, often one associated with humanitarianism, Darwinianism, Neo-Darwinianism, or one or another special cosmology. Or there may be no articulate attention to a moral code at all. Morality may be thought of as a matter which takes care of itself, and as a matter too individual and private to warrant discussion. At the other end of the secularist spectrum are highly articulate atheistic humanisms, such as that of Sartre, in which the individual is all that matters, his decisions being made with deliberate disregard of others and without any meaning or law outside his own isolated, self-contained act which he is here and now making and which gives his life its validity and authenticity. Among the various kinds of secularisms is the Marxist. Secularism is by no means always Marxist, but in its denial of religious resonance Marxism is a secularist humanism with a secularist morality.

Secularism as a moral program proposing to be independent of religion is not so entirely new as some of its friends or enemies would make it out to be. It has discernible connections with Christianity and with Judaism, such as it could hardly have with certain other religions. Many religions consider matter to be evil. Christianity and Judaism do not, and to this extent they have given status to the secular.

Modern secular science, one of the greatest creations of man, has come into being in a civilization conditioned by Hebrew and even more directly by Christian teaching. To other civilizations it is an import. Certainly the Catholic tradition gives an internal validity to the secular world itself, and in more tortuous ways, many Protestant traditions do the same. This world is not independent of God, but on the other hand divine revelation does not necessarily compromise or supersede secular structures. "Grace builds on nature" is a logion of Catholic theologians. In the Christian view, consequently, legitimate attention to things of this world is not anti-religious. But militant secularism goes further, asserting that nothing exists, or at least nothing matters, except the purely secular, that is to say, actuality to the exclusion of anything divine. Morality has nothing to do with God. Secularism is of course not so secular as it often pretends to be. It grew out of a religious view, and often, as in Sartre's case, retains highly dogmatic trappings.

How new secularism is in the United States is not easy to say, for it is not easy to say to what extent it prevailed in the early American colonies. Even with full acknowledgment of increased secularization in many sectors of twentieth-century life, it is not at all evident that earlier Americans as a whole were more preoccupied with religion and morality than Americans are today. Many were religious and highly articulate about religion. And yet it is certain, as Franklin H. Littell's book, *From State Church to Pluralism*, shows, that there are many more Americans affiliated with churches today than there were at the time of the early American colonists. This is so in almost any way one figures the statistics, not only absolutely, but proportionately to the population as a whole, or, if you wish, proportionately to the population of Protestant background (the greater part of the early American population). In other words, the founders of our country on the whole were by no means so occupied in church affairs as their present-day descendants are. We must not, of course, make too much of avowed religious commitment: to assume that church membership is always tantamount to a higher degree of morality is of course not warranted. Church membership can be merely token membership. But it is ordinarily some kind of declaration against pure secularism. In view of the facts of church commitment today, it appears quite gratuitous to assume that secularization has just recently taken over completely in the United States or is about to do so.

To understand the nature of secularist tendencies, one must see the secular phenomenon as it is, without imputing a nonexistent integrity to the past or a nonverifiable decadence to the present. The rise of secularism is in great part not a moral but a noetic phenomenon. It is connected with a changed ratio between man's knowledge of the physical universe and the sum total of all his knowledge. With his usual skill in getting to the heart of the question, Karl Rahner has indicated the noetic bases of the present secular *Problematik*:

> The difficulty of the mission of the Church, since the Middle Ages and now since the end of the modern era when a new age is arising, has consisted especially in this: The nonreligious areas of existence, in contrast with former times, have become of tremendous density, fullness, complication, and capacity for absorption. Simply with a glance at the whole one must ask himself: What could interest the man of former times intellectually and absorb him beyond the satisfying of the most immediate vital needs? And then the answer comes: on the whole only the religious question of existence. For there wasn't anything else really. And what else there was (like art and science) was itself an impelling factor in the religious life.
>
> If we ask the same question for the present-day man, we must answer: besides the religious element there is still almost incalculably much.[1]

Father Rahner goes on to enumerate some of the areas of existence and thought capable of absorbing man's attention and filling his life as never before: secular science, art, technology, economic management. To these we could add others indefinitely, including the whole range of new subjects which have made their way into our universities: sociology, anthropology, literature as a higher discipline, modern cosmology, biology, cosmic and organic evolution, human geography—vast fields of learning many of which only a few generations ago were not even known as possibilities but which now absorb tremendous psychic energies.

It is true that our increased knowledge of the natural world does not answer the basic religious questions. Science, anthropological as well as physical, is basically limited. It gives me, for example, no insight whatsoever into the meaning of my coming death—I must face death as all men have, unpracticed and alone. All our increase in natural knowledge, wonderful though it is, somehow misses the ultimate point. It sheds no light whatsoever on the question as to the ultimate meaning of the universe or of my own consciousness. None of it contains the slightest promise that a thousand years from now or a hundred thousand years from now man will be able to say, "Now I understand the meaning of life itself. I know what existence is all about." We gain more and more detailed knowledge, but the mysterious underlying patterns remain a mystery inscrutable to science. Science can distract us from these mysteries (though it need not), but they are always there, teasing us as they have teased man from the beginning: What is the meaning of existence? It does no good even to say it has no meaning. No one will believe you. Man will continue to puzzle, as he always has.

Nevertheless, if our new increment of secular knowledge does not of itself solve religious questions, it does provide matter for religious reflection. If we feel, as we have some reason to feel, that by comparison with the present the past was in some ways and in some individuals more exclusively absorbed in religion than the present is and was to this extent more moral than the present, we must at the same time own that a great deal of this past absorption was due not to verifiable religious concern as such but to default of worthwhile secular understanding. Instead of giving a fuller dimension to understanding of nature and its processes, religion in the past was often serving as a substitute for natural knowledge. This made religion, with its accompanying morality, attractive, but by the same token it made it vulnerable. Insofar as religion was made to serve as a substitute for science, increase in natural knowledge could directly supplant interest in religion.

In significant ways advance in scientific knowledge of nature has improved the religious prospect. It has lessened the dangers of falling directly into the illusions of the old nature religions with their attendant aberrations, which sometimes went as far as human sacrifice. Early pretechnological man lived close to nature, but his relations with nature were not uniformly comfortable or good. He had very little abstract understanding of its forces. Feeling the power which nature obviously had as mysterious, as almost entirely beyond him, he thought of this power as like that of God himself. This he did, moreover, whether or not he was an idolater. The ancient Hebrews sang in their Psalms of the thunder as *kol Jahweh*, the voice of God. Given the proper Hebrew sense of God's utter transcendence, this was a metaphor and good. The Hebrews were not idolatrous, at least when they remained true to their religion. But without this sense, the mentality here in evidence could readily slip into the crassest sort of nature religion. The power of God and the power of nature could be taken as one. Men could end by worshipping what was not God as a God.

The conviction is not uncommon today that advance in scientific knowledge has itself somehow compromised religion. Earlier, pretechnological man was protected by his ignorance. He was closer to God when he knew less about the secular world, for in his helplessness he felt more dependent on God. Such a conviction overlooks the fact that there was often a fallacy in the way early man conceived of this dependence. He often thought of God as in fact a part of nature, working in the world as natural causes do. This, of course, is not the way God works. However meaningful thunder may be as a symbol of God, Hebrew and Christian teachings do not allow us to think of God as causing thunder in the way in which we might cause sound by muscular action such as beating a drum. God is not a physical body and does not act as one. God's will is indeed realized in the world, even in thunder, but he does not bring about his will through muscular or mechanical action of his own. To think of his action as causative in the way in which ours would be or in the way in which other physical action may be is in fact blasphemous. God is not a substitute for physics any more than physics is a substitute for God.

In his ignorance, early man was all too prone to make him such a substitute. Not knowing the physical causes of thunder, he was inclined to think of God as somehow the physical cause. God was conceived as essentially providing physical explanation. God "did" something to some object in the universe to make this noise. Such a line of thinking not only could lead to gross idolatry by confusing God and nature or nature and God but also could and did set the stage for later withdrawal from God. Since God was thought of as a being bringing about physical results which man could not otherwise account for, the more man found he could account for, or in other words the more knowledge of the natural world advanced, the less this peculiarly conceived God had to do. By the late nineteenth century, there was on hand enough other physical explanation of physical phenomena for him to be permanently retired. This was the context in which Nietzsche could announce that God was dead.

Unfortunately, in the nineteenth century, when the accumulation of scientific knowledge had become truly massive, there were all too many men of faith who had thought that they could prove the existence of God, conceived of as a God of physical explanation, by arguing from man's ignorance. Thunder by this time was better understood, but much else was not. Such persons therefore argued that since for the beauties of a chambered nautilus, an awe-inspiring tree, or a complex galaxy of stars, there was no total scientific explanation, one had to suppose the existence of a supreme being to account for what could not be explained. This is the same thing all over again. One can prove *nothing* from the *absence* of knowledge. If an intricate being surpasses any known physical explanation, this may merely mean that man does not yet know much physics. I believe that a rational case can be made out for God's existence, but such a case can never be based on what man does *not* know. You cannot argue the existence of anything from what you do not know. Proof for

God's existence must be based on the *known* existence of something in our experience and on *insight* into the implications of
that existence.

But that is another story. The point here is that earlier man's ignorance of the natural, secular universe was by no means a religious boon. He was badly off because of this ignorance. His
ignorance in the long run was a threat to his faith. It was a
religious liability, for it distorted his idea of the true God.

It is largely because of a heritage of thinking about God as a
physical explanation that man today feels that God is "distanced,"
éloigné, placed further and further from us. If it has become
difficult to talk about God publicly with the immediacy to which
earlier man was accustomed, it may well be that this earlier immediacy was not all that might have been desired. Sometimes it
was confusion. Thus while it is true that the development of
science and technology has weakened man's awareness of God by
distracting from him, as we have seen, with the wealth of secular
knowledge and by giving man a heady experience of greater and
greater control of the universe, it is also true that the "distancing"
of God is in part due to man's faulty way of conceiving of him
in the past, due to man's ignorance of the physical universe. By
removing a great deal of this ignorance, scientific advance has
improved the religious prospect. God's cause is not served by
ignorance as such.

Whatever its manifold causes, the recent "distancing" of God
is an era, not an interlude. Martin Buber suggests that this is an
age when God is "silent." It might be more accurate to say that
it is an age in which man is silent about God, in great part because man has not assimilated to his knowledge of God the new
knowledge of the physical universe which has been recently given
him. God speaks to men today as always—there is really no evidence that he does not, and a great deal that he does. But God's
manner of speaking to man varies somewhat as man moves
through history. God spoke to man in the Scriptures in the days of
Jeremiah, and he still speaks through them in our day. But God's
voice in the Scriptures echoes today through a dense and carefully explored history which has penetrated and formed even our
subconscious and which was unknown to Jeremiah, reaching back,

as it does, not only to Jeremiah but also hundreds of thousands of years before his time.

God has willed that our day know his word in a vaster cosmic context. There is no point in yearning for an outmoded context into which God might speak. There is no point in stinting in our probing into nature. If man cannot yet comfortably relate God's presence to a cosmology connected with atom physics, he will not learn how to do so by abandoning the study of atom physics. To fulfill his role, man must not only retain his hold on the physical but must also continue to strengthen this hold. Man is the bridge connecting the material and the spiritual, which means, under grace, the material and the divine. He must learn to think of the cosmos in all its marvelous detail and of God, too—not as part of material actuality but as its transcendent Creator who is both beyond it and in it.

5. *Exteriorization of media*

The new fullness in the nonreligious areas of existence which has brought on secularism is in spectacular evidence in the physical sciences. But it has probably not had its deepest effect there. The deepest effect has probably been in the arts of communication themselves. These have had a curious history, registering the process of secularization with singular promptness and immediacy. They were in a sense man's first secular possessions to achieve major development. In their pretechnological Western form, as the *artes sermocinales*, consisting of grammar, rhetoric, and dialectic or logic, the arts of communication achieved a high degree of self-consciousness and self-possession in antiquity. This represented a secular development. In the days of Origen and Tertullian, and indeed even earlier, many Christians regarded these arts with the same misgivings and suspicion which some Christians today manifest toward technology and science—grammar, rhetoric, and logic were things too much of this world. Some early church fathers saw the study of grammar and rhetoric as capitulation to secularism, and St. Bernard of Clairvaux thought much the same of the study of dialectic, at least as this was urged by Abélard.

Since then, the field of communication has undergone a vast development which has effected simultaneously man's external control of his physical environment and his own interior psychological structures. Earlier attention to communication gave the whole field a high personal charge. Rhetoric and dialectic—and, yes, even formal logic, as has been brilliantly shown by Gilbert Durand in *Les structures anthropologiques de l'imaginaire* (Grenoble, 1960)—fostered a world view in which quite literally everything, including even the most abstract issues, associated with intellectual parties or "schools," tended to be cast up in terms of praise and blame, the dominent foci of expression. Later developments have changed this situation. Attention to communication gradually freed itself from the oral-aural point of view which the study of rhetoric had sustained, although at an incredibly slow rate. As late as the late nineteenth century, the pretense was still maintained in places that communication was universally oral, and that writing was subordinate to oratory. But gradually attention was weened to writing, then to typography, and now in our day to the fantastic display of mechanisms and techniques which go into the mass communications media in all their forms. The present problem of the media is quite the opposite of the overpersonalization which was the problem from antiquity through the eighteenth century. The media have become detached from the human person to a degree, externalized, depersonalized, made into "things." So we are told, and so we feel.

Something has taken place here comparable to what we have called the "distancing" of God. The properly human has been "distanced," and with it morality itself. Because of the sheer size and complexity of communication operations, the structure of communication itself has become a special field for study and research. Efforts at communication absorb vast amounts of psychic energy. Operations tending to focus on the mechanism of communication tend to neglect the interior of the individual, where all true communication takes place. In mass communication, the result is inevitable. Father William F. Lynch has protested in *The Image Industries* that films and television chronically tend to confuse fantasy with reality, weaken the sensibility, enslave the imagination, and project spectacular dreams which wipe out the true lines of human actuality. But more than this, since the "thing," the structure itself, demands so much attention, the human, the moral, tends to lose definition and to be minimized.

6. *Interiorization of conscience*

Attendant on these developments in the field of communications there has been another kind of "distancing." This has been between the public expression of morality and private moral performance. We must be somewhat careful in stating what the situation is here, for it is not at all true that in earlier ages the public picture of morality was uniformly high. One has only to think of the base domestic and sexual standards which were accepted as characteristizing the public behavior of the rulers of purportedly Christian Europe for well over a millennium and to compare these standards, for example, with the public image associated with the Presidents of the United States or the governors of our states or with the rulers of present-day Great Britain and other Western European countries. I do not mean to say that all these later public figures have in fact been uniformly edifying by natural or Christian or Jewish moral standards, but only that the public image associated with them has tended to be. All our public images have not by any means morally deteriorated. Some have definitely improved. One could also, for example, make out a good case for the position that the public image of the businessman in the United States has in many ways improved since the era of the robber barons of nineteenth-century industry.

Nevertheless the pluralism of our society and the depersonalization effected by the mass media have resulted in a cleavage within our outlook: today there is much more tolerance for the public expression of views clashing with the values which individuals lived by than earlier society allowed. If one holds absolute standards of morality—as I do, although I do not hold, or do not wish to hold insensitive standards—one finds these standards controverted or openly denied in part (never, I believe, in their entirety) in the public press. Even those who would hold that morality is relative have to act in any given instance according to one or another pattern, and this pattern is open to public attack, too.

Conditions were otherwise in earlier, tradition-directed societies, to use David Riesman's handy term. Here we find more
exact correlation between the kind of standards which society
allowed to be publicly aired and the behavior of its members.
But this condition was not, in fact, entirely happy. Earlier society
tended to expect everyone to behave alike and to be intolerant
of discrepancies between publicly aired moral views and the
commonly expected behavior not merely because it felt itself in
possession of a coherent code, but in great part also because it
tended to identify the good with social conformity. Between the
surface of the individual's life and the interior conscience, there
was no great distance. Interior conscience there was, but it did
not stand so much on its own. Man confronted actuality in a
pattern of behavior which was simply given him. He tended to
be morally satisfied by conforming to the pattern rather than by
examining its merits.

The work reported by Marvin K. Opler in his *Culture, Psychiatry, and Human Values* and by J. C. Carothers in *Psychiatry* for November, 1959, on the lack of individual analytic
powers in illiterate societies is relevant here. In such tradition-
directed societies, it appears that the individual does not venture
into private speculation. The thoughts he thinks are the community's thoughts rather than his own. The ancient pagan Roman
principle later appropriated by Christian princes for political purposes under the formula *cuius regio eius religio* provides a case
in point. Other countries, other gods. Religion *was* conformity.
When the outside changed, the inside was expected to be changed,
too. This strikes us as unprincipled and hypocritical, as it struck
early Christian and earlier Hebrew martyrs. But it sounded less
strange in more primitive ages.

Gradually, as primitive society changed and the structures of
the individual psyche with it, the individual conscience became
more and more clearly the immediate rule among thinking men—
the acknowledged rule, at any rate, if not by any means always
the operative one. Even in the Old Testament, which stresses
conscience from the very beginning, one can see a development
of this sort. The pressure on the interior, individual conscience
achieves a new urgency in late medieval and Renaissance con-

centration on the examination of conscience, and another kind of maximal development in certain forms of Protestant pietism well-known in early American history. In our day this interiorization has reached a new intensity, and it is evident that its development is related to a pattern of interiorization marked in other areas of the conscious life: more today than ever before the literary and graphic arts deal directly with interior states, rather than exterior activity; the social sciences join with psychotherapy to stress interior development of the individual; philosophy becomes concerned with intersubjectivity, as the lines which hold society and knowledge itself together are traced to their deepest sources in the individual's awareness of self and other.

7. Interior versus privacy

In focusing attention more directly on interior states, we have become more and more aware than conscience itself is an interior and personal thing. This does not, however, mean that morality is no longer relevant to externals, to the surface of life, or to the social structure. We are learning in our time that the fact that conscience is personal and interior does not mean that conscience is private. When the personal conscience is respected as such, this does not mean that it is reduced to something mute, incommunicado. Quite the contrary. The interiorized conscience wants very much to be heard. Interiority of its very nature is social. It drives toward communication.

Moreover, the fact that one conscience does not wish to do violence to other consciences does not mean that it is not interested in the externals of behavior. Man's intelligence drives toward unity, and it is inevitable that the individual expect that the exterior conform to the interior, that the public expression of morality conform to what he feels called upon to profess himself. If one believes something is true and right, it is only good sense to expect or hope that all others will see the truth and recognize the right. When they do not, one may excuse them, but one is nevertheless under a strain. The strain can be particularly great in the case of not too intelligent, well-meaning persons, and in the case of the young. Pluralism imposes a penalty, which the individual psyche has to pay.

Our pluralistic society is not easing the burden of morality. It is simply reallocating the burden. In a society such as that of medieval Europe or colonial New England or the Communist countries today, society as a whole assumes—rightly or wrongly— the responsibility of establishing and upholding moral norms. Our pluralistic permissiveness throws the responsibility on the individual. It places a great strain on the individual—sometimes more than a given individual can bear, for present American society is permissive to the point of near moral anarchy. The flaunting of moral beliefs contrary to the going consensus of behavior has become by now a convention which certain public figures and groups feel obliged to follow. Under these conditions the individual conscience is forced to defend its own decisions more and more on its own, and it is not at all evident that the individual conscience is always equipped to do so.

Here is the center of the moral crisis in the United States today: how to support the individual conscience while respecting its integrity. Conscience needs support—from family, friends, and religious institutions. It needs this support not merely to be socially effective but to maintain its own integrity. It is the business of a democratic, pluralistic society to favor such support, to encourage its citizens to act not only individually but also in concert on moral and on other questions. By this I do not mean that every group action of moral protest is defensible, or if it is defensible, that it is advisable or effective. But group action itself which does not deny others' rights is to be encouraged insofar as it helps form and sustain individual conviction.

The question of public morality in our society is intimately tied in with that of group action. The problems of public morality cannot be dissolved into personal, individual problems. Life is a moral affair at every point at which decision is in play, and decision is in play in public as in private matters. Publicly, a nation or other group acts necessarily out of some kind of moral consensus. Pluralism does not eliminate the necessity of consensus but rather demands that it be sensitively arrived at, constantly examined and re-examined. Pluralism makes, in fact, for much moral busy-work, for it is less likely than other systems to fix exactly the agency for deciding what a consensus is and for acting on a consensus. Responsibility is diffuse.

A good instance is that of the mass media, which so challenge our moralists today. In his book *Responsibility in Mass Communication* Wilbur Schramm analyzes four approaches to the problem of moral responsibility in mass communication: authoritarianism, libertarianism, Soviet Communism, and social responsibility within the media themselves. The last approach is the newest, the most promising, and the most complex: as presented by Schramm, following Siebert, Peterson, and Schramm in *Four Theories of the Press,* it rests on an awareness that "changes in media" have forced "new thinking by communicators, commissions, and philosophers" and on the principle that "media must assume [the] obligation of social responsibility, and if they do not, someone must see that they do." The "someone" shows how problematic and open this answer really is. "Someone" might even have to be the government.

In the situation in which we find ourselves, we are destined to talk not less about conscience but more about conscience than perhaps ever before. We must not shy away from our task. We are rather well off to undertake it. We are certainly sufficiently equipped, sufficiently knowledgeable about the complications, anthropological, psychological, historical, and other which enter into analyses, not to fall necessarily into superficial rationalization of our behavior. Our knowledge of complexities should not paralyze us but rather liberate us.

We shall need frankness and courage and insight, for in doing so we will expose areas of disagreement as well as of agreement. In America we have a complex of moral traditions which agree in some places and in others do not. It is essential that we realize the maximum agreement where agreement exists and work with it, that we identify misunderstandings as what they are and not as disagreements, and that where we do not agree we come to a clear understanding of our difference. It would not hurt to get down to particular instances, to pay some attention to casuistry, the careful and informed analysis of complex concrete cases. It is in the density of concrete living that morality has its actual being, in the United States as elsewhere.

But most of all we need confidence that this is God's world, that he inhabits it now as always, invisible but not unknown, at home in its new as well as in its old forms. We must not underestimate the difference in the context, nor the sameness in God and his law.

NOTES

1. Karl Rahner, S.J., "The Lay Apostolate," *Cross Currents*, VII (1957), 244.

11

The Lady and the Issue

AUTHOR'S NOTE.—*The following study was done at a time when ecumenism was not so far advanced as it is today. If it were written now, some of the edges of difference which it reveals between Catholic and Protestant thinking would perhaps be presented less starkly in order to promote further the irenic spirit which we find so welcome and promising. As is plain, the study grew out of a less irenic situation. It was occasioned by a "chorus of protest" from outside the Catholic Church about an action she had taken within the economy of her own dogmatic teachings. That this protest occurred should not occasion dismay or discouragement. For, in addition to many basic agreements, there are real differences between Protestant and Catholic teaching, not only in what is explicitly stated but often enough in more darkly grounded matters which stubbornly resist statement. It is well at times in the interest of ecumenicism itself to bring such matters to the light of explicit formulation and to state frankly the reasons which can be urged for one's own position and against the opposed stand. This is what "The Lady and the Issue" undertakes to do. In a friendly but frank spirit, the study is thus presented* *here as it originally appeared in England (*The Month*), in the United States (*Cross Currents*), translated into German in a Munich journal of intercultural exchange (*Dokumente, now published in Cologne), and translated into French in a Paris professional anthropological and psychoanalytic journal (*Psyché). Readers will be able to correct any emphases which today appear untoward.*

Of the works I have seen since this article first appeared, certainly the most relevant one is that by the eminent physician and psychiatrist Karl Stern, The Flight from Woman *(New York, 1965), which develops on a wider scale themes so close to those in this article that it must be mentioned here. W. Lloyd Warner's volume,* The Living and the Dead: A Study of the Symbolic Life of Americans *(New Haven, Conn., 1959) likewise presents much other relevant material.*

As psychologists now know only too well, issues concerned with authority and submission move in the labyrinths of human consciousness through passages which are often cunning and corridors which are often secretly contrived. The chorus of protest in non-Catholic circles which has followed on the definition of the Assumption provides a case in point—perhaps the finest laboratory case that could be desired from the point of view of theological speculation.

In the protest, there is a curious tension observable between the preoccupation with authority on the one side and with the matter defined on the other, so that the continued insistence that the latter is "non-essential" becomes a phenomenon of considerable importance. Here we have the strange tendency to associate in the act of protest two apparently irrelevant things so often associated in separatist movements: resentment of authority and a desire to write Our Lady off the record. In the present case, this latter manifests itself in the assertion that the actual content of the definition is, after all, quite a negligible matter—an assertion both so insistent and so calculatingly offhand as to hint that it conceals issues too urgent psychologically to be brought out into the open. And so, bring them out we must.

The revolt against the Catholic Church in the sixteenth century was not the simple revolt against authority that it is often made to be. Psychologically and in every other way, the symbol of authority is the father image. But the father image and all the apparatus that goes with it was not only kept by the separatists but inflated by them in a way it could not be within the Catholic economy. The Calvinist's God carried authority to the extreme of sheer whim, and Jonathan Edwards was in the main current of two centuries of separatism when he terrified the citizens of Massachusetts with his sermon on the praiseworthy horrors of divine authority as he conceived it, "Sinners in the Hands of an Angry God." Indeed, the father image is one of the most viable points of the separatist tradition. Attenuated and vestigial, it remains in the feeling about the Fatherhood of God and the brotherhood of man which is one of the last snippets of dogma to persist in the most advanced stages of liberal Protestantism.

Devotion to a stern, unflinching authoritarianism, become an attribute not of a group but of individuals, split the separatist movement into countless sects. The real, deeply felt, but little understood difficulties of separatists were and are not with such authoritarianism, but with the mitigated, mediated authority, the symbol of which must be feminine, the initial experience of which each human being ordinarily knows in his relations with his mother. The Church which the separatist berated he saw, significantly, not as a cruel father but as an outcast mother. In anti-Catholic propaganda, even the Pope became only the Scarlet Woman of the Apocalypse—a title hardly the staple in denunciations of dictators.

The question to which the separatist returned the answer No was not, Is there a stern Master over us all? Rather, it was, In my dealings with this Master is there something involved which asserts itself not by authority so much as by inescapable continuity, which does not dart forth bright words of command but simply dwells with me, something which I do not pretend particularly to understand, which is so immediate that I hardly think of trying to understand it, but which is definitely and ineluctably a datum of my consciousness, which is unmistakably *there?* The matter concerns not a father, who appears at unpredictable intervals, to be sure, but, after all, only occasionally, who is assertive from time to time, but also in a relatively abstract way. The matter concerns a mother, to whom I first awoke, who was there all the time. The father's commands are intelligible, his dealings tend more to be in words, and I know him by them. They are sharp, distinct, and clear. Not so the presence of this other being. She may indeed give an occasional command, but radically she is known to me as the one who is there alongside me, who binds together all my fragments of days and years in the simple continuity of her material presence.

The mother does not operate in terms of authority, which she is inclined to disavow as her own and refer to the father, for her first experience of this child was as he grew in her womb, and she had little enough authority over him there. She continues her work as she began it then—darkly, mysteriously, and with her own being in complete subjection. She must assert authority, yes, but in a curiously obverse way. When she threatens, it is to say that, if necessary, ultimately a father will punish. She is a permanent occasion of humiliation and shame to those she commands, for her dealings, being based always on derived sanctions, not her own but the father's, keep always at the focus of attention the matter of subordination and subjection. Her very commands are in terms of her subjection to the father, whose sanction must rule all, so that it becomes matter for taunts to have to do what *mother* says.

Both by this subjection and by her way of bringing children into the world, which is not by commanding them nor by explaining them, but by bearing them, she is the symbol of submission and of death. She is, of course, the dark lady of the romantic poets and the mother-goddess of the mystery cults. Her role as representative of the dark, material principle of things determines her action with regard to authority: she flowers and discovers herself when completely and totally subject to it, and she gives it continuity and existence in time and space. Without a mother to transmit his authority into the real world of the child's life, the father is a sorry performer, a practical nonentity, and his authority is matter more for humor than for anything else.

This economy in which the female component is a vital factor is the economy against which the separatist mentality rebels. In its attitude toward this economy, the separatist reveals one of the deep, basic drives of his being which gives separatism—from Brownism and Anabaptism and Evangelicism through High Anglicanism—its characteristic twist. Depending on how thoroughly separatist it is, separatism from the sixteenth century to the present stands for a Christianity which, in various degrees, is in a fundamental sense unsexed.

Almost every characteristic tenet of separatist bodies can be charted in terms of the impulse to insulate religion from the femininely polarized aspects of reality. To catch sight of this fact, one must forget the contorting perspectives conjured up by the past few centuries out of the stale smoke of the courtly love tradition, and reconsider the view which makes woman, as against man, a kind of abstraction, the antithesis of all that is earthly, a dweller in a realm of "ideals." This view is ultimately untenable. Woman's relation to ideals is in function of the male's mind. Dante, not Beatrice, wrote the poem. Beatrice may have occasioned the vision, but he *had* it. From the poetic and from the "idealistic" point of view, Dante was inspired, while Beatrice, in a sense, had only to pose for him.

Dante's symbolism and his apotheosis of Beatrice as a kind of incarnate ideal has indeed a certain indubitable validity, but this is not by any means straightforward, and it must not be allowed to obscure the still unimpeachable vision of the old earthcults and of the Scriptures themselves, which see in woman the very opposite of abstraction, the symbol of body rather than of mind, human nature (all of us, that is, and not woman alone) in its material polarity, the passively oriented, the conserver, the saver of odds and ends, the custodian of material possessions (modern advertisers prefer to say the world's great buyer)— adaptable, like matter itself, so that the stock charge against her is frivolity and fickleness, but adaptable in her own sweet way, so that in function of her very pliancy itself, she becomes the great resistant to change in any environment in which she subsists. Many a man has set out to rule a woman and succeeded, but he has neither made her into what he thought he would, nor come out himself unaltered.

The dread of bringing this feminine, passive polarization of reality into the terms which fix one's relationship with God has been an obsession of separatists. The obsession is radically unaffected even by the violence of revivalist preaching and "getting religion," although these phenomena owe their existence and erratic manifestations of self-surrender impulses to the torque which the obsession establishes. One is tempted to say that this dread is more than one of the obsessions: it is *the* obsession which has constituted separatism, seen simply from a particular point of view. The impulse which inspires attacks on Mary, however it may disguise itself here as a defense of God's honor against that of a mere creature, as it sets darkly to work elsewhere reveals its secret springs of action.

Perhaps the most explicit manifestation of the impulse is the fact that with the rise of modern separatism, the concept of the Church as Mother is immediately liquidated. "Holy Mother Church" is heard of only in some few of the least separatist of separatist bodies. She is replaced by such notions as that of the invisible, purely spiritual union of the Elect, whoever they may be, disengaged from any material commitment, or that of the "congregation" based on a contractual union of wills by covenant—a more abstract and masculine sort of business, and something moreover that could perhaps pull its own weight in a court of law.

Ceremony and images are more openly sabotaged. "The coverlet of her bed was made by her own hands, the clothes of lawn and purple that she wears" (Prov. 31:22)—but there is to be no lawn or purple in God's service any more, as William Fulke and other anti-surplice agitators insisted, nor any of the abundance of material objects which the author of Proverbs works into his encomium of the virtuous woman. This is trumpery—or symbolism, which, to the mind confronting us here, is the same thing. The sense of mystery, which shows its psychological implications by its regular association with female priestesses and sibyls in pagan cults, must of course go, too, as the ground is cleared for a tidy Unitarianism and the claims of the fully plausible universe.

The separatist's automatic set against the sacraments is of a piece with his set against the feminine polarization in the world of material reality, and his attack on the sacraments instinctively works itself up to its most furious frenzy in hostility to the Real Presence, where the involvement of God with designable material reality reaches a kind of *ne plus ultra*. To this mind, burning candles are particularly loathsome, for, whether or not he can say why, he bridles at the symbolism with its high feminine charge of submission and consuming death. Beneath the flame, he sees shadowed forth the same reality which makes the Catholic today feel that votive lights can never be adequately replaced by electric lamps, which do not burn themselves bit by bit away. And the notion of sacrificial action, where a material gift—and, what is worse, most often a gift somehow consumed—is in *rapprochement* with spiritual reality, is particularly abhorrent to him.

And yet, perhaps in many ways more significant than any of these reactions of his—certainly more real in its psychological effects today—is the secularization which the separatist from the very beginning instinctively seeks to impose on matrimony. It is a sociological and psychological and physiological commonplace that marriage is, in a very real way, a more crucial issue for woman than for man. Attitudes toward it affect women more than they do men. Marriage is bisexual, but the relationship of the sexes to it differs. In the Scriptural way of speaking, Eve was made for Adam, not Adam for Eve. Adam was indeed not self-sufficient. He needed a helpmate. But his dependence on her is not of the same order as hers on him. If the sexual situation is posited given the existence of the human male, the female is created to fit the situation. Thus, in a bisexual world, woman is destined to be the symbol of sex in a way man himself cannot be. The medieval diatribes against woman are outcries, valid for man and for woman, against the tyranny which sex can exercise. It is no accident that, although the cinema audience is more female than male, sexiness in cinema advertisements—and indeed nearly everywhere—turns on the display of the female body.

An attitude toward marriage, the sacrament of sex, thus tends to be a correlative of an attitude toward woman, and the compulsion that the separatist, from early times, has always felt to keep marriage from being too religious, to deny that it is a sacrament at all, is of a piece with his compulsion to insulate his dealings with God from association with the femininely polarized aspects of reality. Religion must be unsexed, and marriage must go. When she returns to religion, woman must now come alone, unescorted, pretending that she is a man doing the things men do— and one has the female evangelists and ministers who are a persistent, if sporadic, phenomenon in separatist groups. Within the past few years, they have started up immediately in some state-engineered schismatic churches behind the Iron Curtain.

Against the total background of what it is to be a human being, one's sex is in a way a minor incident, and an incident subject even to chemical control. But psychophysically, and metaphysically, it is an incident which, if it repays study, remains always inexhaustible in its implications. Like the law, sex is a bottomless pit with ramifications everywhere. Thus, in their tendency to deny specifically religious relevance to marriage, the separatists have of course denied the religious relevance of virginity. The wife's giving herself to her husband being no sacrament, neither is there any virtue in man's or woman's refraining from all that has to do with this kind of surrender—-saving up everything connected with the self-surrender impulse—to give oneself in a genuinely analogous, but more sublime way to God. The analogy has no force. The Canticle of Canticles is robbed of meaning, and so is the espousal of the soul to God which dominates the whole corpus of non-scriptural mystical literature. Professor Kenneth Murdock's study of the New England Puritan's devotional poetry has made the point that only one writer, Edward Taylor, the least separatist and nearest to Catholic—and, incidentally, by common acclaim far and away the most competent poet—features the traditional espousal motif in his works at all.

The term "Puritan," which establishes itself as the proper name for an arch-separatism, is mortally accurate, if unwittingly so, in its sexual overtones. The "purity" which the Roundhead proposed for religious service meant removing from this service all that bespeaks feminine polarity. Woman and sex being surrogates for one another, the religious economy of the Puritan thus entailed a curious kind of sexual restraint—rightly styled an inhibition for being not the restraint of a frank chastity but the tortured mobilization of heavily disguised drives.

But beyond and beneath all the other manifestations, the most unequivocal sign of the ill-balanced sexual doctrine of separatist movements remains the attitude toward Mary. This attitude is suspect because it is all out of proportion to its announced objective, that of preventing the apotheosis of a creature, which is hardly even aimed at when it comes to the case of a Christ degraded to the rank of mere man. There is no scandal taken when those who no longer think Christ is God elevate him above all other creatures, naming whole ecclesial communities after him, Christian. But recent polemic finds something horribly sinister in the Catholic practice of dedicating individual church buildings here and there to Our Lady. Mary has obviously become a symbol, as it is indeed natural she should, and her symbolic valence is a matter not of her person nor of her mere creatureliness, but of her sex. As is the case in relations with woman, the reaction of her enemies to her is something they feel much more intensely than they understand.

The separatist mentality has not grown up in the world unattended by other related attitudes toward sex. Blood brother to this mentality is the repression of the knowledge that there is tragedy involved in every woman's existence by the simple fact that she is a woman. This repression, a kind of unforeseen sequel to the warped medieval cult of courtly love, has tyrannized for several centuries more and more over men's minds, particularly in "liberal" circles, where insistence on the motif of complete independence as a rule of life is constantly embarrassed by the scandal of subjection within the sexual framework of the race itself. The glossing over of woman's tragedy accounts for much of the unsettling effect on the contemporary mentality produced by Freudian insights, which once more at least frankly face the implications of the relationship between the sexes. The same glossing over is tied up with the obsessional hostility toward Mary and the inability, often enough experienced even by devout

Catholics, to catch the implications of her role in the economy of the Redemption.

Perhaps this repression has seen its heyday. D. H. Lawrence seems to have felt it his mission in life to attack the lies abroad regarding the relations of the sexes, and, from a quite different quarter, a novelist such as C. S. Lewis has used the theorem of the subjection of the female as a kind of leitmotif. It is certain that the temper of the "liberal" mentality would profit by a renewed acknowledgment of the tragedy of woman's lot, and quite as certain that the temper of Catholic devotion to Our Lady would only gain by the same acknowledgment.

Woman's tragedy is due ultimately to the fact that her body is ordered to others in a way that man's is not. For each of us, our mother's body was at one time at our command, and the whole routine of her living was ordered not to herself, but to us. Woman, corporeally speaking, which is to say as woman, for spiritually she is the equal of man, is not so self-possessed as she might be (if she were man). She is built to be an offering to others, to feed them, to be consumed in their use. Her most spiritual aspirations are dominated by this orientation within her. She cannot ordinarily build a kingdom around herself as a man can—she must build it around others. She can be happy only when involved in a certain amount of self-destruction. This is not a godlike quality. It is a humbling and all but indecent protestation of finiteness. Yet a woman is compelled to it by all the physiological, psychological, and sociological drives in her life. As a result, this is a man's world.

The role of woman as mother involves all this, and it involves all this for the radical reason that to be a mother means ultimately that woman must furnish out of herself material for another's body. Woman is deeply committed to the lowliness of matter. The sentimentality and "momism" which is endemic, we are assured, in America today (but sure by that very fact to be epidemic in the world tomorrow) and which is only another aspect of the silent conspiracy to suppress the tragedy of woman's lot, has so warped the meaning of mother that the simple statement that this is what it means to be a mother comes almost as a scandal. Yet Catholics who forget that motherhood is radically a traffic in

matter can realize only dimly the pitch and meaning of Our
Lady's elevation in grace, the full implications of the *Magnificat*
—*et exaltavit humiles*. To speak plainly, Mary is endowed with
the graces which make her the chiefest of mere creatures because
her body was made use of by the infant Christ's.

This is only to say that she was given the graces she was given
because she is the Mother of Christ, the Mother of God. An
angel can generate his thoughts, father them, produce them as a
father. He cannot mother them. Thoughts are not that sort of
thing. There is paternity in the Godhead—more perfect than
human paternity, which functions, however slightly, in terms of
matter, and thus has in it an admixture of maternity—but in the
Godhead there is no corresponding maternity. Nothing higher
than a human being can be a mother. Nothing higher than a
woman can be. Motherhood, woman's greatest glory, is something
that does not exist in the strict sense elsewhere except lower on
the animal scale. Yet it is because of this that she was made full
of grace. Because of the tragedy of woman's lot.

It is because precisely so lowly a creature is proposed as the
greatest person in all creation, exalted above all the angels, exalted, be it known, above every created male person (God is
jealous of masculinity and reserves its exaltation to the case of
His Own Son, where it lodges safe from pride, assumed to the
Divinity)—it is because of this that Mary remains for eternity the
stumbling-block to overweening male pride, whether this be that of
the man who refuses to have woman preferred to him or of the
woman who refuses to have anyone preferred to her but a man.
Mary says nothing, but merely for being what she is, she sets up
a state of crisis. In this state of crisis, one tiny prayer to Mary
signalizes a whole psychological revolution and the opening of
the soul to grace. It is a warrant of, not perfect, but essential
humility. For God will have neither man nor woman on any other
terms than complete submission. Authority is not evil, but good.
Yet no one is rewarded for exercising it. Only for submitting to
God's directives in its exercise.

In that she is woman and exalted for her womanly function as
mother, the exaltation of Mary is a kind of apotheosis of tragedy

and of the will to die. It is, in a very real sense, the exaltation of the material, passive principle in human existence—Newman, whose flashes of discernment here are most rewarding, has observed that heresies which attack Mary are likely to end by asserting that matter is evil, or what is the same thing, by explaining it away. And it is in function of her engagement with matter that the Assumption of Our Lady reveals itself for the critical thing it really is.

The Resurrection of Christ, St. Paul insists, is the keystone of Christian belief. Yet, in a way, the Assumption of Mary focuses the issue raised by the Resurrection more sharply than even the Resurrection itself. It is a quite impossible feat of historical exegesis, but one often attempted, to explain away the Resurrection of Christ as simply a way of speaking indulged in by his pious followers. The spirituality of Christ's message, His obvious desire to sublimate the material as far as possible in the spiritual, while it does not lend any substance to this exegesis, can be used to make the exegesis somewhat plausible. The Church's insistence on the historical verity of the Resurrection of Christ can thus fail to impinge very really on the consciousness of those outside the Church because they can lose it and forget it in the great wealth of purely spiritual items in His teaching. But Mary's womanly function as the symbol of the material world will not allow her Assumption to be thus dismissed in a genial misinterpretation. Mary's whole *raison d'être* is the Body of Christ—she did not give Him His soul or His graces or His spiritual message. What is more, her role is underwritten here not by abstract dogma but by the archetypal symbolism in which psychiatrists deal and which involves the human consciousness in the toils of real existence so deeply that by no flights of abstraction can the toils be spun away.

Mary does not submit to abstraction. She cannot be quite liquidated in the mazy flow of thought. She cannot de distilled into a purely spiritual message. Mary indeed stood for much spiritually. But, rather differently from her Son, who was the Word of God and spoke accordingly, she functions hardly at all in terms of what she says. In a strange way, her spirituality is keyed to her material role, her divine motherhood. To focus a theological issue on Mary is inevitably to engage oneself inex-

tricably with matter and its sanctification. To say that her body is
no longer on earth is to fix the issue once for all. Like all human
beings, her Son had a body, it is true. But His role here is not
hers and cannot be. Mary, in a peculiar way, not only has a body,
but *is* body—being woman, the symbol of body, important as
the mother, whose claim to glory lodges in her having been prepared to give a body to her Son.

Thus the doctrine of the Assumption, far from being anything
"new" or "non-essential," has the very desirable effect of pre-
cipitating Catholic doctrine quite really in the face of the persistent tendency to distill it away into vaporous nothingness. Now
it is less possible than ever to pretend that the Catholic position
means less than it means in fact, or to pretend that a sufficiently
elaborate theory or a proper economy of explanation would make
the Catholic position much less a commitment than it is. The
commitment here, like any commitment, is made not in terms of
theory but in reality. In the case of the doctrine of the Assumption,
the commitment and the crisis is fixed within reality in terms of
the concrete material of Mary's body. The Assumption does not
engender theory so much as create a situation, like that created
by the question, This God you speak of, do you mean that, like
human persons, like you or me, He is really *there?* (the implication being, of course, not by spatial but by personal presence).

The proclamation of the Assumption has been cited outside the
Church as an obstacle to the unity of Christendom. The nervousness here perhaps betrays the dream of a unity without commitments. There is another kind of unity which dominates Catholic
thinking: the unity of the Mystical Body, a unity grounded in the
material here and now, where, after all, the material and the
spiritual meet—Jesus Christ yesterday and today and the same
forever, grasped in the designable actuality of those making up
His Church. Generally speaking, attention to the Mystical Body
and attention to Mary are functions of one another, although
here again Mary underlines the bodily component more urgently
than her Son does.

Perhaps one can go further still. The Mystical Body has been
lately a favorite topic not only of Catholic theologians but of

many outside the Catholic Church, who even hope to implement
out of this topic their theories of a loosely connected Christendom.
Would it be accurate to suggest that the nervousness concerning devotion to Mary which haunts even such minds seriously interested in the Mystical Body betrays a torque in the application
of the Mystical Body doctrine itself? The nervousness is there. It
is a strange psychological fact that, when he has agreed with the
Church on all points of doctrine, even on all points regarding
Mary, there persists for the non-Catholic a curious uneasiness
regarding his personal relationship and that of others to Mary, a
psychological block which may even keep him from praying to
her as his Mother and which at least warns him to tread somewhat
warily here. The state of affairs is quite different from what obtains within the Catholic Church where complete lack of inhibition regarding adulation of Mary is one of the characteristic attitudes which Catholics who have hardly a glimmering of abstract theology bear about in the deepest depths of their being.

Unsteadiness regarding Mary is a psychological symptom of
an imbalance regarding the Mystical Body which is radically a
tendency to slur over the material component, the Body, and to
concentrate too much on the "mystical." Neither component
should be sacrificed. Christ's Church is both mystical and Body,
with that which Body bespeaks, possible wounds and sufferings,
but always a continuity which is not only spiritual but somehow
materially assignable as well. *You shall not break a bone of him.*

By virtue of the archetypal symbolism in which her whole being involves her and which brings St. Thomas to maintain that it
was thoroughly in keeping with the nature of reality that Christ
should have a human mother but no human father, Mary is inextricably involved in the notion of the Mystical Body and thereby
in the structure of the Church itself. Attitudes toward her become
attitudes toward the Church and toward all reality. The point
can be made in two theorems which can perhaps now be advanced. First, anti-Marianism tends to generate separatism and
separatism anti-Marianism. Indeed, in many cases the two are
no more than surrogates for one another. Secondly, the Mystical
Body of Christ is to be found only where there is no nervousness,

no uncertainty regarding matter and material continuity, not as an abstract bit of theory, but as both detached from and set within the complex of all other issues by means of the symbol which is woman. This last theorem can be elaborated in another and perhaps more telling formula: The Mystical Body of Christ is to be found only where such a concept as that of Holy Mother Church exists as a natural frame of thought and as a real determinant of mentality. Groups and individuals which cannot use with confidence and genuine relevance this concept of Holy Mother Church, whatever they may call themselves, are in fact separatist movements. Dogma develops, but it never repudiates itself. Assured possession of this age-old concept of Holy Mother Church is a *sine qua non* of contemporary orthodoxy. Those who cannot manage the concept with assurance are somehow off balance regarding that continuity and unity and that sanctification of the material component of things which the doctrine of the Assumption makes patent as nothing else quite would today.

Index

203

204   *Index*

O'CONNOR, William Van, 41
Ong, Walter J., *The Barbarian
    Within*, ix–xi, 15, 39, 40, 41, 59,
    145; *Ramus, Method, and the
    Decay of Dialogue*, 146
Opler, Marvin K., 8, 59, 184
Oral-aural, 4–16, 24–26, 54–56; *see
    also* Communications; Language;
    Word
Origen, 181
Orwell, George, 13, 100
Osborn, H. F., 63, 82
Ouspensky, P. D., 115

PACKARD, Vance, 13
Parkinson, Thomas, 12
Parry, Milman, 24–26
Péguy, Charles, 113
Person, human, evolution and, 76–
    78, 90–91, 95–96, 121–24;
    providence and, 160; *see also*
    I-thou relationship; Interiority
Personalism, 14–15; *see also*
    Interiority
Peterson, Theodore H., 187
Plato, 6, 88
Platonism, 79–81, 139
Poe, Edgar Allen, 35, 109
Politian (Poliziano, Angelo), 20
Pope, Alexander, 36, 101
Potter, Stephen, 18
Poulet, Georges, 109, 112–14, 126
Pound, Ezra, 12, 30–31, 112, 116–
    17, 143
Presence, 13–16; *see also* Interiority
Printing, *see* Typography
Privacy, interiority versus, 185–88
Protestant-Catholic tensions, 50,
    188–202

QUINTILIAN (Marcus Fabius
    Quintilianus), 20, 39

RACE relations, 48, 169
Rahner, Karl, 162, 176–77, 188
Ransom, John Crowe, 30
Reinhardt, Ad, 93
Religion, nature, 129–31, 155–60

Religious traditions, divergent, 171–
    74, 188–202
Richards, I. A., 30
Riesman, David, 184
Rilke, Rainer Maria, 137
Roppen, George, 99
Rosenstock-Huessy, Eugen, 138,
    142

ST. THOMAS Aquinas, 171, 172–73
St. Augustine, 171
St. Bernard of Clairvaux, 181
St. John of the Cross, 117
St. Ignatius Loyola, 71, 149
St. Francis Xavier, 149
Sartre, Jean-Paul, 137
Scaliger, Joseph Justus, 29
Scaliger, Julius Caesar, 29
Schelling, Friedrich von, 65
Schramm, Wilbur, 187
Scoon, Robert, 82
Scotus, Duns, 121
Secular, sacred and, 159–61
Secular knowledge, advance in, 50–
    51, 176–81
Secularism, 174–81
Sender, Ramon, 93
Shakespeare, William, 35, 36
Shapiro, Karl, 108, 126
Shaw, George Bernard, 100, 113
Sidney, Sir Philip, 33, 40, 117
Siebert, Fred S., 187
Simpson, George Gaylord, 98
Singleton, Charles S., 29
Sitwell, Edith, 112
Slote, Bernice, 108, 126
Smith, John Maynard, 98
Snow, C. P., 38
Sound, meaning and, 2, 56; *see also*
    Oral-aural
Space, use of in communication, 7–9
Speech, *see* Communications;
    Language; Oral-aural; Word
Spencer, Herbert, 82
Spengler, Oswald, 68, 85, 115
Spenser, Edmund, 107
Spiller, Robert E., 68
Spitzer, Leo, 6, 29
Stern, Karl, 47, 189
Stevens, David R., 40

Imprimi potest: Linus J. Thro, S. J., Provincial Missouri
Province, St. Louis, Missouri, February 28, 1966

Nihil obstat: William M. Drumm, *Censor Librorum*, St. Louis,
Missouri, March 3, 1966

Imprimatur: Joseph Cardinal Ritter, Archbishop of St. Louis,
St. Louis, Missouri, March 3, 1966